**OUT OF CHINGFORD
ROUND THE NORTH CIRCULAR AND UP THE
ORINOCO**

Deep in peaceful Chingford is a semi-detached house. Inside, surrounded by maps, machetes and murals, Tanis and Martin Jordan plan their next expedition. In 1970, having saved up, they took a freighter to Trinidad before making their first jungle expedition by hitch-hiking into Surinam. Since then, they have been to Venezuela, Surinam again, Peru and Brazil.

OUT OF CHINGFORD describes the extraordinary adventures of an 'ordinary' suburban couple who finance their travel bug quite independently, and have survived to tell the tale with terrific humour and highly individual detail.

About the authors

Tanis is a hairdresser and writer. Martin has always painted pictures for a hobby and houses for a living. Recently he reversed the situation and became a full-time artist.

The focus of their lives is the South American Rainforest. To date their expeditions total two and a half years spent in the parts that other people don't reach. They are dedicated to the protection of forests. Both are Fellows of the Royal Geographical Society and have lectured there.

Out Of Chingford Round The North Circular And Up The Orinoco

Tanis & Martin Jordan

CORONET BOOKS
Hodder and Stoughton

First published in Great Britain in 1988
by Frederick Muller
an imprint of Century Hutchinson
Limited

Coronet edition 1989

British Library C.I.P.

Jordan, Tanis
  Out of Chingford : round the North
Circular and up the Orinoco.
1. World. Description & travel
I. Title II. Jordan, Martin, *1944*–
910.4

ISBN 0 340 50819 1

Printed and bound in Great Britain
for Hodder and Stoughton
Paperbacks, a division of Hodder and
Stoughton Ltd., Mill Road,
Dunton Green, Sevenoaks, Kent
TN13 2YA (Editorial Office: 47 Bedford
Square, London WC1B 3DP) by
Cox & Wyman Ltd., Reading.

For Mum.
And
for Rudy, who had faith

ACKNOWLEDGEMENTS

To our families, friends and all the people who helped, advised, inspired and encouraged us in the planning and execution of our trips, we will always be grateful.

Out of Chingford came out of 'Brazil'. For this we thank Jo and Bryan Hanson, Hilary Bradt, Adam and Nicky Cole, Byron Rogers, Christopher Pillitz, and the London Ecology Centre. To Lavinia Trevor and Paul Sidey, thank you for your confidence and guidance.

Special thanks to June and Jack Tomlinson, Dominic Jordan, and that midnight reader of manuscript, commiserator of crashed discs and constant voice of encouragement, Patti Taylor.

CONTENTS

PROLOGUE

While I was drowning I thought of Martin, and wondered if he was drowning as well. But in the urgency of my predicament there was no time to worry about it – I was being whisked along beneath murky water by a relentless current and my senses were spinning out of control. The day hadn't begun very well, and it certainly wasn't improving.

Early that morning, in the second week of our journey, we'd emerged from our jungle camp to survey the river. Downstream stretched the mile of rapids and fast water we'd struggled up the previous day. Upstream there was no visible end to more of the same.

Martin lit the wrong end of a cigarette, and spluttered over the smouldering filter tip; I could tell he was nervous. Our anxieties concerned not just the unseasonably high and turbulent river, but also our twelve foot fibreglass canoe that was overloaded to the point of instability. With only two inches of freeboard we were forever bailing water out of it.

'Let's put our lifejackets on,' said Martin, and I was eager to comply. Lifejackets were things we normally used as pillows: sometimes we inflated them to sit on; this day, well into our fourth South American river trip, would be the first occasion we'd used them for their intended purpose.

Mid-morning, while paddling away like a pair of demented river turtles, my fingers became numb with the effort and I dropped the paddle which snagged against a rock a little way downstream. The canoe spun into the bank beneath a mass of overhanging foliage. Unfortunately we'd parked in a residential area and the alligator whose exit we'd blocked chose that moment to emerge, suddenly and violently like a cannonball shooting out straight under the boat, tipping it sideways. In that fraction of a second, water flooded in and the bow sank beneath me. Martin, unconcerned in the back, had no idea what was happening until he was unceremoniously tipped out, a look of utter astonishment on his face as he was whipped away. I hung onto a branch, water up to my chest. There was a fleeting glimpse of brightly coloured equipment floating away, then the branch broke and I was sucked under water.

And now I was drowning. I tried to surface but was caught under a mass of roots. The current snatched me back, swished me around as if in a washing machine, regurgitated me and flung me against a submerged tree trunk. There was the canoe upside down. I clutched at it, trying to right it. It turned, but with a mass of slimy green muck on top, and sank under the weight. Once more I was swept off and flung around like flotsam until I hit the slippery trunk of a submerged tree with a rib-crunching smack. The water dragged my body under the tree and as I struggled to anchor myself I began to lose my grip. Driven by fear I launched myself up to a position of relative safety.

Everything looked blurred. I had lost my contact lenses but I could distinguish the bank, about thirty feet away. My nose was running and I wiped it with my hand; it was covered with blood. All I could hear was the ceaseless roaring of water as it broke over me. I yelled for Martin but he was gone. Nothing moved except the water. It wasn't meant to be like this. One of us wasn't suppposed to die. It was just another trip, like the others. It was supposed to be fun, an adventure. That's what we did it for, wasn't it? It was dangerous of course, and we'd often talked about getting killed. Usually we joked about it, confident it wouldn't happen to us.

CHAPTER ONE

I'd never thought about travel until I met Martin.

I hadn't had time to think about much at all; if I thought of the future I probably imagined marriage and children. I was fifteen, he was seventeen, and the minute we met we fell in love. Not long after, Martin's parents died. When we married six years later he'd never stayed in a job for more than six months. He painted as well, huge, tormented canvases. A dreamer, my parents said, always miles away. A genius, I thought, and worked as a hairdresser while he painted.

'A sea of shifting sand!' Martin read aloud. 'Let's save up and go to the Sahara,' he said. 'It can be our honeymoon.'

'You'll need a reliable vehicle,' said my father, who was in the motor trade, 'I've got the very thing.' A four wheel drive, super-equipped Land Rover was what we'd have liked, but as we could only afford a hundred pounds, a Morris Minor was what we got. 'Don't worry, it won't let you down. The only thing you may need is a spare fan belt and there's one in the boot,' he said.

A year later, on a bleak and icy January morning with a snowstorm whipping through London, we drove to the coast bound for Morocco.

As we left Ceuta for the open Moroccan countryside, two youths in flowing robes stood high on a mount, silhouetted against the sun, watching as we approached. 'It's like being transported back centuries,' I said. 'They look quite biblical, don't they?'

CRASH! A bottle broke on the bonnet.

Our first Moroccan town was like another world; one of robed men, veiled women, and donkeys. It all seemed so foreign, as if we'd crossed an ocean rather than the narrow strip of water which separates Morocco from homely Europe. In the bazaar, people haggled over exotic merchandise. Haberdashers peddled their wares, pausing eagerly as veiled women, showing nothing but one mysterious eye, stopped to examine the goods. Food was covered by a crawling, black mat of flies. The vendor waved a whisk, allowing tantalising glimpses of pastries, sweets and cakes. Even the bread we bought contained a few freshly baked specimens. Butchers utilised modern technology in the interest of hygiene by liberally spraying buzzing, bloody carcasses with aerosol fly-killer. Adults took little notice of us but children created a great hullabaloo, clambering over the car, excitedly grabbing at everything that wasn't tied down as we tried to close the doors without amputating little arms and legs.

Driving south along a country road, past caravans of robed men leading camels and heavily laden donkeys, we were off to see the legendary sand dunes of the Sahara desert.

Night. We slept in the car parked beside a narrow road high in the Atlas mountains. It was so cold we took turns to warm our fingers over the camping Gaz stove. When at last we could detect the first faint light of dawn our spirits rose with the prospect of a rise in temperature. Daylight revealed the towering peaks above us, shining orange and gold where sunlight struck. Below us the deep valley was filled to the brim with mist, like an immense bowl of steaming milk. In the darkness of the previous evening these hills had appeared stark and forbidding, but now, in the soft morning light, the rocks had a magical glow.

We crossed the mountains into the foothills on the edge of the Sahara. It was days since we'd left the last town but each evening as the great orange sun slipped down, a speck would appear on the horizon, bobbing in the shimmering light. In an unerringly straight line it came at us, gathering size and stature until, lungs puffing and robes flapping, an Arab stood at the door. A few minutes idle conversation before he turned, satisfied, and strode purposefully out into the desert.

'Tanis, we're being attacked!' The car was shaking violently. There must be a dozen men out there. We'd read that there were bandits in the region, but the book was old and we had laughed. I wasn't laughing now as I pulled my trousers on with one hand, frantically groping in the blackness with the other to locate some sort of weapon, talking loudly all the while in three different voices to give our attackers the impression that the car was full of men. I sprang out onto the road, wheel wrench held aloft, blood pounding with adrenalin ready for the first blow. There was not a soul to be seen anywhere, yet the car was still bouncing about as if it was alive. So was the ground, vibrating to deep rumbling noises. An earthquake. Legs braced against the quaking earth, we clung to the car as it started to slide towards the rocks. And then it was quiet and still. I relaxed my grip on the car. Another violent tremor and a hail of rocks showered down around us. Then it was over.

Next morning we wove our way along a road marred by deep cracks, strips of tarmac lay neatly severed along the verges. The road ended abruptly. All that remained of the bridge was a ten foot concrete projection, sticking out forlornly over the ravine and twenty feet below, a pile of rubble.

Out of the foothills we turned west towards the Atlantic coast. Apart from the intense heat and the absence of vegetation the desert was quite different from our expectations; gently hilly rather than flat, and rocky with not a sand dune to be seen. With the royal blue Atlantic Ocean on our right, we drove towards Spanish Sahara.

Camped outside Goullimime was a tribe of desert nomads, their squat brown tents blending with the terrain. We drove through the gates of the town and a crowd of curious onlookers gathered round, staring and talking excitedly. A man in voluminous, cornflower-blue robes stepped forward. The crowd fell silent. 'I am Jordi Ali, welcome to my town, you will take tea with me, please?'

His house was a rambling complex of white painted buildings and low-walled enclosures. Throughout the afternoon we sipped hot, syrupy, tooth-decaying mint tea from tiny glasses and attempted to discuss, in French, eighteenth-century Italian painting for which our host had a passion!

That night there was to be an important dinner party for the elders of the nomadic tribesmen. Women were forbidden to eat alongside men but our host promised an exception would be made in Tanis's case. We were led away to be dressed in silky blue robes, cool and perfumed. A door opened and Jordi Ali invited us in; first we must remove our shoes. We entered a carpeted room where eight men waited, some in blue robes, others in dark brown, blanket-like cloth. Their names registered not at all but their faces, lined by age and hard living, left a marked impression.

We were seated on embroidered cushions in a circle on the floor; our host clapped his hands. I was half expecting the carpet to take to the air and fly out of the window. Servants entered bearing a huge tureen containing a rich spicy stew of mutton and vegetables, with sprigs of mint floating on the surface. Side dishes of pulped apricot and fried eggs followed and after chanted prayers we were ready to begin. I was ravenous but nobody moved, each man stared expectantly at Tanis. 'They're waiting for you to start.' I said.

Reaching out she plucked a piece of meat from the dish and ate it. On cue a dozen hands descended on the food. The meat was big lumps of fat and gristle and I watched sympathetically as Tanis chewed reluctantly, horror registering in her eyes as she forced herself to swallow something she abhorred. 'Just eat the vegetables,' I suggested. But our hosts seemed positively pleased to have a woman dine with them and kept passing her the most succulent morsels of fat, watching with delight as she dutifully forced them down. At last, having suffered enough, she sat back feigning repletion. The group looked up in horror, the dish was still half full, they were still hungry. I was still hungry. We all waited expectantly.

'Eat a bit more,' I entreated. She struggled on until the oldest man, while chewing a piece of fat, decided it was absolutely *the* most delectable thing he'd ever tasted. He opened a cavernous mouth, exposing blackened stumps of teeth, and generously passed the semi-masticated, hair-encrusted delicacy around the group to Tanis. By the time it reached her the saliva on it had ceased foaming. I was truly impressed by her expression of enjoyment as she swallowed it.

On a deserted beach called Tan-Tan Plage we erected our tent for the first time. It was luxurious to stretch out fully without becoming impaled on a handbrake or strung up on a steering wheel. In the middle of the night I was woken by a violent prodding from Tanis. I rolled over to be greeted by the sight of a large unidentifiable form framed in the doorway. Stories of wolves and rabid dogs filled my mind. I hissed loudly, attempting to impersonate a venomous snake. The creature started, then ambled away. Creeping to the entrance I peered fearfully into the blackness but it had gone. In the morning we found our nocturnal intruder breakfasting on a straggly bush. A large solitary goat.

Wherever there was a scrap of vegetation goats grazed. They climbed the few stunted trees which managed to survive in the harsh environment, and walked to the very end of the branches to strip away the remaining leaves. To us this seemed picturesque and amusing, great stuff for photographs in glossy magazines, but we were witnessing an ecological disaster; these few remaining trees would soon be dead with no chance of being replaced by a new generation of plants. What little soil that was left would dry up, blow away, and the lifeless desert would become a little bit larger.

Turning inland we headed toward the south-east corner of Morocco, crossing desert composed of a dark mixture of gravel and pebbles, often sufficiently well consolidated to drive a car across. Searching for the elusive sand dunes.

It was a holiday when we arrived at Figuig to cross into Algeria. White buildings grouped around a square were all shut. People thronged the pavement, dozens of children surrounded the car before we came to a halt, climbing up the bonnet onto the roof, making faces at us through the windscreen. A policeman appeared, waving his gun. The children crept away.

'Algeria, *s'il vous plaît*?' Martin asked.

'*Beni Ounif*,' he said, pointing to a gap between two buildings.

The children crept back. Laughing, he shook his fist at them, then beckoned us to follow. With children hanging on to the car we drove slowly behind him. The desert stretched ahead, there were no signs, no other cars and no road. He pointed to tyre tracks on the dusty surface, shook Martin's hand and returned to the festivities.

'This is a bit unorthodox, aren't we supposed to go through customs?' I said.

'I think we just did.'

We followed the tracks. The desert was dotted with barbed wire and bits of rusty machinery. Here and there were tall poles with notices nailed on and barbed wire coiled round them, looking like supports for newly planted trees. 'Perhaps it's a reforestation programme,' I suggested, stopping beside one for a better look. We walked around to read the sign. CHAUSEE DE MINES. We were in a minefield.

Hardly daring to breathe, let alone move, we stared around us with renewed interest at things we'd noticed earlier; bits of machinery scattered across the desert had once been motor vehicles. The rusty wheels and twisted engines had not been dumped there, they'd been blown to bits. It was deathly still. 'Tan, concentrate on what I'm saying, can you turn the car round?' I looked at the tyre marks we'd followed so confidently. Now they were barely visible.

'You must be joking, there could be mines either side of it,' I said. It seemed safest to go on. I inched the car forward. 'I can't see anything,' I squeaked.

'Calm down, you're doing OK, just keep going slowly.'

'Anyway if we do hit one we won't know anything about it. We won't even hear the bang.' Martin is always so reassuring.

Palms slipping sweatily on the steering wheel I drove on, waiting for the car to explode beneath us. At last we pulled up in front of huge metal gates festooned with barbed wire. The end of the track, but the gates were shut and a large padlock gleamed at us smugly. Martin opened the car door. 'Don't get out, Mart.'

'Don't be silly, Tan, we can't just sit here, anyway the padlock might be unlocked.' He walked towards the gates.

'Don't touch them,' I shouted. He looked perplexed.

'Why ever not?'

'They might be electrified. If this was a war zone there could be booby traps around.'

'But they're not at war now, are they?' he countered crossly.

'Then why are there bloody mines everywhere?'

'I don't know, Tan, calm down, don't get so excited,' he said tensely.

'Excited? I'm not excited. You're just ratty because it was your idea,' I said, smarting.

'If you remember Tan, you said it was a short cut. Some short cut.'

'You shouldn't have listened to me.'

'Don't worry, I won't in future.'

'Right!'

'Right!'

We sat in hostile silence.

In the distance a rider appeared, wobbling towards us on a rickety bicycle. He stopped at the gate. A thin, black man in a shiny petrol blue mohair suit, his pockmarked face partly obscured by mirrored sunglasses. Without dismounting he examined us and the car. 'Passports,' he demanded. Martin slid them through the wire. He turned and rode away. 'Hey, come back!' we cried, but he'd gone.

'People at home won't believe this,' Martin said. I was sure they wouldn't, I was having a job believing it myself.

Just before dark in the intense desert silence . . . creak . . . rattle . . . creak. The man was coming back. He pedalled up and without a word opened the gates and beckoned us through. I turned on the ignition. The battery was flat.

Spurred on by the thought of being stranded in a minefield we pushed the car through, and as it gathered momentum, bump-started it, then followed our guide to the frontier town, cruising to a halt outside a single storey concrete building. It was the police station and we were put in a cell.

Next morning we met the chief of police, who was called Tariq. He was twenty-eight, slickly handsome, very well-educated, speaking French, Italian and English fluently, and he was charming. He was also a little unhinged. 'Please understand that you are not my prisoners, but driving across this border is suicidally dangerous. Tourists do not cross here, so you might be spies. Do you have Algerian money? No? I am also the bank here, I will change money for you, give it to me.'

Tariq dashed away with our money leaving the cell door open. We wandered outside to find our belongings heaped in the road while his minions searched the car. Triumphantly one held up a flat, sealed package. 'What this say?' he demanded, shoving it under my nose. I read it aloud. 'Full fat processed cheese.' He confiscated it.

That evening Tariq took us to a café, bought us a bottle of wine, then reviled us while we drank it. 'That is poison. Forbidden to we the faithful!' His chin was high in sanctimonious arrogance as he waved his hand at the bottle of *vin rouge*. Then proceeded to tell us that in France, he regularly consumed large quantities of cognac. Clearly, his adherence to that aspect of Islamic law could be geographically determined.

His unpredictable changes of mood made us nervous. To steer him away from touchy subjects Martin pointed to the plastic tablecloth, gaily decorated with pictures of fruits. 'We get all these in England,' he said.

Tariq, eager to demonstrate his command of English, pointed. 'Banana, orange, apple, I know all fruits, all fruits!'

'Pineapple, strawberry,' continued Martin.

'Strawberry, what is strawberry?'

'This thing is a strawberry.'

'That is pimento,' Tariq declared abruptly.

'No. It's a fruit we have in England called a strawberry.'

'It is pimento.' I could see his insistence was irritating Martin; why did there have to be a strawberry on an Algerian tablecloth?

'It's not a pimento, it's a strawberry,' Martin said firmly.

'IT IS PIMENTO!' Tariq shouted, fists clenched and trembling in anger. A knowing silence came over the place. Clearly, Tariq was a despot in this little town.

'Well, so it is,' Martin agreed, trying to sound surprised, as if he'd just seen the logic of a well-reasoned argument, 'so it is!'

Two days later we asked Tariq for our passports and money. 'Impossible,' he announced, 'today the bank is shut.'

'We want to leave now.'

Tariq opened a drawer, withdrew a revolver and inspected it, spinning the chamber. Flicking a speck of dust from the barrel he laid it on his desk. 'Do sit down,' he invited. All day he kept us there with no food or drink, not even allowing us to visit the toilet. At seven-thirty that evening he took our passports and money from a drawer and without a word, tossed them contemptuously on his desk. We took them and left.

At Colomb Bechar we took the car into a garage. It wouldn't start without a push and now the electrics had failed. Between us in our dreadful French we explained our theory. We'd been stuck in a minefield and somehow the mines had drained the battery. The mechanic looked startled then bemused. He opened the bonnet; even an inanimate object would make more sense than us. The fan belt had broken.

Driving in a straight line across the flat, grey landscape toward Tarhit, we felt like two motorised Lilliputians in the middle of a vast empty car park. On the horizon a range of craggy hills appeared, apparently floating in water with a mirror image reflected beneath. The hills were thirty miles away and it was half an hour before the optical illusion was resolved into hills, rising out of solid ground.

In the hills, with low cliffs on each side, piles of wind-blown sand filled dips and gullies and lay heaped around boulders.

The road turned sharply and there, beyond a strip of flat desert, were sand dunes; not gold, not yellow but a rich, deep orange. We'd expected dunes as big as houses but these were mountains of sand five hundred feet high. Dwarfed beneath them was a village with a chain of oases and clumps of date palms. It took us half an hour to climb to the summit. Standing on the knife-edge ridge in the searing midday heat we looked across an endless sea of motionless sand (which no doubt shifted occasionally). The silence was so intense that we could hear the blood pumping around our brains. The dunes, like petrified waves, had an unexpected and exquisite detail – a hair-line crest, stretching for miles into the stark wilderness. This was our triumph, not the stuff of epic journeys, but we'd come to find the sand and we'd found it.

'I wish we could stay longer,' I said wistfully.

'We'll come back again.'

'Maybe we could buy a van and drive round Africa.'

'We can go anywhere you know, Tan,' said Martin confidently.

'What do you mean?'

'Well, we could go exploring in South America if we wanted to, like Colonel Fawcett.'

'But we don't know anything about exploring, you need guides and things, helicopter back-up, we couldn't afford all that.'

'I don't think you need all that stuff. Colonel Fawcett didn't have helicopters.'

'And look what happened to him, he disappeared,' I pointed out.

'Yes, but that was different,' said Martin, avoiding the issue. 'I really fancy going to South America now. Think of it, Tan, jungles and rivers, places nobody has ever seen, imagine seeing a jaguar in the wild.'

'Just don't tell my mum about Colonel Fawcett!'

Back home it was expected that we would stop travelling now that we had got it out of our systems (rather like food poisoning). But we were just beginning. Eighteen months later we set off for South America.

UNDER THE KAN-KAN TREE

CHAPTER TWO

The taxi driver had six fingers on each hand. His name was Kwisi and he told us that he too was a foreigner, from Surinam. He had married a Guyanese lady, they'd moved to George-town and lived there ever since. But he'd never taken to the town and yearned for a quieter life, for jungle villages and wide rivers, a life remembered from his childhood. 'My people are Bushnegroes,' he said, turning to Martin. 'Many years ago my people were brought from Africa for slaves, but they escaped to the bush and fought the white man till they were free, now they living deep in the jungle by the rivers.'

Kwisi knew that we'd noticed his extra fingers; we'd been covertly glancing at his hands since we got in the car. 'A lot of Bushnegro peoples have six fingers,' he explained, adding thoughtfully, 'some of us have six toes as well.'

Veering sharply to avoid an ox-cart, the battered old taxi bounced in and out of deep potholes, its innards scraping the dirt surface as it rattled along the country road that led from Timehri airport to Georgetown, the capital of Guyana. Our belongings, disgorged by the conveyor belt item by item, (minus the duty-free), now burst from the hastily re-packed rucksacks and flew round the car as if bewitched, adding to the general confusion of our arrival in South America.

Everything was a shock to our senses. It was so hot and humid that it felt unnatural, as if a hot wet blanket had dropped over us; the damp air pervaded by smells of woody decay and vegetation, earthy and sweet like compost and new-mown hay. It was all so incredibly, luxuriantly green; even the telegraph wires had plants growing on them. We gazed in wonder at the unfamiliar world beyond the dust-spattered windows. The road was bordered by a wall of vivid green bushes. Here and there stood huge trees, spared from the axe when the road was pushed through the forest. Great masses of coiling twisting creepers dangled from their mighty limbs and mingled with the greenery below. The constant buzz of insects invaded the car.

On we went, past little villages of wooden houses, whose occupants sat impassively on their verandahs, while barefoot children stopped their play to stare as the taxi trundled by; past plantations of tall dark-green sugar cane rising on both sides of the road, hiding the horizon. A sinuous green snake wriggled across the road; we grinned at each other excitedly. With a grunt, Kwisi swerved into the bank determined to squash it flat. This hostile attitude to wildlife was something we'd have to get used to. We came out again into open countryside past flooded rice fields where lean, sinewy men in ragged shorts toiled in the noonday heat.

Kwisi knew about the jungle, he'd lived there for the first twenty years of his life. Martin asked what it was like. 'Very nice, very nice. Better than here,' waving six fingers at the red dirt road, the palm trees and tin-roofed, grey-board houses surrounded by waist high weeds and steaming puddles of water. 'Sweet water in them rivers, get plenty fish, plenty animal in the bush; monkey, pig, bush-cow get sweet meat, tiger living there too.' Tiger?

Georgetown was colourful and picturesque in a quaint, run-down way, without the high buildings and traffic congestion of a European city. Wide tree-lined avenues flanked by colonial-style timber houses gave way to garbage-strewn backstreet slums; donkey carts and bicycles jostled among the beat-up cars and trucks. The taxi dropped us at the central market, Stabroek, a huge bustling place full of stalls selling fruits and vegetables; sugary cakes, pastries and wedges of thick, luminously-coloured jelly dripped stickily next to Amerindian artifacts: bows and arrows, blowpipes and feather headdresses. A jovial black lady, spotting us for the innocents that we were, thrust a fruit in our hands and collapsed with laughter at our expressions as we dutifully bit into it; it dried every drop of saliva leaving us purse-mouthed with surprise.

So began our education, passing from stall to stall sampling more fruits than we had imagined existed, valiantly attempting to assimilate all the information offered. 'Don't eat this if it green.' . . . 'this one bad if it pink.' . . . 'never take this one with crabmeat, you don' get no childrun then!' (this accompanied by much giggling and winking). 'You don' never eat him with alcohol,' holding up a large green pomegranate type fruit, 'else you be stone cold DEAD!'

With a good feeling of bonhomie and juice running down our chins we made for the exit. A tiny wizened lady waving a parasol barred our way. 'You all from England?' she accosted; we nodded. 'Then you all know my son Selwyn, he living in Huddersfield.' Without waiting for a reply she carried on, 'You tell that boy to write his mother, I don' hear nothing from him in eleven years, you tell him write me when you go home.' She hurried off and was lost in the crowd.

That first day in Guyana ended less happily than it had begun. After waiting fifteen minutes to be served in a shop, it dawned on us that we were being deliberately ignored. Our packs were ridiculously heavy as we trudged around looking for a cheap place to stay. Away from the main street the hostile looks we drew from groups of youths made us bad-tempered with each other. Sweating like mad in the unaccustomed heat, we needed to sit down, calm down, and gulp down a cold beer.

Drinking bars in Georgetown were strange places, completely devoid of furniture, with stout metal grilles from behind which the barman would slide you a drink through a tiny opening, watched over by a shotgun toting protector. There were several men in the bar, propped up against the walls; they watched in silence as we crossed the room and ordered two beers. 'Money first!' snapped the barman. Martin paid and two bottles were slid under the grille. Conversation in the room resumed but the atmosphere was unpleasant.

'Drink up, Tan, and let's get out of here,' Martin said, draining his beer. A man lurched over to us. He had yellow eyes and breath that stank of rum.

'Americans?'

'No, English,' Martin answered.

'Ah, British,' he sighed. 'I am very fond of the British, I worked for the British when this country was British Guyana, they are good people. Two beers for these British people,' he called to the barman, slapping a note on the counter.

'Oh, no thanks, we really must be going,' said Martin.

'Why?' he demanded. 'You too proud to drink with me?'

'No, no of course not.' Martin shot me a look; trouble. The man passed us the beers and picked up a tumbler of rum from the counter, tossing half the contents down his throat in one go.

'The British,' he continued, 'this country was rich under the British but since they gone it get poorer, why you think that so?' Slurp, down went the rest of the rum. 'We are independent now, In–De–Pen–DENT, and the British are rich, the British are rich with Guyana's money, they don't leave us nothing. People in Guyana don't like the British, you see why?' He raised his left hand; he was holding a piece of wood and he tapped it against the bar; one end was driven through with half a dozen six inch nails. 'But I like the British, I proud to drink with you.' He cleared his throat and spat a glob of phlegm at Martin's feet. He was dangerously drunk. Martin pulled a note from his pocket.

'Let us buy you a drink?' he said pushing the note into the man's hand. Momentarily distracted the man turned and leant against the bar.

'Run, Tan!' ordered Martin, pushing me towards the door. Run? With seventy pounds on my back it was all I could do to walk, but fear is a great driver and I scuttled out and was off down the road like a stampeding elephant with Martin close on my heels. Back on the main street a beggar asked for money but when Martin offered some he demanded more, hobbling crookedly after us shouting, 'White shit, White shit.'

Dusk was falling when we found a boarding house. Mrs King, the owner, was a kindly, well-intentioned old lady who constantly harangued her guests on the folly of wandering Georgetown after dark. Criminal fashions change frequently and the latest, she told us, was 'choke and rob', a particularly unpleasant way of relieving the unwary of money and goods by semi-strangulation. Taxis were not to be trusted as a villainous driver could take you out to the lonely bush, rob and dump you there. A permit was required to travel to the interior and we, as foreigners, would probably not be granted one. Her list went on and on. No, it was not the place for us. We had very little money and our one, rather vague ambition was to spend some time in the 'jungle', a word which conjured up kaleidoscopic mental images of an environment I'd read about and pictured in my mind as we'd planned this trip.

With no road link to either Venezuela or Brazil and no money to spare for air fares, we decided to travel overland to Surinam. We rode the train out of Georgetown. With a will of its own it wobbled along at jog-trot speed, slowing its pace occasionally so that people could alight without risking life and limb, but never actually stopping at stations.

The countryside was dotted with villages of dilapidated wooden shacks with rusty tin roofs. These dwellings were raised several feet above the ground on stout poles. This being the rainy season the land beneath was flooded and though only inches deep, the clear reflections in the unrippled surface gave the illusion that the villages were planted in wide lakes. At this time of year, fish leave the main waterways for the flooded countryside and children sat with fishing lines trailing from windows and verandahs.

At the end of the track we tagged on to a queue of more than fifty people, countless chickens, birds in cages and piles of sacks, boxes and bags, all to be crammed into a single-decker bus. Our rucksacks joined a mountain of luggage on the sagging roof rack and we were driven at lunatic speed along narrow dirt roads with pigs, hens, goats, dogs and children scattering in panic as we roared along, horn blaring. The road follows the coast through a narrow strip of well-populated country between the coastal swamp and the immense forests of the Guyana Highlands. For considerable distances there was no public transport and private motorists provided a cheap, unofficial taxi service, squeezing as many as ten people and their luggage into a vehicle designed to carry five. The atmosphere was friendlier outside Georgetown and we felt far less threatened.

At Springlands Skeldon, a small port on the Corantijne river, we boarded the ferry for Surinam. Twelve hours later, after a plague of mechanical breakdowns, it docked at a wooden jetty below a huddle of white-painted, tin-roofed buildings. The tide was out, the river low, and we had to 'walk the plank', a board fifteen feet long, tied at an incline between boat and jetty, shifting unpredictably as the boat bobbed in the swell. Way below the plank was the soft brown mud of the river bed; anyone unlucky enough to fall in would surely disappear, like a spoon dropped into custard.

It was comforting to see that the other passengers were as nervous as we were, though as the only foreigners we attracted most attention, hardly surprising as we looked quite ridiculous. Before leaving England we'd formed the peculiar notion that our normal clothes would be unacceptable in South America. Tight jeans and tee shirts were out. Instead we wore huge, baggy, sludge-coloured trousers and big, ugly leather sandals. (Among my wardrobe was a pair of culottes that came well below my knees and were guaranteed to be sexually unprovocative.) We both wore men's shirts. Huge old rucksacks, each with pots, pans and sleeping bags tied on at rakish angles ensured that our ensemble did not go unnoticed.

Passengers crossed the plank in all manner of ways: on their behinds, on hands and knees. One cocky young man out to impress the girls strolled out, hands casually in pockets, whistling nonchalantly till a sudden movement had him down on his knees, eyes rolling with fear and all composure gone. Last as usual, we wobbled across, acutely aware that the seventy pounds on our backs would hasten our demise if we fell. When it was apparent that neither of us would plunge obligingly into the mud, everybody grabbed their belongings for a mad dash to the customs shed. The search was ruthless. All food was confiscated. Bags and baskets were turned upside down to reveal bananas, bread, pickles, vegetables and chunks of dried meat and fish. A burly Chinaman in khaki shorts gathered up everything in a canvas sheet and hurled it unrelentingly into the river, oblivious to all protestations. Our only problem came at Immigration when having explained to the officer that we were backpacking, he declared with a beaming smile, 'Ah ha, so you are hijackers.'

The town of Nieuw Nickerie looked little different from a Guyanese town, steep-roofed wooden houses with the same verandahs and balconies, Chinese shops on street corners, but the place had a different feel: people seemed more relaxed and shops didn't have grilles over the counters or bars across the windows. Here our cautious entry into a café was greeted with friendly curiosity and within minutes, a steaming plate of spicy fried chicken and rice was placed before us and a bottle of 'Parbo', the potent local beer, was presented 'on the house'.

Feverish from over two hundred mosquito bites I had collected along the way and suffering from a dreadful cold, I needed to rest up for a day or two. Martin made enquiries about a room and before we knew it, a middle-aged Asian-looking man seated himself at our table, introduced himself as Denny and explained in broken English that his friend had a guest house, and what's more, he would take us there on his motorbike. I was happy to stay at the café, cooling my fever with the beer and let Martin sort it out.

Leaving Tanis to drown her sorrows and scratch her bites, I climbed on the back of the bike. Surinam's towns are laid out with mathematical precision in rectangular blocks, all roads ruler straight and every turn a right angle. Several lefts and rights later I'd lost track of the route and was reduced to searching for conspicuous landmarks. Finally we stopped outside a three storey house where I was introduced to a Chinese man who would provide us with a room for an absurdly small fee. We shook hands and he produced a bottle of rum which we sat and consumed between us, thus finalizing the deal. The inscrutable Chinese man stood swaying slightly on the verandah. In an alcoholic haze, Denny and I floated down the stairs and in a muddle of arms and legs settled ourselves on the motorbike.

Weaving from side to side of the road, Denny drove so near to a group of pedestrians that I accidentally kicked a girl with my outstretched leg, evoking cries of anger from her and a wild increase in speed from Denny. We reached the café in a state of mild euphoria. After a lot of hand shaking and shoulder slapping and a few more beers, Denny went back to work. It was the hottest part of the day. I lay on a bench outside the café in the shade of a giant silk-cotton tree and promptly fell asleep.

Thump. Thump. Thump.

I awoke with head pounding and lungs playing a medley of accordian tunes. As on a hundred other occasions I vowed never again to drink to excess and to quit smoking that very day.

I lit a cigarette. 'Come on, Tan, let's go to this guest house.' Knowing it was all of two miles away I was wondering whether I would be able to find it. Wearily we trudged along. Half an hour later, worries ceased when I recognised the house and gratefully climbed the stairway. Entering a large room we dumped our baggage on the floor. There were now six Chinese men sitting cross-legged in a circle on the floor playing cards. They glanced at us for a few moments when we entered then returned to their game. It seemed impolite to interrupt them, particularly as I couldn't quite remember which was the man I'd met earlier.

After sitting on our bags for half an hour getting more tired and tetchy we began grumbling loudly to each other; after all, we only wanted to be shown to our room, cheap or not it was the least we could expect. Eventually the game ended, the men rose and five of them left, nodding politely to us as they passed. Ah, the remaining man must be the landlord, I was sure I recognised him now. He spoke to us but we didn't understand. I attempted to mime that we wanted our room, we needed to sleep. A vacant look appeared in his eyes. I reminded him of our earlier meeting, elaborately pouring imaginary rum down my throat and staggering drunkenly. He stood there looking more glassy-eyed. If he didn't remember me he must remember Denny? Feeling a bit foolish I imitated a motorbike revving up, holding the handlebars firmly. At this he took a step back as if he thought I might run him over.

'This is ridiculous,' I said to Tanis, 'I drank rum with this man, I sat in this room in that chair with . . .'

'Hold on,' she interrupted looking round, 'what chair?'

There were no chairs in the room, there wasn't anything in the room. As the truth dawned I squirmed with embarrassment. This was a private house. My attempts to explain only seemed to convince him that he was in the company of a madman, and one with an hysterical wife to boot. We fled down the stairs leaving him gazing thoughtfully after us.

In the days that followed we headed east. Because of the rains, some roads were impassable and public transport had taken to the rivers and canals. So it was that one morning we sat beneath a thatched shelter with a large number of men, women and children, all waiting for a boat to carry us onwards. Tethered to a pole among the passengers was a dangerous pig, which lunged threateningly at anybody who went near it: anyone that is, except a lady in a red cotton frock who owned the animal. It nuzzled her legs affectionately when she spoke to it.

After five hours the boat arrived, a large dugout canoe with an engine on the back and a canopy over the top. The instant that the canoe touched the bank the placid, well-mannered group of travellers, who had waited so long and so patiently without complaint, suddenly broke loose in a crazed scramble down the muddy bank. Casualties were ignored and stepped upon. Excited by the commotion, the pig panicked and rushed towards the river, jerking hard on the rope, which broke. The pig, unable to stop, slid on its back and descended squealing into the water, disappearing beneath the surface, closely followed by a splash of red as its owner, desperately trying to save it, overbalanced and hit the water in a belly flop. As usual we were last on, failed to get a seat beneath the canopy and for the next few hours were forced to burn in the fierce afternoon heat.

Before leaving Guyana we had studied a map and chosen, by name alone, a place in Surinam where mail from England could be sent. We selected a town called Totness; a nice familiar name. Three weeks after choosing the place we got off a bus on a dusty road with ramshackle dwellings on one side and coconut palms on the other. A wonky, handpainted board announced 'Totness'. It didn't seem the sort of place that would have a pillar box, let alone a post office. Setting off in search of a human being we came upon a group of men who sat in the shade of a mango tree, playing cards and drinking beer, a combination of activities we'd come to regard as the national pastime. They looked up in surprise as we approached. A plump, elderly man stood up. He spoke English well, despite being so drunk that he swayed alarmingly, lurching forward and grabbing me to avoid falling down. But his wits were in far better shape than his sense of balance and he astonished us by asking, 'You are Mister and Missis Jordan from London, England?'

It transpired that he wasn't psychic; he was the postmaster and had received some letters for us and had been wondering when we'd turn up to collect them. He was delighted to meet two people from the Kingdom of Great United Britain. 'English is taught in schools in Surinam,' he explained, 'and we know much about the Great British Bobby.' The Great British Bobby apparently has no need of a gun due to his skill with the truncheon, a wooden club he can hurl with deadly accuracy a distance of one hundred and fifty feet to bring down a criminal, rather in the way Australian tribesmen use boomerangs. The bobby wears a tall helmet beneath which he keeps his spare truncheon.

As it was Sunday we would have to wait until Monday for our mail but the postmaster suggested we go for a swim in the local pool while he fixed us a room at the hotel. It seemed amazing that this tiny hamlet should have a swimming pool but sure enough, just outside town was a white-tiled open air pool with diving boards and brightly painted changing huts all within a wire enclosure. There were no people to be seen and we gratefully shed our clothes for a dip. Sitting on the edge with our legs dangling, we gazed into water so black that we couldn't see the bottom, the surface as smooth as glass. Just as we were daring each other to jump in, a ripple spread from the far end towards us and a fish three feet long appeared from the depths and hung beneath the surface, gawping at us before sinking away out of sight.

Back in town, tired and still dusty, we headed for a tall dilapidated wooden building we were told was the hotel. The ground floor windows were boarded up giving the place a derelict air, but Nathan, the proprietor, who'd been alerted by the postmaster, welcomed us warmly. His best double room was a pound. As only the cheapest hotels fitted our budget we no longer expected much, but nothing had prepared us for Nathan's establishment.

Dragging our rucksacks behind us, we followed him up three flights of rickety stairs, the air getting hotter and hotter, like climbing up a chimney, until we reached the very top of the building where he unlocked a door. It creaked open to reveal a scene straight out of a Dracula movie. Through the shutter slats a dim light fell on several inches of grime. The floor was covered with bat droppings and cigarette stubs. Heavy black cobwebs draped the walls and ceiling. The air was thick with the odour of decay. Throwing open the shutters did little to improve the room; if anything it looked worse. Shreds of mosquito netting hung sadly at the window promising an itchy night. Only the cobwebs were holding the cracked plaster on the walls; Nathan was lucky to have such industrious spiders. There was an ancient double bed, with a rumpled stained sheet half covering a mattress with something resembling horsehair bulging out of its holes. A three legged chair comprised the 'fittings'. Martin switched on the light but nothing happened.

Nathan was charming though, and so pleased to have guests that we tried to hide our dismay as he bustled around the room flicking dead cockroaches off the bed, smiling happily as the dried carapaces hit the walls like bullets. After satisfying himself that all was in order he shuffled down the stairs to return minutes later with a bottle of cold beer and two glasses on a tray, handing it to us with the flourish of an efficient host.

The bathroom was downstairs on the second floor. An open shower stall, a cracked basin without taps but with a mirror above it, so old that most of the silver had worn off. I peered dispassionately at my reflection, a dirty-faced hobgoblin stared back. Was that me? Though the toilet had no seat at least it flushed. Beside it was the obligatory receptacle for used paper. South American plumbing is often dreadful and the system cannot cope with paper – particularly the large amounts that foreigners seem to need. Sometimes the bin is absent and fear of being held responsible for blocking the hotel's drains can present an uncomfortable dilemma. The bin in Nathan's bathroom was full to overflowing.

Lying on the plank floor was a dead moth, emerald green and white with a wingspan of six inches. It looked like a thing made from coloured paper, an invention by an imaginative child. Looking closer, I noticed a trail of tiny ants was busy dragging it slowly and jerkily across the boards towards a hole in the wall. On the ceiling a lizard crept about upside-down catching insects. Two bright green frogs sat on the wall. I watched them all with fascination as I showered. Such commonplace things as frogs, lizards and giant moths in bathrooms were still a novelty to me with my limited experience of tropical South America.

Back in the attic while Martin showered, I unpacked as few essentials as possible and began a letter home. By seven o'clock it was too dark to write and not daring to light a candle in this tinderbox, we lay on the mosquito-net-less bed in the stifling heat and eventually dozed off.

Dreaming of clean sheets and cool English nights we were rudely awoken by a loud, insistent hammering on the door. 'Christ Almighty, what's happening?' muttered Martin, slipping into reality. Bang, bang.

'Wake up, Mister,' called Nathan.

'Yes, what is it?'

'Fire, Mister, fire!' came the electrifying reply.

Simultaneously we leapt from the bed, me to grab our belongings and stuff them into our rucksacks, Martin frantically to wrestle with the rusty door lock. We were thirty feet above the ground in a house made of wood beneath a tin roof.

'Fire, Sir,' repeated Nathan.

Oh my God!

His courage and integrity was admirable; he was, after all, risking his life to save us. Just as I was about to hurl our bags out of the window Martin threw open the door. 'Here is your fire, Sir.' Nathan said, staring in astonishment at Martin's nakedness. An equally astonished Martin accepted the light bulb he proffered.

CHAPTER THREE

On Monday, with long dawn shadows sliding imperceptibly towards the postmaster's house, Martin and I solemnly awaited the opening ceremony. In Surinam even ordinary, everyday acts are conducted with some formality. The postmaster appeared. Gone were the ragged shorts and canvas sneakers of the weekend, he was resplendent in a blue uniform with perfectly pressed trousers, peaked cap with badge, and shiny black shoes. After closely examining our passports and confirming our signatures he handed us three letters. Formalities over, he produced a bottle of rum and we drank a toast to the Great British Bobby.

The bus was loaded with parcels, boxes and sacks of mail. Ramajam the driver, a serene and considerate man, had kindly squeezed ten passengers in as well and they obligingly shuffled us along to a seat at the back. Soon we realised why; Ramajam's personality underwent a metamorphosis the moment he sat behind the steering wheel, his shoulders hunched, his eyes squinted in a maniacal glare, one hand hit the horn, the accelerator hit the floor and the old van was transformed into his getaway car and it was us in the back he was escaping from. He bounced over potholes at such speed that Martin hit the ceiling, cutting his head open. Ramajam was apologetic but was clearly far more worried about the luggage that had fallen off the roof rack.

The pounding headaches we endured for the rest of the ride receded as we arrived in the capital, Paramaribo. Ramajam stood on the brakes and the bus slammed to a stop. Like a man emerging from a trance he turned to us and inquired politely, 'Why-ica?'

'Why what?' we asked, puzzled.

'Why-ica, oo wani go why-ica?' he repeated, raising his eyebrows and nodding his head as if to force some understanding into us. We shrugged helplessly, we couldn't even make out what language he was speaking let alone what he might mean. With a good humoured grunt of exasperation he drove through the busy streets and pulled up outside a three-storied wooden house. 'Why-ica,' he said, and disappeared inside the building returning minutes later accompanied by a tall, bespectacled lady who spoke English. 'Why-ica', she explained, was the local name for YWCA (Young Women's Christian Association) guesthouse, but it was neither necessary to be female nor Christian to stay there.

Our explorations started with the town. On the waterfront we watched the muddy Surinam River swirling towards the Atlantic, accelerated by a falling tide. An iron ferryboat with hundreds of passengers bobbed past the rusting hull of an enormous ship that stuck out of the water like a dead whale. 'A German battleship' we were told, 'abandoned at the end of the war.' Vultures strutted by the river but the streets were full of familiar pigeons, seeming almost as out of place as vultures would have done in Trafalgar Square. The three-hundred-year-old city of Paramaribo has its share of ugly modern concrete and brick, but many areas have wide avenues lined by ancient mahogany trees and magnificent timber houses from an earlier period. Elsewhere, in the poorer districts, badly constructed barn-like buildings lean so daringly over the sidewalk that it feels perilous to walk beneath them. The ubiquitous Chinese shops stand on every corner.

As we came closer to the market, the din of traffic and people was fast becoming dominated by that of music, a blaring cacophony of American Soul, Asian classic, Asian pop and a sprinkling of Latin Samba. 'It's a mini-bus rally,' said Martin as we entered a square where scores of vehicles were parked, all painted in garish, multi-coloured designs. 'Or is it a Carnival?' as he absorbed the scene. It was a 'wildbus' terminus. Privately owned vans, each with an elaborate speaker system playing music at deafening volume, were waiting to fill with passengers to be transported here, there and everywhere.

The racial diversity of the people in Paramaribo was astonishing: Chinese, Indonesians, East Indians, Amerindians, Creoles and Europeans. There were men with turbans, men with pigtails, tall Africans and tiny Orientals, ladies wrapped from head to toe in patterned silks smoking roll-up cigarettes, portly pipe-smoking women in wide hats and long cotton frocks, young people with Afro hairstyles and trousers made from brilliantly coloured Crimplene. Bushnegroes from villages in the interior selling intricately carved wooden artifacts, jostled confidently past the few glossy-haired, copper-skinned Amerindians who, by comparison, looked ill at ease in the bustle of the city streets. Dutch was the official language, but most people spoke Taki Taki, a pidgin dialect made up of English, Dutch and many other languages from around the world.

A man with a big tortoise under his arm pedalled by on a bicycle. A child pushed a dilapidated handcart, loaded to overflowing with watermelons. Two golden-skinned boys forced a way among the pedestrian throng carrying between them a catfish five feet long, and were shouted at by the elderly companion of an Asian girl who stared aghast at the slimy fish scales smeared across her red and silver sari. Street vendors sat in a line along the pavement behind piles of chilli peppers, aubergines, yams, paw-paws, pineapples, plaintains and bananas, neatly set out on clean linen cloths, shrieking as we clumsily tripped over their wares and almost squashed the day's profit. Along the kerb, stalls displayed spicy cooked meats, noodles and rice.

A row of wooden barrels were filled to the brim with pigs' tails in brine. A man with a fortune in gold teeth gave a glittering smile and, pointing at the barrels said, 'We eat the pigs' tails but who eat all them pigs?' Bursting into laughter he slapped Martin on the back repeating, 'Who eat all them pigs, eh?'

Following our noses we arrived at the fish market where

creatures from the deep were laid out on wooden tables. In addition to familiar looking fish, there were sharks, giant catfish and big-eyed monsters with needle sharp teeth, being gutted and despatched into the waiting barrels with the flick of a blade. The floor was slippery with blood, bones and scales. Scraggy cats shot out from under the stalls, swiping any flesh that dropped before it hit the ground, their turn of speed encouraged by the occasional missing paw or tail. It was a busy thriving place, but one that would give a health and safety officer nightmares.

At one o'clock in the afternoon, the shutters came down and the town went to sleep. Every shop, stall, bar and house closed up. The policewomen, deftly directing traffic at every cross-roads, pocketed their whistles and strolled away. People disappeared up stairways and down alleys until the streets echoed with emptiness. It seemed that while we were part of a sea of bodies, the fierce heat had been dissipated, but now, alone on the street with just a few sane-looking dogs about, the midday sun concentrated on us. We thought we'd burst from the heat as we searched for the YWCA. We couldn't even remember the name of the road it was in.

There were other European travellers at the YWCA, but one in particular should have stayed at home. Kurt was a frail, thirty-year-old German whose long dark hair had spiky patches on top where it was growing back after an outbreak of alopecia or a dispute with a local barber. He wore a sad expression, seldom smiled and when he spoke, averted his gaze and barely moved his lips. Kurt's adventures began in Mexico. Only days after setting off on his once-in-a-lifetime tour of the Americas, he was on a bus approaching the border of a Central American country when he discovered in his bag a carefully sealed package. Puzzled, he looked at it for a moment or two, then realisation dawned. Drugs, planted on him to take across the border. Without opening it he tossed it out of the window. Safe across the border in a crowded street, three burly men surrounded him. One snatched his bag and began rifling through it. They wanted the package and were about to discover it missing. Leaving his rucksack on the pavement and his bag in the hands of the villains, he ran for his life. Fortunately his documents and money were in his belt; he escaped but lost all his possessions. Philosophically, Kurt thought that at least he could continue his journey. He was still positive at this stage.

In Panama he was mugged and was in hospital for two days. 'One man kicked me in the tentacles!' he explained while we endeavoured to maintain suitable expressions of shock and sympathy.

In Colombia his hotel caught fire and he was trapped on a fourth-floor balcony with superheated plaster and ceramic tiles exploding off the walls behind him. Kurt's next ordeal was also by heat, in a cheap Venezuelan pension, while taking a shower. The water supply was linked to that of the toilets and during his shower somebody flushed the cistern. All cold water was temporarily diverted and Kurt, scalded by near boiling water, leapt forward and cracked his head on the tiled wall. Four stitches and hospital treatment for concussion were required to put him right.

His catalogue of disasters was endless. Indeed he was travelling on compensation money received after a vehicle had run over his hand. Somehow he'd managed to get through Guyana unscathed. Or thought he had until a few days after arriving in Surinam, when the symptoms of a strange disease were manifested. 'But I'm over that now,' he assured us, 'the spots have gone and my hair is coming back.' Kurt wanted us to go and eat with him. For our own safety we politely declined. It was clear that we'd all be poisoned, the ceiling would collapse, or the restaurant's kitchen blow up.

It was time to make plans, our money was dwindling fast and we couldn't afford to stay at the YWCA indefinitely. As part of a government project to promote tourism, cheap trips were being offered to a place called Stoelmanseiland, an island on the Marowijne river deep in the jungle interior. 'This is the land of the Bushnegro people; Africans whose ancestors escaped from slavery to European Colonists, and established themselves in the forests of South America alongside the indigenous Amerindians,' the blurb read. 'Here they live today, many thousands of tribal people in villages by the rivers.' Just as Kwisi had told us. It was the chance we'd been looking for, to get away from the modern world.

In the airline office a tall Afro-Chinese man called Horty de Bruin seated us before his desk. Stoelmanseiland was a wonderful place, he informed us enthusiastically, there was a five day tour with full board at the Government guest house included. It was not only way out of our price range, but we'd hoped to camp there for some weeks. Our spirits fell. He regarded us with curiosity as we feverishly calculated our finances on a scrap of paper: even if we slept in the street and ate only twice a week we couldn't afford to go. 'I don't like to see you sad, I try to help you,' Horty pronounced. 'You are people who like to look to the animals and flowers of the jungle yes?' Yes.

'How you think to sleep there?' We explained that we had a tent.

'Ho K, wait here.' He entered another office and a voluble discussion ensued. He came back smiling. 'Ho K. I explain that you are people who look to the animals, not like other tourists. I tell them you will go home and tell about the animals and flowers in Surinam, so that more peoples will come to see them, so Ho K, they say you can go. What I do for you is give a ticket to go one way only to Stoelmanseiland, you live in the little house but you must carry all food you eat with you. It is very cheap. This I think will make you happy.' It did.

With a week to kill before our flight the idea of camping on the coast appealed to us. Golden, palm-fringed beaches, clear blue sky, nights under the stars, a tropical paradise no less. Marked on our map, a few miles from the city, was a road leading to the ocean.

Rucksacks loaded with provisions, we boarded a wildbus, a beaten-up Volkswagen van with a pair of fiendishly glaring eyes painted on the front, called 'Tiger Express'. I was lucky to get a window seat for within minutes the vehicle was filled to overflowing; at least we had an oxygen supply. The heat and discomfort of the journey became almost intolerable. I couldn't get my hand to my pocket for a handkerchief to wipe my dripping face, pinned as I was beneath a grossly fat woman whose folds of flesh completely obliterated Tanis. She sat between us, overlapping, arms folded across her vast bosom and methodically scratched away at my chest. If I wriggled or twisted she would stop for a while, then idly start scratching again. I studied her closely. Her face, only inches away from mine, gave no clue to her motives. I wondered if this was some kind of sexual advance or if, being so large, she automatically assumed that any flesh within scratching reach belonged to her.

An Amerindian family sat opposite. The man wore faded blue dungarees and his hair hung down in two long plaits. The woman had hooked her dress off one shoulder so that their child could suckle her breast. The man called to the driver, the bus skidded to a halt and for several seconds was completely enveloped in a cloud of red bauxite dust. When it settled I could see no sign of habitation, only trees and bushes. The family disembarked, the man in front holding a machete, the woman several paces behind carrying the child, pots and pans, baskets and sacks. They disappeared among the leaves with no visible trail to show where they had gone.

Soon I was unable to bear the stifling heat any longer. I forced the window open wide and, braving the dust, stuck my head out. Precisely at that moment, a man in the front opened his window, put his head out and vomited. To the amusement of the other passengers the stream of fluid hit me full in the face.

The driver let us off beside a straight dirt track with a canal on one side which led into the bush. Our relief at being in the fresh air was tempered by the loneliness of our surroundings as we strode along the path towards the sea. After twenty minutes we collapsed in a heap. The track now ran along the top of an artificial earth embankment, fifteen feet above the canal. The jungle bordering the track had been only a hundred yards wide and we'd soon emerged onto a featureless plain where we sat making the best use we could of the meagre shade cast by a bush. On the horizon lay a dark band of vegetation and that, we hoped, was the coconut palms above our beach of golden sand.

Something was coming along the track from the direction of the road. Fifteen minutes later it trundled alongside, a cart with wooden wheels, piled high with sugar cane and pulled by a great brown ox. The driver was Indonesian, slim and barefoot, wearing only a pair of baggy trousers rolled to his knees and sporting a moustache which hung almost to his chin and curled at the ends. A woman, also barefoot, was swathed in brightly patterned silk and behind her hid four children aged between four and eight. The couple stood smiling at us saying nothing, the woman taking the opportunity to roll a cigarette. The man indicated that we could load our rucksacks onto the cart. With no common language we observed a friendly silence. The smallest child took hold of my finger and trotted along beside me, too shy to permit any exchange of glances but examining me intently when he thought I wasn't looking. A flock of white ibis rose from a bush ahead of us and settled a hundred feet further on. A black snake glided through the water of the canal below. A gentle breeze brought the smell of the ocean.

The trees we had seen earlier in the distance were not coconut palms but a rather sinister swamp forest. The man pointed to his house, half hidden among the trees, its new tin roof glinting in the sunshine. We shook hands with each of them and continued onward to the sea. On either side were trees with white trunks and dark green shiny leaves and ahead was the ocean. We emerged from the confines of the forest as abruptly as from a tunnel. The beach was an endless expanse of brown mud. On the shore, brown, muddy waves rolled over and collapsed with a hollow booming sound. It was the most desolate and hostile place we had ever seen. 'Blackpool,' said Tanis, but she wasn't laughing.

The mud at our feet was cracked into irregular slabs, like crazy-paving, but the crisp baked surface was fragile and we sank to our knees in brown goo when we stepped onto it. There was a fleeting impression of movement over the ground, as when a breeze moves a field of grass. Orderly holes in the mud, thousands of them, and in each lived a crab. As we'd approached, the crabs had ducked into their holes and now were cautiously reappearing; dull-red crustaceans with one normal sized claw and the other grotesquely oversized which they waved angrily in front of them. Fiddler crabs.

While we watched, mosquitoes settled all over us for a feed. A cloud of airborne soot arrived, microscopic flies which took up positions between the mosquitoes and punctured our skins like hot pin-pricks. The place was spectacular in its wildness but hardly resembled the coast we had imagined, and the idea of erecting a tent and sunbathing on the mud with crabs and insects, swimming in the soupy, and no doubt shark-infested sea, had us laughing hysterically at our ignorance of the country we were in.

Albina, Surinam.

Dear Mum and Dad,

Martin has just reminded me to ask you to keep all my letters, we might want to read them in years to come!

The trip to the coast was a disaster so we came here yesterday. This place is very small and is a trading post for all the Indians and Djukas up and down the river. (Djukas are one tribe of Bushnegroes, there are five altogether, Djukas wear their hair high at the front and cut to a point like a peak.) If you look on the map Albina is in the east, on the Marowijne river. On the opposite bank is St Laurent, the old French prison. That side of the river is French Guiana.

We travelled here on a wildbus, with two ferries in between. There were two American men on the bus who've come here to hunt (ugh), cowboy hats, the lot! They wanted to get a Djuka boatman to take them up by river but the price is too high. They suggested we go with them and split it four ways but we couldn't afford anything like that. Now they've gone downriver hoping to hunt with the Indians.

We are staying in a hotel which is owned by a Dutch lady who is a bit odd, if I say she reminds me of Bette Davis in Whatever Happened to Baby Jane *you might get the idea. Long bleached curly hair with a little bow on top, and thick doll-like make-up. She also seems to have sleeping sickness.*

The other day while waiting for a boat and drinking a Parbo beer, a guy came up and started to talk to us about politics. He spoke very good English and it was only when he explained that he was elected Prime Minister but hadn't bothered to turn up that we tumbled. It was he who told President Nixon to get the troops out of Vietnam and on Saturday, he's going to rule the world. It was really difficult to keep a straight face.

When we got on the boat we sat next to a woman who scratched constantly at black rings all over her body, I'm glad we had all our jabs. Martin has gone out this morning to find somewhere to camp while I pack. Three policemen just knocked at the door. They pointed to the window, they wanted to go out onto the roof. Once inside though, they were far more interested in the contents of the rucksacks and thought it very funny when I actually picked one up and carried it. It gets a bit easier every day – or I get stronger. It weighs over half a hundredweight.

I posted the last two letters together, it costs a fortune in stamps as they're so heavy. My cold is going now and I am beating the mosquitoes. I cover myself in thick insect repellent which gets incredibly uncomfortable and gooey when you sweat. Martin has been gone ages so I hope that doesn't mean we'll have to walk miles to get to a camp. We get up before six, it's too hot to stay in bed after that and we only eat once a day now, it's all we need (and can afford!). Martin has started smoking again.

I made the mistake of asking one of the Americans if he'd seen many spiders in the bush. He said no, but he found one as big as his hand upstairs. I suppose I'll just have to get used to it.

More later.

We are camped by the river after a terrible day yesterday. Our own fault though. We walked out of town along the river. After five minutes we had to take our shoes off as they rubbed blisters with the sweat and the fact that we hadn't worn them much. We walked barefoot for the rest of the way. At about noon we found a place to camp in a banana-tree plantation. It was very hot. By the time we'd made camp it was so hot that our clothes were wringing wet. After about an hour it was getting hotter and hotter and we were bitten to death by mosquitoes and the kabouria fly which brings up big red welts. I began to fear for our safety and sanity, thinking we'd collapse with heat exhaustion. So, we drank a pint of salt water which revived us a bit and decided the only thing to do was to go and lie in the river, three hundred yards away. We left all our gear as we couldn't have cared less about it at the time, and we're getting so sick of the weight of it, it might have been a blessing if someone had stolen it all! We rushed to the river, stripped off completely and just sat in the water for about an hour. It was marvellous. Later, there was a tremendous storm and we huddled in the tent. It was full of mosquitoes. I couldn't sleep, it was so hot and dark that I felt claustrophobic and had to light the torch.

This morning we moved into a Carib Indian village (there are three huts here) right on the river, so it's quite breezy. The Indians use hollowed out trees for boats with motors attached which are very fast. We get our water from the river which is very muddy but with sterilizing tablets it's drinkable. I remember Dad saying once that he didn't like the thought of the lack of toilet facilities abroad, there's none here at all, just the jungle, so you have to be careful not to sit on a snake or an ant's nest. Snakes don't seem to come into the villages (at least they haven't yet) but there are hundreds of little lizards about ten inches long. They come and investigate if you sit very still.

We had another big storm today, really strong wind then torrential rain which passed to leave sunshine again.

The domestic animals here are a real sorry lot. They scavenge mostly and are covered in terrible sores, with parasites and worms, etc. They don't seem to belong to anyone, just take up position outside someone's house and stay there. The houses are open thatched huts and the people are very friendly. The whole country seems very friendly and comfortable, everybody speaks to us if just to say good morning. By the way we now have two great machetes, long, curved sword things about two and a half foot long, which are essential for hacking away undergrowth. At first we felt a bit self-conscious walking around with swords but nobody takes any notice.

There are miniscule flies which buzz in our faces and hair but don't bite. It wouldn't do to be afraid of crawly things here, everything you touch is covered with insects of one sort or another.

Later.
Martin went into town yesterday and bought a pig's tail for dinner. It was a mistake. Apart from being too salty it was pure gristle. Today we walked in (two miles each way) and bought some eggs and tonight we'll have an omelette. I did some washing on a stone in the river, very effective but clothes wouldn't last long! We intend to go back to Paramaribo tomorrow to stock up for our trip to Stoelmanseiland.

Paramaribo.
We left Albina at seven this morning after getting up at five o'clock in the pouring rain and packing everything up wet. It was a good chance to wear our macs; they work very well and fit over the rucksacks as planned, we looked like two plastic camels coming down the road. We have found another biting insect, a large black fly with a hard shell whose bite really hurts and brings up itchy blisters. Martin caught a butterfly as big as the palm of his hand this morning, it was beautiful, brown and gold. There are some enormous things here, everything's bigger than we know it at home, ants and flies an inch long. We tried to catch some fish yesterday with Martin's string shirt but they all got away. We found centipedes, termites and a blue crab. The palm trees here are giants and so many different kinds. Pineapples and bananas seem to grow everywhere.

Later.
Have just got back from shopping. The market is a fantastic place. There are voodoo stalls where they'll make you a potion. They have lucky charms and hate charms and they'll put curses on things for you. All these little bottles of suspicious looking liquids, and old women like witches stirring them up! There is no dried food so we'll have to take tins with us. We're only allowed eleven kilos and our rucksacks weigh five empty! The first thing we did when we got back to town was have a long shower, we really stank from the river water. Lots of love,

T & M

CHAPTER FOUR

The crowns of jungle trees looked like cauliflowers as the little plane came into land. Carved out of the forest was a neat rectangular landing strip. Figures clustered along its edge and someone frantically pedalled a bicycle across the middle of it. 'This is the first place we've been to with no roads,' said Martin.

The plane bumped to a halt. The people were Bushnegroes, naked children and women with intricate scar designs on their faces and breasts and strips of material wrapped around their hips. Only one man was among them, an old fellow wearing a loincloth and carrying a handful of arrows. They stared with uninhibited curiosity as we disembarked from the twin-engined aircraft. To say we were surprised by the appearance of this assemblage is an understatement. For a while, I wondered if they'd been dressed up and put there for our benefit. Passengers fumbled in their bags for cameras, snapping away in a frenzy before the photographic Godsend disappeared back into the forest.

The island looked busier on the ground than it had from the air. There were plenty of people around, most wearing Western clothes but a few dressed like those at the airstrip. Their village stood by the river; a dozen wooden huts, extravagantly decorated with geometric paintings and roofed with thatch. There were other buildings, a white-walled hospital, a school and the unfinished guesthouse with its open-air bar. On the edge of the clearing stood the towering omnipresent forest, like a wall between us and another, more secret world. On the wide river, people were paddling dugout canoes.

Our party strolled into the guest house for their pre-lunch drink; we were directed to a tumbledown shelter, beneath which we could erect our tent. It was midday sun time but now we were not alone. One by one, villagers came to watch. It was in our favour that no one in the group had seen a tent before and so couldn't appreciate what a mess we were making of erecting it. I asked a youth to hold one corner and instantly dozens of willing hands came to our assistance. Everyone grabbed a bit of tent or a guy rope, and all pulled in different directions. Finally, the tent was up, lop-sided and sagging but its purpose was obvious, and people drifted away until only the children remained. We opened a tin of sardines and shared them around. Two of the children had six fingers.

'I wonder if we're allowed in the guest house?' Martin said, 'We look a bit scruffy.'

'I bet we can't afford their prices,' I said.

We sidled into the bar, hoping the manager wouldn't notice our crumpled, scruffy clothes. We bought drinks. Motionless on the wall was an orange spider. Martin's curiosity overcame him and we prodded it to see if it was real. It was, it bit him.

It was time for an afternoon siesta. With the fly-sheet over the top the tent was doubly insulated and three hours later we awoke, thick-headed, hardly able to breathe in a dark blue oven. Fighting each other to get out we cannoned from the front and staggered around in the blinding sunshine flapping our arms to cool down. The matinée was witnessed by a youth who introduced himself as August Anapai. He worked for the Anti-Malaria Campaign, based across the river and he'd paddled over to inspect the tent. In no mood to praise the joys of camping in the tropics, we asked how we could cross the river to explore the mainland. He offered to take us.

Next morning, August, Tanis and I paddled his canoe across the river and stepped from sunlight into the cool shade of real tropical rainforest. August carried a machete in one hand and a shotgun in the other. The gun had no stock and his cartridges were too large and had to be forced into the chamber. Tanis and I hastily agreed that if August decided to shoot something, we should throw ourselves on the ground and cover our heads.

Taking up positions behind August, we held our shiny new machetes in front of us and wondered what to do with them. With short deft strokes of the blade, our leader clipped away small branches that got in his way but when I attempted to copy him the branch sprang back and lashed me in the face. Tanis was worried about stepping on a snake and kept hopping about and bumping into me. Eventually she trod on a twisted, fallen branch and the end reared into the air – she sprang forward with a cry and plunged the sharp point of her machete into my bum. After that I insisted she walk ahead of me and thought ruefully that we weren't conducting ourselves in the manner of real jungle explorers.

An undisturbed tropical forest teems with creatures. Nowhere else is populated with such a diversity of living things but we felt deprived, on entering the forest for the first time, not to see furred and feathered fauna everywhere. Our impressions were of green gloom and dampness. Even the diffuse sunlight seemed green and damp. Straight spindly trees surrounded us, their crowns lost in the leafy canopy high above. Here and there stood trees of massive girth, often with wedge-like supports more than ten feet high around the base; these were plank buttresses, a common feature of tropical trees. Gazing towards the top of these giants, I couldn't see where the first branches emerged, such was the confusion of leaves and vines.

August followed a path which was almost invisible to us. This was one of those 'jungle trails' I'd read about but all I could see of it was an occasional cut in the bark of a tree. Subconsciously, I had been expecting a jungle trail to be like a well-trodden nature trail through a British National Park. August was walking quickly and making a lot of noise, jumping over fallen branches and pushing his way through bushes. We wondered why we were not proceeding with caution and looking for snakes? And where were the animals, the monkeys, tapirs and armadillos? After an hour the only forest dweller I'd seen was a small brown moth. Obviously we had a lot to learn about the jungle.

'Aha!' exclaimed August, '*nyang*,' pointing to a spiky palm tree. Food. Scattered around the base were scores of brown nuts the size of walnuts. Holding one against a tree trunk he cracked it open with his machete and removed a white object. Biting off half he handed the remaining piece to me and I popped it into my mouth. It was soft and sweet and melted like butter. 'You've just eaten a maggot,' observed Tanis. August was cracking them open one after another. They *were* grubs. Having enjoyed one without realising what it was, I helped myself to some more.

Seated on a half-rotted log to rest, we looked around. The forest was still, the quiet broken at intervals by bursts of distant sound, hoots and howls and shrieks and wails that made us tense-up during the intervening silences. August pointed to the ground near our feet. 'Tiger.'

Big cats are called tigers. Small ones tiger-cats. There, clear enough even for us to see was a footprint made by a very large cat. It was an exciting moment. It was a real jungle we were in, a jungle where wild animals roamed. Only recently a jaguar had walked past the very log on which we sat, a fact so unremarkable to August that he virtually dismissed it as being of no consequence.

Our faith in August as a man who knew the South American jungle like we knew Epping Forest, was rudely shattered when he stopped, turned to face us and said. 'We loss, Mister!' I'd read about people getting lost in the jungle and had gathered the impression that it ranked in seriousness along with being lost in the desert, or at sea. There was no sign of the sun to give us direction; the ground was flat with no gradient to walk down in the hope of finding a stream at the bottom. Mentally I handed over all responsibility to August. It was quite pointless for Tanis or me to start making suggestions, we would only confuse matters.

For the next three hours we sweated through the forest, first in one direction, then retracing our steps to go in another. August paused for a moment and I took this opportunity to roll a cigarette, but before I could light it he stopped me, explaining that deep in the forest live Indians who would smell the smoke from a great distance and come looking for us. So clever were these people that they could chop down trees with their bare hands and if an Indian thought you'd spotted him among the foliage, like magic, he would disappear. I pocketed the tobacco.

There did seem to be some system in our search and eventually August gave a triumphant shout and pointed to a knife-cut in the bark of a tree. He had found the trail. Safe now, we laughed and joked. August seemed as relieved as we were and told us about his uncle who had lived his entire life in the region but had gone hunting one day and become lost.

'What happened to him?' I asked. August shrugged his shoulders. 'Do you mean he never came back?'

'No,' replied August. 'Him never come back. Him loss.'

Our first jungle experience had primed us for more. My mind was full of images of plants with big shiny leaves in lurid, unnatural-looking hues of green; plants that looked as if they were made of plastic. Although we hadn't seen a single mammal, we had seen blue morpho butterflies. Few things can be more breathtakingly beautiful than a morpho in flight, its wings radiating a blue as intense as stained glass with sunlight shining through. The delight of that first vision fixed a picture in my mind that will stay for ever.

Just as we'd emerged from the forest there was a noise near my left ear, a noise I'd heard before, without seeing what produced it, something between a buzz and a whirr. The tiny creature hovered two feet from my face inspecting me, wings a blurr but body stationary and glinting in the sunlight like a multicoloured jewel. With incredible rapidity it moved from one station to another; left, right, up, down, then it was gone, so quickly I didn't see which way it went. I'd discovered why humming birds are called humming birds, it's the sound their wings make. Humming birds dance in the air pretending to be insects. They make you fall in love with South America.

Once we had been introduced to the jungle, life on Stoelman-seiland became a little constricting. Within a day or two we had explored the island. There were very few places to walk, and our days were spent sitting by the river or wandering to the villages and chatting to people, improving our Taki Taki.

Martin was content, but gradually, the enforced idleness made me listless and lethargic. I began to wake in the mornings feeling unhappy and my stomach would knot at the thought of the long day ahead. Martin was quite happy to spend long periods sitting dreaming or sketching; he couldn't understand my despondency and urged me to write up my diary, but there was nothing new to say. I knew I was a misery but I couldn't help it.

One morning, lazing in my sleeping bag sipping a mug of the thick, grouty liquid we called morning coffee, listening to Martin preparing breakfast (porridge with water and one spoon of sugar), I remembered that the second group of tourists were leaving that day. We had shared beers with them the night before. In a few days they would be back in their respective countries, reunited with their families, while we were to stay here for weeks and weeks, stuck on an island in the middle of nowhere. Waves of homesickness washed over me. What was I doing here? I wanted to go home. I longed for our flat, to be cooking meals, hoovering, washing up, going shopping, all the ordinary things of my life at home. Mostly, I didn't want to be here. Suddenly I hated the jungle; hated the inactivity of wandering around the island all day, making chores like washing clothes last as long as possible for something to do. Why had I let Martin drag me out here? It was completely irrational, I'd been as keen as him to come, but I hadn't expected to be homesick and now that I was, I couldn't, or wouldn't control it. Tears streamed down my face and I felt sorry for myself. The tent flat opened and Martin's head appeared in the doorway. 'Breakfast's ready.' He was cheerful. I snuffled loudly. 'What's the matter, Tan?' concerned now, 'you're not ill are you?'

If homesickness could be classed as illness then I was, I wanted sympathy and attention. Martin put his arm round my shoulders, lifted me up and handed me his handkerchief. 'Ah, Tan, you poor little thing, what's wrong?' Blowing my nose and wiping my eyes I told him.

'I ... *sniff*, I'm homesick, *sniff*, ... I want to *sniff*, go home,' I snivelled.

'Oh, is that all?' he said relieved, dropping me with a bump. 'I thought you were ill. Come on, come and eat your porridge, you can have some extra sugar to cheer you up.'

At first it appeared that the majority of Bushnegroes went about their day-to-day business of fishing, hunting, farming and boat-building in much the same way as before the twentieth century ventured up their river, but soon it became clear that their lifestyle was changing, rapidly and profoundly. Many of the canoes were now propelled by outboard motor engines making long journeys easier. They had acquired the mixed benefits of modern medicine, tinned food, pop music and money. Young men went to the coastal regions to work on construction projects; with their earnings they could buy outboards, guns and transistor radios. Many of them settled in the towns. The ancient, tribal way of life which had successfully withstood the trauma of a violent upheaval from the forests of West Africa to the forests of South America, was defenceless against the temptations of a modern world.

I was inside the tent washing the groundsheet when I heard voices outside. 'Excuse me, mister.' I peeped out to see a young man shaking hands with Martin. He was dressed like a man from town, but he wore the high-topped hairstyle of a Bushnegro. Smiling self-consciously he shifted his weight from one leg to the other.

'My name is Rainier,' he said. Like August, he worked for the Anti-Malaria Campaign and explained how teams of employees travelled to remote villages, distributing sacks of salt laced with medicines and spraying dwellings with insecticides, part of a project designed to eradicate malaria and other diseases transmitted by mosquitoes. 'The boss say he fix it for you to go with us, you can bring the little house with you.' We piled everything into Rainier's boat, homesickness fading at the prospect of useful activity. The boss insisted we should erect the tent in a prominent place where everyone passing on the river would see it.

Packed into two canoes along with sacks, boxes, gasoline drums and an extraordinary assortment of shotguns, we motored up the Tapanahoni river. Fifteen in number, the crew were cheerful and boisterous, having Tanis and mé along was a novelty. The boats were powered by thirty-five horse-power outboard engines and cut through the water at high speed, motoring through rocky fast-flowing stretches without stopping, passing settlements in riverbank clearings where people waved to us.

Several hours later we arrived at a village of about thirty huts. A small crowd gathered on the beach to observe us; women naked to the waist in wraparound skirts, men in loin cloths. In the centre of the village, looking bigger in isolation than if it had been surrounded by forest, stood a mighty tree more than a hundred and fifty feet high with buttress roots ten feet tall. The long tapering trunk stretched eighty feet before the first branch emerged. These trees, called 'kan-kan' by the Bushnegroes, have religious significance. The site for a village might be selected for the existence of just such a tree. Beneath this one was a sacred shrine – a miniature hut on stilts, a wooden frame with cloth draped over it and a number of beer bottles planted in the earth.

Rainier explained that the pre-arranged purpose of our visit was to collect blood samples. These villagers had not given blood before and were a little suspicious of the idea. Wading through the shallow water, we heaved the canoes onto the sand. Like everybody else, Tanis and I were barefoot and were breaking one of the commandments in our jungle survival handbook: 'Always wear adequate footwear, especially in native villages'. The author obviously attached a great deal of importance to this, because he'd put it between instructions on how to make a tent out of your parachute and the rule in capital letters which said, LEAVE THE NATIVE WOMEN ALONE. As we were already into the habit of eating fresh fruit and swimming in rivers – both forbidden activities – we felt a lot more confident about breaking rules.

I stepped from wet sand onto compacted earth and experienced a searing pain in the ball of my big toe, as if I'd stepped on a red-hot coal. I jerked my foot away and an angry wasp flew out of a hole in the ground where it had been passing the time of day until I had inadvertently blocked up the exit. Apart from Tanis, nobody seemed to have noticed the incident. I ignored the pain in the hope that it would go away. Exquisitely carved wooden stools, about ten inches high, were brought out for us and I endeavoured to make myself comfortable, though the entire sole of my foot now felt as if it was on fire.

The village headman is called a captain and his second-in-command, a basha. Some fifty villagers gathered round as the Captain, an elderly little man with a mischievous face, made a speech in Taki Taki. Long and chant-like, some of it I could probably have understood but my attention was focused on the wasp sting; the pain had now travelled from foot to ankle and on up to my knee, leaving both joints feeling as if they had been severely sprained. The Basha made a short speech followed by a lengthy exchange between the Captain and Rainier. I didn't attempt to pay any attention as by now the pain was racing up my thigh towards my crotch and I was becoming alarmed. Tanis nudged me and I looked up to see the Captain point first at me and then at a young, beautiful woman who stood near him.

What happened next shocked me out of my preoccupation with my groin. The young woman gasped, turned and fled, sending two children sprawling in her panic. The Captain shouted something and the escapee was pursued by all the other women. Rainier explained that the lady who had run away was the Captain's wife and she had been chosen to supply the first sample of blood. Furthermore, I had been granted the honour of obtaining it. As if this were not enough to cope with, the pain now felt as if a horse had kicked me in the balls. The Captain's wife had been captured and was being dragged towards me, kicking and struggling every inch of the way.

Doubled over in agony and with a grim smile on my face to show confidence to the expectant crowd, I was presented with a triangular steel blade to puncture the donor's skin, and a glass microscopic slide on which to put the droplet of blood. The victim was hauled before me. Several women held her while others took her arm and forcibly unclenched the fingers.

With my best 'this won't hurt a bit' manner I took hold of her finger but as I pricked the flesh, she jerked her hand away and I sliced open her whole fingertip. I stared in horror. Blood flowed freely, dripping off the glass slide onto the ground. Silence. I looked at the Captain. He stood up, turned and disappeared into his hut. 'Christ, you've done it now,' Tanis muttered. 'Why didn't you just cut her finger off and be done with?'

Before I could answer, the Captain emerged, carrying a full bottle of rum to celebrate my demonstration of surgical skill. The crowd clapped, children shrieked with excitement. As I drank, the pain from the sting gradually eased into a dull ache and I began to enjoy myself. Half an hour later I'd almost forgotten about the Captain's wife when Tanis pointed her out, sitting in the doorway of a hut, nursing her finger and glowering at me. Each time I looked in her direction she half rose, getting ready to make a run for it.

Dear Mum and Dad

I am writing this in the tent by candlelight, Martin is asleep with a hangover! We are still with the Anti-Malaria Campaign and have made a really good camp, with a fire outside to keep snakes away at night. This is something you have to be really careful about (and we are!). Last night just as it got dark I went to the river for some water; there's a big fallen tree by our camp with one end on land and the other submerged. As I stepped onto it I saw something moving at the other end, half in and half out of the water. It was a huge snake, about the thickness of a telegraph pole, it slid across the tree and kept on sliding. I couldn't believe it, it must have been at least twenty feet long. I was so surprised I dropped the saucepan in the river. I wouldn't mind but I'd spent all afternoon scrubbing it clean. The women who cook for the crew came to see us while I was making coffee and were horrified when they saw my pots and pans. They explained that you have to scrub the outside (which is thick with burnt-on soot after every use) using wire wool. They gave me some, but now all my hard work is at the bottom of the river and we have to boil water in the frying pan.

By the time you get this it will be too late for you to worry about us being eaten by twenty-foot snakes. There are the biggest freshwater fish in the world in these rivers, up to ten feet long.

This morning the boss sent us out with the men, going to Djuka villages, either spraying or taking blood (yes, they still let Martin). At some places the villagers simply refuse to allow anything to be done. Today, at one village the Captain took a liking to us and went off and cut us some sugar cane. You cut the bamboo-like pole and chew the white fibre inside to extract the sweet juice, it's delicious. At another village they gave us breadnut. It looks like a pale green melon with blunt spines all over it, you cut it open and inside the white flesh are nuts, about twenty or thirty. You boil and shell them and they taste like chestnuts, but not so sweet. We ate them with cassava bread which is made from cassava root, grated and pressed to remove the poisonous juice, then dried in the sun, mixed with water and baked into pancakes, half an inch thick and the size of bicycle wheels. It's filling but rather like chewing cardboard. We also got some limes, which we really appreciated as we have no fruit at all.

This afternoon I washed all our clothes in the river, kneeling on the tree and Martin walked by and knocked the whole pile in the water, we had to fish it out with sticks before it sank. At sundown we take toothbrush and soap to the river, everyone has a scrub up until spotless from head to toe, then we sit in the sun to dry, telling stories and watching the sunset. Tonight we had homemade bread made with flour and water only, spread with Bovril.

Sitting in the sun all day has burnt my scalp so I have to wear a scarf. Today we saw parrots flying above us and thousands of yellow butterflies, it's called the butterfly river. Some Americans killed the orange spider, it's a shame as he didn't come off the wall and was quite high up. He'd lived there ages.

I must condense this letter as we're running out of paper. More later.

CHAPTER FIVE

What a pity Tanis isn't here, I thought.

In the forest was a clearing. In its centre, ten yards from me, a circle of gigantic mushrooms, the caps brown domes two feet across, on stalks four feet tall. There were dozens of them. Resisting an urge to rush forward and examine them at close quarters, I savoured the moment, admiring them from the spot where I'd seen them, convinced I'd made an important botanical discovery, for I'd never heard of mushrooms like these. I went closer. They were large gourds, fixed upside down on the tops of poles, stuck in the ground by people. I'd discovered a Bushnegro graveyard. There had been an outbreak of malaria along the Tapanahoni River and many had died, mostly children. The spot seemed lonely and sad then, and I crept away.

Back at the village an old man came to talk to us. With a sing-song nasal delivery that was a delight to listen to, he chatted away in Taki Taki for several minutes, in the mistaken belief that we understood every word. 'We no sab Taki,' I tried to explain.

'Oo no sab Taki?' He was astonished. 'Oo, . . .' pointing at me, 'no sab,' waving index finger back and forth '. . . *Taki*?' pointing to his mouth.

'No.'

Now he looked distressed. He patted me on the shoulder and left, shaking his head sadly. Perhaps he'd misunderstood, thinking we meant that we had no language at all. Later he returned with a bowl of peanuts, giving them to me without a word.

Usually, interest and kindness was shown toward we

Bakrahs (white people) but not always. Occasionally we were regarded with suspicion and sometimes ignored, hardly a surprising attitude when it's realised that they have a lively interest in the historical events which brought their ancestors to South America in the first place. Passed on by story-tellers from generation to generation, their tales expose the harsh fact that for centuries white people treated them abominably. Indeed it was the English who claimed the land of Surinam in the early 1600s and they who first brought slaves from the West African coast, taking captives from the countries between Senegal and Angola.

The Spanish who had discovered Surinam were not greatly interested in it, but the Dutch were, and after a war with the English in 1667, followed by some complicated negotiations, an exchange of territories was agreed. This resulted in the Netherlands acquiring Surinam and the English, Nieuw Amsterdam, later to become New York. The years of slavery continued and with increasing colonisation, the numbers of transported Africans required to work the plantations increased as well. Inevitably, there were many escapes and by the 1680s large numbers of Africans were living free in the remote forests of the interior.

Soon there was more war between the Colonists. The French and Dutch were busy slaughtering each other and the chaos that ensued facilitated mass escapes of slaves until they became sufficiently numerous to muster a highly motivated, formidable army. Eventually the Dutch regained control of the colony over the French but then faced a more serious menace from the slaves, (the ancestors of today's Bushnegroes) who, supremely well adapted to life in their new environment and nursing bitter memories of barely imaginable cruelties, waged a war against their former captors which lasted a hundred years and very nearly succeeded in driving Europeans from Surinam's shores.

During the decades of war, the Bushnegroes had spread out and divided into various, largely geographically determined groups, most notably the Saramaccas, Matawais and Djukas. In 1772 the Netherlands organised its final onslaught against the troublesome rebels, among whom several great leaders had emerged. 'Joli-Coeur' and 'Baron', both escaped slaves with first-hand experience of oppression and torture, and 'Bonni', a Mulatto born in freedom of an escapee who despised the white component of his genetic heritage.

The Dutch troops were losing their war against the Bush-negroes. By 1778 they gave up and went back to the Netherlands. There followed a restive truce between the Bushnegroes, who now ruled vast territories in the interior, and the colonists, still growing crops on the narrow coastal belt. After a hundred years of war, both sides were weary. Bonni and his tribe disappeared into French Guiana but emerged again in the 1790s and engaged in an uncharacteristic battle with their former comrades-in-arms, the Djuka tribe. Bonni was killed and much fascinating mythology surrounds this historic event. Since that time, inter-tribal peace has reigned along with the sometimes uneasy truce between the Bushnegroes, the Dutch and the various other immigrants who have continued to arrive.

Headquarters.

Dear Mum & Dad,

It's 3.30 p.m. and we've just got back after an amazing morning. We went way upriver. The first village we stopped at, the Captain insisted that the crew pay him for each blood test. There were a lot of people with malaria there as well. In another village a girl came up with a bowl of peanuts she'd shelled for us. I had nothing to carry them in, so she tipped them into my bag, pounds and pounds of them; peanuts everywhere. But it was the final village that was incredible; we were the first white people they had ever seen! First of all they simply stared open-mouthed, then curiosity got the better of them and they began touching and examining us. I think they thought we'd been skinned or painted, they kept licking their fingers and rubbing our arms and legs to find out what we were like underneath. We were amazed, it shows how far in the interior we are. Corned beef for dinner tonight, it was horrible. Martin says he's going to throw the remaining tins in the river! More later.

Yesterday we went off into the bush on our own. It was exciting, we had to mark each tree with our machetes so as not to lose the way back. We went about three miles. In some places we had to hack our way through, it was so dense. We wore the denim puttees I'd made. Did I tell you before we left, I phoned the army and asked where to buy puttees? There was a long silence, then muttering, followed by peals of laughter. 'Madam' he said, when he could stop laughing, 'we haven't used puttees since the Great War.' I can see why they laughed, the puttees were useless, kept coming undone and trailing along behind us, catching on everything.

If you go very quietly you see a lot more wildlife, mind you, it's almost impossible to creep in the jungle, every footstep breaks twigs and rustles leaves. But we did see caterpillars with big plumes on their heads, enormous dragonflies all different colours and I found a frog that looked just like a dead leaf. We lit a fire and had frankfurters and bread for lunch before making our way back. You have to be very careful not to lose the trail, if you step away from it you can be lost in seconds. The Bushnegroes just nick a piece of tree bark and bend it over or snap a branch of a bush so it hangs down, and all the time they look back to be sure it will be visible on the return. We didn't need to worry too much, our trail looked like a motorway.

Later.
It's now the thirteenth and it hasn't been lucky. This morning I dropped my lighter in the river. Martin climbed down but sank up to his ankles in soft mud and got bitten by a fish; and I've been so careful with it till now. Then I went to get the frying pan to make coffee. We hang our rucksacks on a dead tree and keep the plates, pan, etc. in them, you can't leave anything on the ground here. Well, as I pulled it out, the whole bag turned into a black moving object; ants had made a nest in it. It was terrible, hundreds of them ran up my arms, Martin dropped the bag on the ground and they made straight for the tent. We spent three and a half hours getting rid of them, in the end we had to dig a trench round the tent and fill it with water.

This afternoon there was an incredible racket from the crew's hut, banging and crashing. We shot out just in time to see one of the boys come charging out the door closely followed by two others, who grabbed the first and held him on the ground. He was going berserk, yelling and moaning and making odd noises. Then they locked him in the hut and he wrecked it, throwing things out of windows, including himself. First we thought he'd had a fit, then when it went on for another hour, we reckoned he'd gone mad. People from Stoelman-seiland came across in boats to see what was happening. The two boys *holding him could barely keep him down, everyone was suggesting remedies and some were chucking water over him, it lasted about three hours. Now he's perfectly OK and we realise he was drunk. The boss is away at the moment! More later.*

Today is Martin's birthday, I made him a card and as a present we ate one of our emergency ration dried omelettes. It was very good, we'll have the other one tomorrow on my birthday. Rainier went to the guest house yesterday and got me some beers, so we had a celebration lunch. Unfortunately we then went to sleep in the tent and woke feeling awful.

This country is really wonderful, so much wildlife, so much forest. We hope to come here again but well organised next time. We have serious thoughts of setting up a small expedition to go really deep into the forest, places where no-one has ever been. The Government here encourages that sort of thing, it's something to think about anyway.

Later.
Quite a lot to catch up on. In the last few days we've visited more villages, we stopped at one on the French side where there was a shop. All it sold was red balloons and Chanel No 5. We've made quite a few lone forays into the forest, but our food supplies are very low now, we're out of porridge so it's rice every day, and a tin of spam every three days. We'll soon have to think about leaving. The boss has told us that the normal price back to Albina by boat is seven and a half guilders but the guest house charges tourists two hundred, isn't that ridiculous? He's promised to get us on the delivery boat for the cheap price.

Yesterday afternoon we discovered that the tent was full of dead termites, they are from all the wood I pick up in the forest to bring home. Today there's an enormous ant in here with me, picking up the bodies and putting them in a corner, quite helpful really.

Last night in the tent Martin found an insect two inches long crawling up his leg. He grabbed it and threw it at the opening, but we thought he'd missed, so we had to turf everything upside down to try to find it. (Did I tell you I'd packed the torches with the batteries in them and they got turned on in our bags, so we don't have anything but a little candle?) Anyway we couldn't find the creature and by now we were convinced it was a scorpion, not a good bedmate. Not a restful night either.

Everything must be banged, shaken and kicked before opening here, in case a snake or tarantula has crawled in during the night. We hear snakes hissing near the tent every night, and rodents scurrying around. They call them rabbits, but they're nothing like the rabbits we know. We've been having very heavy storms and the river has risen eighteen inches in the last week. By the way, we found out that there are piranha fish in the river but they so rarely bite that you needn't worry. The main worry we were told, are anacondas which usually only go for children. I wish I was a bit taller!

My hair is a most peculiar colour now, and suffering a bit from bad treatment. When we arrived here and I unpacked Martin's rucksack all fifteen tubes of insect repellent had lost their tops and oozed out, and a whole bottle of iodine had leaked its contents in mine.

Earlier I said that one of the boys got drunk. Well today they all did. They came back from Stoelmanseiland and were wobbling and turning the boats in circles. Even drunk they're fantastic boatmen. They lived it up all afternoon then collapsed and we haven't heard a sound since. More later.

The boss has just told us that there's a boat leaving tomorrow and there's room for us. If we don't take it, the next won't be for two weeks and we're virtually out of food. Evenings in the tent are spent drooling over thoughts about all the delicious foods we have at home, I can't believe that sometimes I didn't know what to cook, with all that choice! I'll finish this in Albina.

Paramaribo.

The boat left at daybreak. Rainier took us across the river, it was very sad saying goodbye, but he is sure we'll be back as we have drunk from the rivers of Surinam and that ensures our return. After an exhilarating ride down some treacherous rapids we arrived at Albina. Everything was shut and there was nobody about. Martin went off to look for a bus and came back with bread (real bread) and cheese (wonderful) and the news that there wasn't a bus to Paramaribo until next morning. As we sat eating and wondering where to camp, I heard a car coming, the only noise in town. It was a Witboi lorry (Witboi is soap powder) which I ran out and stopped. The driver agreed to give us a lift so we squeezed in the front seat with our gear for the three hour journey. On the way, I told him we were keen to get to the post office to collect our letters and he screeched through the city streets and delivered us outside at two minutes to six. There were six letters from you. We came to the YWCA, bought some cold Parbo and sat and read them all, it was lovely.

Later.

Well, this is our position. In a couple of days we leave Paramaribo and *begin making our way back to Trinidad to get the ship home. If, as you say in your letter, the engines have failed and it's laid up, it may miss a sailing. Just in case, could you please send some cash to Trinidad? We're on such a tight budget that if we have to wait a month in Trinidad, we'll come home very thin indeed. Which reminds me, can we put in an order for a Sunday dinner please? Roast chicken with stuffing, potatoes, cauliflower and peas please, and Martin says a plum duff to follow. Lots and lots of love, T & M*

We were ten weeks in Trinidad waiting for that wretched ship!

CHAPTER SIX

South America haunted me. Tanis was back at work, but I couldn't settle down. There was so much to see, I wanted to get out there and see it. The waiting made me restless.

Early one mild November morning I walked in the forest. A cobwebby mist still floated here and there among the trees. Many times in the jungle I had been reminded of Epping Forest and now, surrounded by familiar hornbeams and beeches, I was seized by an overwhelming need to visit the jungle again.

Relentlessly we saved, comparing such luxuries as newspapers, new clothes and visits to the cinema, with our desire for another trip. Every penny was squirrelled away. All we required was a large chunk of remote forest with a river we could disappear up for a few months, as far away from modern man as possible. We pored over maps. In South America, we were spoilt for choice, so much so that I couldn't decide where to go. I searched for inspiration but it eluded me.

On the day before New Year's Eve, the inspiration was provided. Surrounded by mince pies and sausage rolls, we sat with Tanis's parents watching a television programme, *Around the World in 80 Minutes*. There was Kenneth Alsop in a plane, flying over dense jungle, deep in the heart of Venezuela, attempting to film the Angel Falls, the highest waterfall in the world. I sat up and watched intently, aware that Tanis was doing the same. Now Kenneth Alsop was talking to a man named Rudy Truffino who had a vast knowledge of the area.

'Sure, there are plenty of jaguar here,' Rudy was saying, 'we even get the black jaguar, just last week I saw one upriver.' The black jaguar! What I'd give to see one of those. Dense cloud obliterated the falls; one of Rudy's films was shown. There on the screen was a sight that removed all thoughts of mince pies and sausage rolls and transported me to a wonderland where a waterfall, half a mile high, dropped from a mountain into a jungle that stretched from horizon to horizon. As Kenneth Alsop said, 'Who knows what might live down there?'

Tanis's parents weren't so impressed by the dense, tropical forest with its promise of black jaguars, nor the vicious rapids that stretched for miles up to the falls. 'I hope that's nowhere near where you're going,' remarked Emmie.

'Oh no, I shouldn't think so.' There was no point in worrying her prematurely.

As soon as we left the house I turned to Tanis, 'What did you think?'

'Could we do it?' she said.

'Tan, we've got to go there, we can take our own boat and explore wherever we like. Did you see those canyons? Nobody knows what's there, just imagine it!'

'It did look fantastic, didn't it?'

'There'll be a tremendous amount of organisation. How soon do you think we could go?'

'Well, for a kick-off there's the fare, then equipment and food for three months,' she said.

We were home now and I handed her a glass of wine, anticipating her reaction. 'Hmm, actually Tan, I hadn't thought of going for three months.'

'What do you mean? You always say it's not worth going for less.'

'Yes, well, I think this should be a proper expedition, you know, really organised . . . and I think we should go for . . . at least a year.'

'WHAT!' I thought she was going to choke. 'A YEAR, I can't go away for a year, what about Mum and Dad? What about the shop? I can't leave for a YEAR, we'd be away for Christmas, I can't be away for Christmas!'

I knew that I was asking a lot. She wanted to go as much as I did but her family was a close one and she was thunderstruck by the thought of leaving for a year. 'Must it be a whole year, wouldn't a few months be long enough?' she pleaded.

'Well, definitely not less than nine months,' I capitulated.

'Oh Martin, Mum's going to have a fit!'

At midnight next evening, with our family and friends we saw in the New Year. Clinking glasses, we drank to the Venezuelan trip.

It was all very well for Martin to have these outrageous ideas, but we hadn't the faintest idea how to mount a proper expedition. We began by writing letters: to the Venezuelan Government to see if we needed permission to enter the area; to embassies, ministries, tourist boards, to boat and tent manufacturers, outboard motor companies and the suppliers of dehydrated foods. If a company in the phone book had South America or Venezuela in its name it received a request for information and advice. The most important letter was to Rudy Truffino.

Our plan was to take our own motor-powered boat up the Carrao river, (a sub-tributary of the Orinoco), to its source, and on the return journey turn up the Churrun river and visit Angel Falls. Neither of us knew much about boats or boating but from our experiences on the rivers of Surinam we knew we didn't have the expertise to handle a heavy dugout canoe. The boat we would use must be light, strong, easy to repair and capable of holding equipment, food, and us. An inflatable rubber dinghy seemed the best choice, and we settled for an eleven foot Avon Redseal. To have time to practise with it, we needed it soon, but couldn't afford a new one.

'Martin, we've got our boat.' I rushed upstairs to tell him. 'I phoned the Avon Rubber Company direct. They were a bit taken aback but eventually put me through to sales and I spoke to a really nice man called Paul Gammon. He was enthusiastic about our trip and has offered us an ex-demonstration model, for a quarter of the original price, we can collect it as soon as we like.'

That weekend we went to Wales and met Paul Gammon. He was still enthusiastic. 'I've had a think,' he said, as we shook hands, 'there are lots of other things you may need and perhaps we can help. Let's go and look at the boat.' By the time we left, we had acquired lifejackets, oars, several repair kits, a large strip of fabric for major repairs, and the name of an outboard engine firm who would loan us a motor to try out with the boat.

My brother Graham, his wife Ginny and four-year-old daughter Gabby became involved with our plans. They borrowed a boat and motor and on a cold Saturday in March we camped in a field beside the River Wye (at a stretch marked 'For Beginners' in our book on white-water canoeing) and set off to reconnoitre. At first, we couldn't find anything that resembled a rapid, then we spied it, near the bank. The drop was all of eighteen inches. 'It's not very big,' Ginny voiced our thoughts.

After dinner, while Gabby slept in their tent, Graham and Ginny sat with us and over a bottle of wine we discussed tactics. As the wine diminished the rapid grew.

'Better wear lifejackets,' Martin said, 'especially Gabby, just in case.'

'Mustn't forget to tie the outboards on,' said Graham.

'Don't forget to aim for where the water channels to a vee,' I said.

'What happens if we miss the vee?' asked Ginny.

'That's when you could be in trouble, the boat could turn sideways in the current.'

'Perhaps we should go first as we've had a bit of experience,' said Martin, 'and then if we get into difficulties, you can decide whether to take Gabby.'

'Gabby's really looking forward to it,' said Graham.

Next morning Gabby watched as we assembled the boats. Without warning she was violently sick. 'What's wrong, Gabbs?' Graham asked, alarmed by her pale face and trembling lip. A tear slid down her cheek.

'I don't want to drown in the river,' she burst forth.

'Oh Gabbs, it's not a real rapid, look, it's a tiny little drop, do you think I'd let you drown, we thought you wanted to try,' Graham was solicitous.

'I heard you last night, you said it was dangerous and I'm scared.' Shuffling our feet in embarrassment, we looked sheepishly at each other.

'That was only messing about, Gabbs, honestly,' Ginny said.

Gabby had done a lot in her four years and didn't want to be left out now, but even a little rapid looks big when you're four.

We went first then waited for their boat to make the descent. It was singularly unremarkable. 'Gabby didn't come then?' I said to Ginny.

'Yes she did, we stashed her under there.' A face emerged from underneath the bowdodger.

'I fired it!' she grinned.

'We need a really good tent,' said Martin and off we went to a camping exhibition. There were tents with awnings, tents with windows; I was entranced by a tent complete with kitchen, living room, bedroom and toilet, imagining such luxury in the jungle. Martin was more practical.

'I've found the perfect tent, Tan, come and look.' In the corner of the field was a small, green, igloo-shaped thing.

'But it hasn't any windows,' I said stepping inside, 'there isn't even a sewn-in ground sheet.'

'I thought we might ask Mum to put in some windows of mosquito net,' he said, 'and perhaps she could sew in the ground sheet?'

Poor Mum, she wasn't exactly elated about the trip but since we worked together at the shop, she was learning to live with it. Because of her skill with a sewing machine, she had been inveigled into making a cover for the boat and all our kit bags.

'But I thought you wanted windows!' she exclaimed when we put it up in the garden.

'We wondered. . . ?' said Martin.

She did a wonderful job.

As we planned to use a more powerful engine than recommended, Graham modified the boat. Our ineptitude at grasping more than the bare essentials of engine maintenance exasperated him. 'Can I give you some advice?' he asked. We nodded eagerly. 'It will be a new engine and there's no reason why it should go wrong, but if it does, *please* don't take it to bits. Just clean the spark plugs and try it again. Unless you have absolutely no choice, DON'T TOUCH IT.'

'We ought to find out if we deviate,' announced Martin from the depths of a jungle survival book.

'I beg your pardon?'

'Deviation; when people get lost in the jungle, they don't walk in a straight line but tend to go to the right or left. If you deviate too much you can end up walking in a circle. If you are aware how you deviate it's possible to correct it. Come on, let's go to the forest and try it.'

Two hours later after staggering in countless semi-circles, I bumped into an elderly couple walking their dog. 'Excuse me dear, but what are you doing, is it some sort of game?'

I pulled down the blindfold and looked around. Numerous groups of people were watching my progressive stumblings but Martin was nowhere to be seen.

The Venezuelan Government were proving to be extremely helpful. Our knowledge of the language was limited, so we enlisted the assistance of a Spanish relative and soon numerous letters and forms whizzed back and forth across the Atlantic. We learned the value of the obsequious approach and added a touch of perfume to the envelopes for luck. In this manner we obtained a shotgun permit. Though we had no intention of hunting, it seemed advisable to be armed. There was still no letter from Rudy Truffino; we wrote again.

Food was a problem. Most firms catered for large expeditions but a two pound pack of dehydrated food would begin to absorb moisture once opened; for just two of us we needed small quantities. I found just the thing in my local super-market, Vesta Dried Dinners were meals for two in a sealed pack. They came in a variety of mouthwatering recipes: chicken curry, beef curry, chicken supreme and chow mein. I bought three every week. Unfortunately, they also came with their own pack of rice and by the time I'd bought a hundred and fifty, everyone who visited us left with packs of rice. I knew how important treats could be in the jungle and as fast as Martin made our packing crates, I filled them with Angel Delights, packets of custard powder, tins of Golden Syrup, Bovril and Marmite. Staples such as rice, flour, pasta, beans and oats we would buy in Venezuela.

Our intention was to fly from Caracas to a jungle camp called Canaima and from there, set off on our own. A letter was dispatched to the airline that serviced Canaima: could we obtain petrol there? Also, could they inform of any size restrictions for freight? There was no reply. We wrote again, and again. At last the information arrived; they had no idea about petrol and the width of the door was nine inches. We chose to ignore the latter.

Our flat resembled a battle station at the height of activity. When Martin was sure that I enjoyed my role as Commanding Officer and was unlikely to de-bunk, he decided to drop his bombshell. 'Tan, I've changed my mind, I think five months in Venezuela is long enough.'

After all the mental and physical adjustments I'd made! Secretly, I was quite pleased he'd eventually come round to my idea and decided I could afford to be suitably indignant. 'I don't believe this,' I said, 'I told you nine months was too long and now, after all our preparation, you want to cut it to five? It will be difficult altering the boat tickets you know.'

'No, Tan, you don't understand. I think we should spend the last four months exploring Surinam.'

I stared at him in disbelief. 'When did you decide this?'

'Er, well, I just thought while we're in South America we may as well go back to Surinam, two trips for a single fare. Don't you think it's a good idea?'

'You rotten sod, you planned it all along didn't you?'

I had to admit it was a good idea.

Previously, the only petrol containers we'd seen in South America had been plastic. Here, this was considered dangerous; some plastics slowly dissolve while others spark when the lids are turned. Gifts became essentials rather than luxuries; for Martin's birthday I bought him six ex-army metal petrol cans and the next day on mine, he gave me a box of anti-snakebite serum imported from America.

At Christmas, the last before we left, our presents were all for the trip, and highly ingenious they were: rubber torches that would float, a battery-operated lantern, cycle-clips (instead of the ludicrous puttees), a miniature game of draughts for jungle evenings, magnifying glasses, knives, whistles, jungle hats and a Union Jack to fix to the boat. Ginny bought a tiny mending kit and filled it with extra strong needles and cotton. Mum had made us money belts and lots of waterproof bags for odds and ends; and from my sister, tiny gold St Christophers.

Two years had passed since we conceived the trip and we'd enjoyed hundreds of evenings planning and anticipating the things we would see. Now, conversely, fears flooded in. The approaching trip was daunting, might actually prove impossible. All the information we'd gathered confirmed that in reality we had nothing to fear from animals or Indians, but our subconscious minds remained unconvinced and every night we woke, sweating, from nightmares. Martin's dreams were of a jungle floor so full of snakes he could barely take a step, mine were of fearsome river creatures grabbing my legs.

There were six weeks to go and still no word from Rudy Truffino.

Accident and illness were next on the worry agenda. 'Have you had your appendix out? No? Too late now,' said our family doctor who had entered into the spirit of things with a relish and began pumping us full of vaccine.

'Dr Brace, are you sure we'll need all these?' groaned Martin, clutching his bum as the second tetanus jab was administered.

'Can't be too careful, Martin, can't be too careful, especially where you're going. Now, that's tetanus, typhoid, yellow fever, polio, have cholera just before you go. Hepatitis? Right, you need gamma globulin today, bend over and turn the other cheek. What are you doing about diarrhoea? We've covered malaria, haven't we? That's it, take a walk around the waiting room a few times to disperse the fluid, that's what's causing the pain. Have you thought about burns?'

Like Topsy our medical kit grew and grew.

Martin was decorating a room.

'Venezuela?' his customer said, as he explained our plans. 'I know someone in Venezuela, Bishop Marshall, he's the Anglican Bishop of Caracas. His wife is in England now, visiting her family, I'll ring her up.' By the end of the call Mrs Marshall had generously offered to receive our mail, book us a hotel and help us when we arrived. It seemed heaven sent.

Three weeks before we sailed, our crates of equipment were to be taken to Southampton. 'Tickets must be shown on delivery,' the docket stated. Our tickets hadn't arrived yet. A message came from the Venezuelan Consulate in London, our visas were ready. 'Visas will be issued on production of Return Tickets,' the form said.

A call to the shipping company brought the alarming response, 'Tickets will only be issued on production of visas.' At first we laughed at the silliness of the situation, but days of fruitless negotiations posed a serious threat to our plans. In the end a shipping clerk was bribed to lend us the tickets for a day. We dashed around, flashing them where necessary and the situation was resolved.

Two weeks before we left, a telegram arrived at the shop. It was for Mum. PLEASE TELEPHONE ANDREW FYALL DAILY EXPRESS IMMEDIATELY.

'What's it all about?' I asked.

'Well,' she said, 'I know you think it's silly but I'm worried about you going, all on your own, miles from anywhere, no radio. How will we know if anything happens to you. Suppose you have an accident, we won't know what to do if you need help. So, I thought that if a newspaper knew what you were doing, well, they've probably got people and offices out there, they'd know what to do.'

The *Express* published an article about us. The very notion that a national newspaper could have any interest in us was incredible. Radio programmes invited us on to talk about our plans. Mum was relieved, the worry wasn't solely on her shoulders now. We were anxious; what had begun as something we wanted to do, now seemed almost obligatory. Suppose things went wrong, all those people who'd helped us would be let down.

'Aren't you brave?' said some people.

The cashier in the bank where I collected our travellers' cheques said, 'I think you want your brains tested!'

Every night, in the week prior to departure, I looked around our flat and thought, what have we let ourselves in for? Martin was cheerfully nervous, he couldn't wait to go.

There had been no word from Rudy Truffino.

I dreaded saying goodbye to my parents but they surprised me. 'Now come on, don't get upset, think of it as a lovely holiday,' said Mum sounding chirpy. Didn't she realise she might never see me again?

'Get a move on or I'll be late for work,' Dad quipped.

Graham, Ginny and Gabby were taking us to Southampton. In the car Gabby gave me her favourite teddy bear as a mascot. It was only an inch and a half high and called Orinoco. They'd dressed him in a safari suit and plastic mac for the rains. In one hand he held a fishing rod. I cried all the way down the North Circular Road. Then I realised I'd forgotten the camera bag.

'A word of advice from the war,' our landlord said as I rushed back in, 'always keep some toilet paper in your pocket!'

THE RIVER THAT
FALLS FROM THE SKY

CHAPTER SEVEN

Our ship was called the *Montserrat*.

The lounge was pervaded by smells of brandy, coffee, cigars, cologne, and suntan oil; evocative scents for a dismal January day in Southampton dock. That night we set sail for South America. We entered the Bay of Biscay with a storm brewing and next day the crew were battling against fierce winds to secure deck cargo. Passengers were not allowed outside. After lunch we retired to our cabin, hardly bigger than a cupboard though it did have a porthole. I was not allowed the top bunk any more as the night before, sound asleep, I had crashed to the floor, whacking Martin in the nuts on the way down.

Sleepily, I opened my eyes. I felt strange, as if I were being rolled around. With a start I realised that I was indeed rolling across the bunk. The cabin was tilted to an angle of seventy degrees and going further and further over. At the bottom of the roll there was a great 'WHOOMPH' as our side of the vessel was submerged and the ocean closed over the porthole. Now the sky was whizzing by as we rolled back the other way. I was scared. 'Martin, you awake? It's very rough.'

'Ummm, I expect it's OK.' Martin doesn't panic easily. I heard a rustle as he leant across to look out of the porthole. It was like being on a scenic railway.

'I don't like it, Mart.'

Silence.

'Nor do I.' Was that panic in his voice? Simultaneously we leapt from our bunks and dragged on our clothes, falling over each other in our haste. If the ship was going to sink we wanted to be up top, near the lifeboats.

We hauled ourselves up the stairs and tottered into the lounge. There was ample evidence of acute seasickness among the passengers, vomit dripped from the walls, but the entire area was now deserted. Behind the bar, casually polishing a glass, stood an elderly Spaniard, sucking a cheroot. He sounded as though he'd learnt his English in Brooklyn. 'Dis ain't nuthin, doncha worry,' he assured us without removing the cheroot, 'you wanna drink?' He reached for a bottle of brandy. At that moment the vessel lurched violently and bottles, glasses, ashtrays, cups and saucers slid from shelves and tables and cascaded to the floor with a deafening crash, followed by a succession of distant thumps, crashes and yells from other parts of the ship. 'Jesus Christ!' exclaimed the barman, hauling himself upright.

Fortunately, the bar stools were fixed to the floor and for the next three hours we sat clinging to a pillar. The rest of the lounge furniture broke from its moorings and slid across the room to hit the opposite wall; sofas, chairs and tables travelled back and forth, back and forth, like some relentless industrial process, splintered fragments flying in all directions. The door leading to the deck had been barricaded shut with timber, preventing the ever growing pile of wreckage from crashing through them into the sea.

We stared through the windows in horrified fascination at waves that towered high above, then slammed down upon the deck in a cloud of spray that obscured all sight of the ocean for several seconds. When it cleared, we were perched high on the crest of a wave preparing for another downward plunge into a deep, awful, grey valley of water. 'Do you think we've had it, Mart?' I asked, seeking reassurance.

'I think we might have!'

The door burst open and a high ranking Spanish officer fell into the room. He looked pale and fearful. After speaking to the barman he turned to me: I expected the voice of confident authority to dispel my fears. Placing his hand on my head he said, 'We are in the hands of God, my dear,' then raised his eyes towards heaven and made the Sign of the Cross before leaving, clutching his rosary.

But the old barman was a tower of strength and his more down-to-earth approach helped us believe we might survive. 'Dis aint nuthin,' he would exclaim at intervals, dismissing contemptuously the world of howling wind and mountainous sea outside. 'Blow itself out Goddam quick,' he would mutter, then relight his cigar and puff away silently for a time.

By sunset, the wind had dropped and scores of seamen were rushing around cleaning up the mess. It was still very rough and no more than fifty out of five hundred passengers appeared when dinner was served two hours later. It was soup.

Listing badly, we limped into the Spanish port of Vigo. The hull of the ship had a split over ten feet long and was laid up for four days. Several of the crew admitted it to be the worst storm they had experienced. The waves had been over fifty feet high, they told us, several ships had sunk, with at least a dozen others badly damaged.

Repairs conducted and nerves of passengers and crew restored, we departed from Vigo at four in the morning towards the African coast. Two hours later six bells rang out. 'What does six bells mean, Martin?' Before he could answer a steward rushed past our door shouting 'Fuego! Fuego!'

'Oh no,' yelled Martin, hurtling from his bunk, 'the fucking thing's on *fire* now!'

Doors burst open all along the corridor and people cascaded out into the narrow passageway dragging bags, suitcases and children. A naked woman ran out clutching a towel, which she ineffectually attempted to wrap around her body as she headed for the stairs. On deck, all was chaos. Crowds of people, many in pyjamas and all furious, were pushing their way back down the stairs against the panic-stricken hordes fighting their way up. A message came over the tannoy, 'Please not to take notice. It is not fire. It is to train the crew.' Later that day it was discovered that the cables holding the lifeboats were welded solid with rust, and for the rest of the week dozens of men worked with oxyacetylene cutting equipment to free them.

Since leaving Vigo we had crept along at half speed. It was evident that the ship was still in bad shape, but since it neither sank nor caught fire, with the gradual improvement in weather came a gradual relaxation among the passengers. We neared the Canary islands beneath a clear sky with flying fish skimming ahead of the bow wave. Tenerife became visible as a hazy hump on the horizon. It was the hottest part of the day, almost sunbathing weather, and passengers were out in force, sprawling in deck chairs or lying half dressed by the tiny pool. Abruptly the engine stopped. The unexpected cessation of deep throbbing vibration was as much of a shock as an explosion would have been. For ten seconds it was eerily silent. People sat up looking quizzically around, then a great 'WHOOOOSH' came from the funnel as it belched forth a cloud of black soot and ashes which rained down upon us. The engine had produced its terminal fart.

For two days we drifted aimlessly off the African coast with flying fish and dolphins for company, before the auxiliary engine could be cranked into life. Then after three days of repairs we set sail from Tenerife to cross the Atlantic. 'Do you realise?' said Martin as the harbour lights twinkled in the dark, 'according to the schedule, we dock in Venezuela tomorrow!'

> *The very deep did rot: O Christ!*
> *That ever this should be!*
> *Yea, slimy things did crawl with legs*
> *Upon the slimy sea.*

Ancient Mariners we were becoming when, for the third time the engines failed, this time in the Sargasso sea. Now we drifted in waters where clumps of floating, olive-green seaweed nudged the hull, in water a deep and extraordinarily transparent blue, a phenomenon indicating an absence of suspended life, an unproductive, sterile sea.

Fresh water ran out. Salt water to wash in and only wine to drink.

A passenger jumped overboard but was recaptured.

The Captain fired a pistol through the ceiling of the bar to quell a riot.

At half speed the Monster Rat chugged on.

Then one morning we sailed into the 'Bocas del Dragon', a narrow channel between Trinidad and Venezuela. On the Venezuelan side the sea was brown and muddy from the outpourings of the Orinoco river; the Trinidad side was a clear cobalt green, as if an invisible barrier existed between the waters. Around us, tiny jungle-covered islands, dark green and lush in the dawn sunshine. It was three years since we had seen jungle. It was like coming home after a long time away.

Caracas.

Dear Mum and Dad,

Well, today is D-Day and we are now in Caracas. First of all I'll explain our day. All cabin luggage had to be on deck by five in the morning and we docked at La Guaira half an hour later. Our ten day journey had taken twenty-one days.

After breakfast an officer came to tell us that the Bishop was waiting for us in customs. We couldn't believe it, we hadn't expected to be met at all. Thanks to Bishop Marshall, we sailed through customs, though he was slightly alarmed when we told him what we were carrying; particularly the medical kit. He didn't think they'd have let that past without some problems. Our hold luggage won't be unloaded until this afternoon so we'll return later.

It's a beautiful drive through the mountains but you should see the shanty towns. They are like cities stretching away in the distance, occupying whole valleys and mountainsides, all made of corrugated iron, plastic sheets, cardboard and other junk. No water, no sanitation, lots of kids crawling around in the filth. When it rains, rows of houses get washed down the mountainside.

Caracas wasn't anything like we'd expected. It's more like Barcelona than New York and quite safe, contrary to what we'd been told. It's not very big and the weather is fairly cool, like an English summer. It's in a valley and from anywhere in the city you can see green hills. But it's fast, noisy and modern though; crossing roads is a nightmare.

First we went to the British Embassy to register; next of kin and religious denomination (none). At this the Bishop said, 'Well, perhaps being friends with a Bishop is the next best thing.'

On then to a hotel. He had five letters from home for us. Tell Gabbs that Orinoco is fine, just glad to be off the boat!

11.30 p.m. our time.
Customs was the most amazing thing we have ever been through! Apparently the Bishop had already arranged to meet an agent who would help us sort it all out and we found our crates and unlocked them. Here we had a nasty shock. The agent asked for our papers from the Consulate in London. He went quite grey when we said we didn't have any! It seems the letter of permission from the Venezuelan Government may not be enough. The agent went away and came back to say he can get us through customs without being checked, for 100 Bolivars (£10). We didn't ask how, just paid up. Later, up comes a customs official who glances at the unopened crates and stamps them. Meanwhile the Bishop made enquiries about storing them some-where. When the agent found we were going to Canaima he said, 'Take them to Avensa and they'll store them.' He found a lorry that would take them and off we went. On the way we had to pay to get out of customs, pay to get through a gate and pay to get out of the port. Tariffs and taxes they're called! At the airport we went straight to freightage, weighed the crates, paid, and they reach Canaima tomorrow. So, all we have to do is book our seats, buy our gear and we're off.

The Marshalls have a friend called John Forbes who has flown the length of the Carrao River and knows the area well. We spoke to him on the phone and are meeting for lunch tomorrow. Everything has gone like a dream and all thanks to Bishop Marshall. It's hard to believe it's all happening now.

Next day.
How can I start to tell you the wonderful things that have happened to us? If ever two people had a Guardian Angel it would seem it's us.

John Forbes arrived at noon and said he had somebody in the car who we should meet. He introduced us and we nearly fell over. It was Rudy Truffino, the man who was in that TV film with Kenneth Alsop. Over lunch they asked loads of questions and seemed to be assessing us. At first Rudy was abrasive and critical, mostly about our boat, saying it wouldn't be anywhere near fast enough. We said we didn't care how long the journey took. Then he said we couldn't live off the land. We said we'd brought all our food with us. Then, that we'd never get permission to go. We showed him our letter. Now he said we'd need a gun and we wouldn't get a permit. We showed him our permit. He threw every problem at us and each time (luckily) we had an answer, until he asked where we planned to get our fuel? That, we couldn't answer.

'What the hell,' he said, 'I can sell you as much gasoline as you need.' Rudy has his own camp, upriver from the tourist camp run by the airline, Canaima. He's Dutch, mid-forties but looks thirty, very slim and sun-tanned with piercing blue eyes. He speaks seven languages and is married with three children, all at school in Caracas. Rudy's camp is called Ucaima, he and his wife have lived in the jungle nineteen years.

Now that he's thoroughly assessed us, he's entered into the spirit of the trip. We spent the afternoon with him. He's in Caracas to have treatment for a back injury sustained in a canoeing accident. He's helped us buy a gun, and will buy it back from us when we leave. We can stay at Ucaima, Canaima is grotty he says, full of tourists and miners. Rudy has a low opinion of them, saying most are outlaws or screwballs (I presume he means the miners!).

Rudy's start in the jungle was quite spectacular. He heard about a company that wanted to open a tourist camp in the interior, so offered his services. They dropped him by plane, with two weeks supply of food to start clearing an airstrip. At the end of the fortnight they would collect him, but they forgot. When they remembered, months later, Rudy had a thorough knowledge of survival in the wild, having swopped his clothes with an Indian for bow and arrows and a blow pipe.

As compensation, he was offered the job of running the camp, he agreed and that was the start of Canaima.

Because it was so difficult to find, Rudy and his friend Charlie Baughn were the only people who took visitors down. Rudy as navigator, Charlie as pilot. They knew they were nearly there when Charlie's cigar, lit at Ciudad Bolivar, had burnt down to a stub, then they would search the ground below for the airstrip. Naturally enough, he was the first person to go to the base of Angel Falls, but he only goes in the rainy season in dugout canoes. Local Indians call the mountain that Angel Falls drops from Auyantepui, Devil mountain, because of the awesome thunderstorms it brews. They claim a river drops from the clouds. We plan to explore two canyons, the Aonda and the Churrun.

Rudy dropped us back here at 8.00 p.m. and we are too excited to go and eat, we had to write it all down first. If we hadn't met him, we would certainly have had a hard time getting fuel, there's none at Canaima as there are no roads. Angel Falls is about forty miles from Rudy's camp and there's no one around up there, the Indians won't live near the mountain and the miners look for gold on the Carrao, so we'll be entirely alone.

Rudy was very envious of our medical kit. We've promised to give him some of it when we leave.

Next morning. I've just re-read this and want to write it again, it's so unorganised and scribbly but Martin won't let me. He has insisted I write on the back of pages as I am using a whole pad per letter.

We fly on Saturday. Rudy is staying in town for a few days but will radio his wife to meet us. I'll stop now and post this and maybe another before we leave. Then, don't forget you won't hear from us for a long time, unless we can get a letter out. Don't worry if you don't hear, it's simply because there are no post offices in the jungle. We'll phone the moment we get back to Caracas.

The plane that we fly down in dips over Canaima (so they can put the kettle on) goes on up to Auyantepui, into the canyon to Angel Falls. The pilots take bets with each other on who can fly nearest to the wall of the canyon. Sounds like fun eh? Lots of love to all. Take care of yourselves, I worry about you. Hope the guinea pigs are fine. Love, T & M

Dear Graham and Ginny,

This is just a note to add to Tanis's letter, but don't show Mum and Dad! We expect to be in the jungle for three to four months and we won't be able to get letters out so we'll leave a couple with the Bishop to send to Mum every few weeks, just saying that all is well and we're still alive.

The only danger Rudy anticipates is trouble from miners, not in the canyons, just on the Carrao. He's told us to keep the gun loaded!

He doesn't see any real danger from animals, except the Bushmaster snake, which by all accounts will actually come out and attack people. It has a heat-sensitive pit on its head which acts as a rangefinder so it's always very accurate when it strikes. Apparently they're very common around Auyantepui. It grows to nine feet, and if it bites you, you'd better send for the priest!

The Carrao river has a high tannin content so you'd be all right

Graham, just add milk and sugar and you'd have a cup of tea. I'm looking to explore a river with a high alcohol content but I can't find one.

Love Martin.

CHAPTER EIGHT

All visible evidence of civilization was behind us. Leaning across Martin to peer out of the plane window, all I could see below was an endless carpet of green jungle stretching to the horizon, splashed with brilliant purple jacaranda trees in flower. A flat-topped mountain resembled a giant's castle, steep cliffs of bare rock, pink in the sunlight and blue in the shadow, with an emerald green summit.

This was the wild country of the Venezuelan Highlands, where strange table mountains called 'tepuis' reach heights of ten thousand feet. A thousand million years ago, these huge blocks of stone were part of a vast continuous plateau, that stretched from Colombia to French Guiana and south into Brazil. Since then, the relentless combination of rain, wind and sunshine has eroded the plateau and now, all that remain are these isolated masses of resistant rock, rising out of the forest. The rocks which form tepuis are among the most ancient on earth.

The plane descended steeply, levelled out, then followed the course of a wide river. Mid-stream the water looked black, but where it flowed over sandbanks it was bright orange. At frequent intervals the water whipped into white foam as it surged across rocky barriers. Dipping its wings over Camp Canaima, the plane headed toward Auyantepui. A massive rock bastion rose before us, grey and forbidding. We entered a vast canyon, it felt as if we were flying into a tunnel with four thousand foot cliffs forming its walls and a ceiling of swirling clouds.

Auyantepui's summit is a swamp and forest-covered plateau, as big as the Isle of Wight. The mountain acts as a giant condenser of atmospheric water. As a result, thirty feet of annual rainfall (compared to Britain's three feet) make it one of the wettest places on earth. Ephemeral waterfalls cascaded down the vertical rock face in silver streams. The plane banked and turned sharply, trees and rocks appeared in horrifyingly vivid detail and there, to our right, was an immensely tall column of water, seemingly suspended in space. Angel Falls. The highest waterfall in the world.

It's recorded that the falls were first reported in 1910 by Ernesto Sanchez La Cruz, but it was Jimmy Angel, a North American pilot-prospector who rediscovered them by chance in 1933 and gained immortality. Romantics owe him a debt of gratitude for possessing such a suitable name. We'd seen photographs of him. 'Jimmy Angel looked like Dad, didn't you think, Martin?' I mused. 'Blimey, that river looks a bit rough.' It was like a staircase fashioned from rock.

Forty miles downriver we landed at Canaima. Facing a magnificent horseshoe of waterfalls dropping into a wide, red lagoon, the setting was superb, but the camp was disappointing, packed with noisy holiday-makers on weekend excursions, transistor radios blaring pop music, the sand littered with Coke cans and other junk.

In the bar we met a goldminer called George, a soft spoken Canadian with a passion for the BBC World Service. A few years before there had been a goldrush on the Carrao, four thousand miners arrived and for a year this lawless community had worked a small, rich section of river, regularly murdering each other in knife and gun fights and committing suicide by descending the rapids blind drunk. When the gold ran out, most went elsewhere but a few stayed, working the Carrao in the dry season and retreating to Canaima when the rains came.

'This guy, he's crazy, he's got worms in his brain,' George said, inclining his head at a man approaching our table, 'Hi Willard.' Willard was a lean, fifty-year-old North American with a mass of dark curly hair and a permanent grin, unrelated to his mood. A dedicated loner, he had last been seen six months earlier. 'Where you been?' asked George.

'Oh, just sort of, over there.' Willard waved vaguely at the forest.

'Any luck?'

'Nope. Well yeah, a little, um nope, nothing much, don't rightly know.'

'Want a beer?' said George, pushing a bottle across the table.

'Nope, thank you kindly. Well maybe, yeah, I could use a cool beer. Hell no, but thank y'all the same.'

Willard had been in Venezuela for about twenty years but five years before, he'd suddenly become homesick, sold his gold and returned to live a life of luxury in the USA. After a year he was fed up and returned to the jungle. Before his last trip he had bought a new aluminium boat and outboard motor, but the outfit had been stolen (he was sure) by an Indian from Canaima. 'Now I'll find out who took it,' he assured us.

'How?'

'The guy who took it'll come and tell me.'

Local Indians have a tradition of sharing. Seeing miners as mean-spirited, they like to make mischief. But after a few months have passed they perceive the incident as forgotten and would be surprised still to encounter anger.

'What will you do?' Martin asked.

'Nothin, no point in doing anythin. He'll have got rid of it long ago and nothin I do'll get it back now, will it? I think I'll go get a beer.'

'See what I mean,' said George. 'It's the mercury does it.'

Willard seemed neither mad nor dangerous and we wondered if George had been serious. 'Those guys there,' indicating a group of men at the bar, 'are real mean bastards. The one on the left, he knifed three men one year, French he is, looks real friendly, don't he?'

Not any more he didn't!

'See the guy on the end, next to that tourist?' He looked like everybody's favourite uncle. 'Colombian, chopped up his best buddy with a machete. Can't find a partner now.'

'I'm not surprised,' said Martin. 'How come they're not in jail?'

'Who's gonna arrest 'em? No police down here. So long as they don't bother the tourists or cause trouble here, nobody cares what they do to each other in the bush. I kinda remember hearing they took over this place at gunpoint some time ago. Maybe just a rumour I heard. You got a gun?' We nodded. 'Keep that quiet here, and watch out up there on the river, they'll steal your gun soon as look at you, and your outfit. Just stop any trouble before it starts.'

I took a deep breath and plunged in, 'How do we do that?'

'Shoot 'em! There's plenty of places to bury them.'

'WHAT!' we said in unison. 'You're not serious?'

'Sure, but don't bury them right by the river, when the rains come the river'll wash bodies down here, tourists don't like that. And don't put no little crosses up neither.'

I looked at George in a new light. *He* knew we'd got a gun.

'Don't you fret,' he said drily, 'I'm going up the Caroni.'

Rudy's wife Gerti arrived with the Land Rover to take us to Ucaima. In a straight line, their camp is only a couple of miles from Canaima, but the road winds across grasslands taking wide detours to avoid thickets of trees, with the last half mile through dense forest. 'We had one hell of a job cutting a way through here,' said Gerti.

'You and Rudy made this road?'

'Rudy was manager of Canaima, but after they enlarged the airstrip and all those trippers came down, he decided to make another camp up here. Much more peaceful.'

Our inflatable dinghy lay on the beach, plump and sleek in the morning sunshine. Rudy looked at it doubtfully. 'I tell you that's a fast river. There's one hell of a bunch of rapids up there. The first ones you hit are the Mayupa, seven bitches in a row, just around that bend,' he pointed upriver. 'A couple of years ago a whole lot of American guys in two rubber boats, twice the size of that, set off from here,' he chuckled wickedly, 'they capsized on Mayupa, lost everything, and gave up. Broke a few bones too I think.'

There was no changing things at this late stage and Tanis and I began loading equipment on to the boat while Rudy dropped snippets of advice.

On went thirty gallons of gasoline. 'When you fall in, turn on your back, face downstream, legs out in front, then you don't bust your skull.'

Followed by kit bags full of food. 'Don't hunt; then the Indians will leave you alone.'

Tent, sleeping bags, spare clothes. 'Don't camp on islands, a flash flood will wash you away.'

Engine spares, repair kits, oars and boat-cover. 'You get some fun on the Churrún river, the one that goes to Angel Falls, there are seventy-nine sets of rapids. Counted them myself.'

Engine oil, tool-kit, rope and ammunition. 'When you're past Mayupa, try out the gun, see if it works!'

Medical kit. 'Jesus, where are you two going to sit?'

Machetes, pots and pans, gun. 'Keep the gun hidden in the boat, but handy, listen for outboards, that means miners. Indians, they won't trouble you. Remember, get back before the rains set in. OK? So have fun.'

The small crowd of Indian workers from the camp had assembled to watch us depart. They waved as we began to move upstream, but we were going so slowly that it was ten minutes before a bend in the river hid us from view. Our arms and faces ached from waving and smiling. Feeling elated but very alone, we made our snail-like way up the Carrao river in our overladen boat, admiring the scenery and feeling a bit overawed. From the overhanging trees, vines trailed in the river, tugged into sweeping curves by the current. The water was spectacular; crystal clear and stained deep amber by humic acids leached from the vegetation, resembling wine in the shallows, black ink where it was more than a couple of feet deep. Tepuis, blue and misty with distance, sat on the horizon. We couldn't see Auyantepui.

'Land of Lost Souls' is the name given to this mysterious country of forest, savannah and mountains. The summits of tepuis are separated from the jungle below. Plants and animals living up there experience a different climate and for millenia have evolved in isolation; this, coupled with the mythology and remoteness of the region, provided the inspiration for Sir Arthur Conan Doyle's *Lost World*.

The river flowed swiftly as we approached the Mayupa rapids. Attached to the rocks, subjected to the fast, turbulent water grows a plant called *podostemaceae*. For much of the year these plants resemble seaweed, but in the dry season the water level falls, leaving them exposed to sunshine. Before they shrivel and die, they burst into flower and as the water level gradually falls more and more plants bloom. Whole stretches of the Mayupa rapids were fast becoming a beautiful flower garden in pink, purple and blue. Drawing closer our progress slowed until, even with engine roaring at full throttle, we weren't moving at all. Though we hadn't imagined we'd be able to motor up rapids, to discover we couldn't even motor up close to them was a shock.

It didn't appear too dangerous, only tricky, so without further ado I took hold of the painter – a long rope attached to the front of the boat – and clambered ahead over the rocks, while Tanis stayed with the boat, guiding it around obstacles. Together we would push and pull it upstream. When the rope was taut I signalled to Tanis and began to pull; meanwhile she hopped from rock to rock pushing the boat into the current, constantly slipping on the wet podos but keeping well out of the river. 'Look, Tan,' I said 'if we're going to do this you'll just have to get in the water.'

'Couldn't I sit in the boat and push it off rocks that way?'

'No. You'll have to get in. I don't know what you're worried about, there's nothing in it,' I said.

'How do you know, you can't even see the bottom?' she said, voice rising, 'and it's not you that'll be up to your neck in it.'

The river was new to us both and though it wasn't creatures lurking underwater that bothered me, I'd found that when the water was only knee deep it was difficult to maintain balance. At anything greater than hip depth, the resistance made it almost impossible to move forward. I wallowed ahead and began heaving on the rope. For two minutes Tanis managed to stay on dry land before the current caught the boat and spun it sideways, leaving her suspended horizontally above the water, feet on a rock and hands clinging to the boat. Eventually she fell, with an ungainly splash and reappeared swimming for the bank in deep water downstream. After that she was all right, which was just as well, because several times I fell on the slippery rocks, let go of the rope, and the boat was carried off by the current with Tanis clinging to its side.

It took four hours to get past that first rapid and we were grateful that nobody witnessed our antics, though when we finally reached quiet water we were inordinately pleased with ourselves: despite our ineptitude we'd done it without losing or damaging anything. Skill would come with experience. For that day we'd had enough. We paddled toward a beach where the sand was criss-crossed with animal tracks and littered with broken shells of recently hatched turtles' eggs. Along the waterline hundreds of butterflies, green, yellow and orange, sucked nutrients from the wet sand and took flight in glorious, multi-coloured clouds at our approach.

Among the trees we cleared a space for our first jungle camp. Erecting the tent had seemed easy in our garden at home, but now, poles that had slotted so snugly together sprang apart with a life of their own at the slightest touch. As we made one side straight and taut, so the other hung slack. Blackflies converged on our bare ankles, their stinging bites leaving itchy blood blisters. I lit a fire and cooked our first jungle feast, beef curry with rice.

At dusk, armed with machetes and torch we set off to explore our surroundings. It was an island. 'That's one of Rudy's rules we've broken,' observed Tanis.

In the darkness, fireflies flashed on and off, like miniature, faulty light bulbs. Held in the torch beam, ruby eyes glared unwaveringly at us. A small spotted cat, a margay. The unearthly, wailing roar of a troupe of howler monkeys echoed across our island. It had been a halcyon day.

The Mayupa rapids took three days to ascend. Our flat inflatable was unable to slip through the narrow channels between rocks that nature surely had designed for dugout canoes. We had to portage; hours spent unloading the boat, carrying everything over the rocks to reload once more. Then the current was slow. The tangled vegetation was like a wall on each side of us, reflected in the still, dark water as in a mirror. Our voices echoed in the still air.

On an overcast morning we rounded a bend and Auyantepui was there ahead of us. The pink, sparkling rock we had seen from the plane had undergone a sinister metamorphosis, to a menacing cold bluish brown, masked by swirls of grey cloud. Standing like an impregnable fortress, we could appreciate why local Indians believe that the Devil lives on top of this tepui. Making camp was time-consuming and we aimed to stop no later than three-thirty in the afternoon. For Tanis, the best campsite was always beyond the next bend and she'd drive on in the hope of finding the perfect spot, which often resulted in a mad scramble to pitch the tent anywhere before it got dark.

At the mouth of a creek, we pulled into a sandbank and for some time the forest around us was quiet, silenced by our noisy activities. Then, just before sunset, cicadas began, increasing in volume and speed until the noise was like the whine of circular power saws. One by one, frogs began to croak; long slow 'GERLOOPS'. Somewhere in the distance a trill-phone rang; a tin bucket was banged with a stick; a random sequence of notes from a violin; a train whistle followed by a burst of insane laughter. Unidentified sounds have a place in the folklore of indigenous forest people: they believe them to be voices from the spirit world. For us, nearly every sound was unidentified.

Aonda, the smallest of the two canyons where we planned to spend a few weeks exploring, had its entrance via a channel, hidden behind an island surrounded by rapids. In the canyon, luxuriant forest sloped away from the riverbank, curving steeply upwards to the foot of turreted cliffs three thousand feet high. The boat stopped with a jerk, nearly pulling me over backwards. I turned to Tanis. 'What the. . . ?' She motioned me to silence and pointed up river to where a thin plume of smoke curled above the trees.

'I'll go and investigate,' I said, 'you load the gun and stay with the boat.' I picked up my machete and set off into the forest.

As soon as Martin was out of earshot I loaded the gun. We'd tried it out and it certainly worked, the kickback nearly dislocated my shoulder. I sat on the edge of the boat scrutinizing the bank. Suppose Martin came back with a bunch of miners in hot pursuit? I checked that the motor was ready to start, though with a maximum speed of four miles an hour and a rocky river, it wouldn't be a high speed getaway.

I wandered up and down. Would I, I asked myself, would I actually shoot someone? Returning to the boat I propped the gun against a tree. The bark moved. I peered at it. There, inches from my nose, was the biggest spider I had ever seen! A perfect camouflage artist, its body an inch and a half in diameter, legs all of four inches long, barely visible, flattened against the tree. It disappeared. This was serious. If it dropped into the boat directly underneath, it could scuttle into a kit bag, emerge at night and cause havoc in the tent. I'd forgotten about Martin when there was a rustling in the bushes and I grabbed the gun. 'You won't believe this, Tan, not in a million years,' he said.

'What is it?'

'Well,' he began.

'Don't lean against that tree! There's a massive spider on it,' I interrupted.

'If you're not going to listen . . .'

'I'm listening, see if you can see it, it's incredible.'

'Tan, if you don't want to hear . . .'

'Sorry, go on.'

'Up there in the jungle is a big canvas awning and, . . .'

'But whose is it?'

'I wish you'd let me finish, I'm coming to it. In a large clearing, weeding tomato plants, there's an old man. He must be in his sixties, spectacles tied on with string, and stark naked!' he ended with a flourish.

Good God, he's got a touch of the sun! 'Go on,' I said cautiously.

'Under the awning is a virtual library, including a copy of *The Naked Ape* in English.'

'I see, Martin. OK. What was it really?'

'Follow me,' he said, and set off along the bank.

'Now do you believe me. I told him you were with me and he's put his shorts on,' he whispered.

Just as Martin had said, there was a canvas awning and a man. He had a craggy, weatherbeaten look, wild sunbleached hair and a beard. He was indeed wearing shorts, knee length, voluminous and full of holes. We shook hands. 'How are your tomato plants?' I asked, as if I'd just arrived at his suburban bungalow for tea.

'Zay are good, yes, good, I think I shall haff many fruits. Come, come to see zem.' The circular clearing was dominated by felled trees. 'I cut zeese to make a camp and every day I burn zem. Zis is how you find me yes?' Neat rows of plants were laid out in well-raked beds. There were a few banana trees but there wasn't enough food here for a man to survive on.

'What do you live on?'

His eyes lit up and he flung his arms wide. 'Fresh air, fresh air!' he shouted, as if we were fools to worry about a little thing like food.

'Are there any other people around?' I quizzed.

'You are the first persons since I am here.'

'How long is that?'

'Zat would be eleven years. Now, you go, I must work.'

Upstream we found a camp site, a high beach littered with driftwood. I began unloading the boat. 'Hold on, Tan,' Martin called, 'this is an island.'

I was too tired to care and extolled its virtues. 'Look, it hasn't rained for weeks, it's higher than the first beach we camped on and it means we won't have to cut a clearing,' I said. 'Go on, let's risk it.'

'It's not high enough,' he complained, 'a flash flood could wash it away.'

'Martin, I'm too tired to move.'

The tent refused to co-operate and we left it leaning drunkenly to one side. A plate of chicken curry and rice, washed down with mugs of coffee did wonders for our morale, but later as we settled down to sleep, Martin said again. 'I still think we should have moved.'

At about one in the morning the sky fell down. Martin was asleep and I hoped he'd stay that way until it stopped. Two hours later, as the storm began to abate, a soft, ominous voice said. 'Tanis, you were wrong. The water's coming in.'

I could believe it.

'The boat,' Martin said, struggling from the sleeping bag, 'the kit bags are in it and they're not tied up. I KNEW something like this would happen.' He crawled out of the doorway, splashing straight into the river, which had risen to the front of the tent.

Rain was pouring through the mosquito net windows too, since we'd left the shutters open. Delicately I suggested that he close them. I could hear him crashing and splashing around the tent, swearing as he tripped over guy ropes in the dark. He crawled back in, dripping wet and very angry. Before he had a chance to speak I said brightly, 'Next time Martin, I think *you* should pick the campsite.'

CHAPTER NINE

Martin stood on the bank. 'I've found a natural clearing, perfect for a campsite,' he said. The clearing was a yard square.

'Oh Martin!' I began, 'it's miles from the river.'

'Don't start moaning,' he cut in, 'we've had a dose of your campsites, remember?'

That morning had been spent mopping up the damage before heading upriver to find a more permanent site, a base from which we'd explore the canyon. By the time we'd finished unloading, the moon had risen with a face so bright and clear, we could make out its features. As we crept along the tiny trail to the tent, blackness descended, all trace of light obscured by the canopy. It was impossible for us to get in the tent without allowing entry to mosquitoes; they festooned the walls. As we zipped ourselves in, they whined in our ears and fastened onto any available flesh. Soon the walls were splattered with our blood, where we'd squashed them.

Night in the jungle, a cacophony of sound. Crashes, bangs, growls, squeaks and whistles. A rustle outside the window then a twang as a creature bumped into a guy rope. Probably an armadillo. From deep in the forest behind the tent came a tremendous commotion followed by a desperate scream. Something had had its dinner. And then came a different noise; a deep ominous rumbling, reverberating through the canyon, growing louder by the second. Not thunder, and not far away. The noise receded, the ground ceased trembling and for a while the jungle was silent. 'There's only one thing *that* could have been,' said Martin thoughtfully, 'a landslide.'

From the river came loud plops and splashes: caimans, South American alligators. 'Let's go out in the boat tomorrow night and look for things,' he said, inspired by the sounds. I lay in the darkness wondering what things we might find.

The boat drifted into the bank, hitting the wood with a dull thud. I put one leg over the side onto a flat, gnarled log. Suddenly it reared up and a massive pair of jaws full of vicious yellow teeth clamped shut on my leg, chomping through my shin bone as if it were wax. A stream of blood and blobs of torn, red flesh dropped into the water. The creature shook its head back and forth, trying to drag me into the river and down to its underwater lair. With clenched fists I pounded on its snout again and again.

'Tan, wake up,' Martin was shaking me. For a moment I was frozen with terror before I realised where I was. 'You were lashing out like mad, you punched me on the head,' he said indignantly.

'I had a terrible nightmare, and I tell you now, I'm not looking for things at night, and that's definite!'

At ten o'clock the next night a clear starlit sky illuminated the water as we paddled quietly upstream, our eyes becoming accustomed to the darkness. After a time, we put down the paddles and let the current take the boat slowly back. For the next fifteen minutes we shone torches at every likely-looking object but they all turned out to be inanimate tree trunks or rocks and we began to feel our quest was in vain. Lighting cigarettes we started to talk, in whispers at first but soon we were having a lively discussion about the food we would eat when we returned to Caracas, all thoughts of caimans replaced by cheese and cream cakes. Suddenly there was an alarming splash, followed immediately by two more, as several large, panicking animals launched themselves into the water a few feet in front of the boat. Capybaras, rodents like giant guinea pigs, four feet long and weighing a hundred pounds. Disappointed that we had missed an opportunity to observe them, we resumed our careful scrutiny of the riverbank.

Soon we were rewarded by the sight of an eight foot long caiman, stretched out on the trunk of a fallen tree, just above the water. Holding torches at eye level, the caiman's eyes shone back at us like embers. It reacted to the light by opening one eye, then closing it and opening the other, as if winking at us. As we passed, it turned its head around so that the long jaws lay along its back, and continued to survey us over its shoulder, one eye at a time. Finally, realising that it hadn't fooled us into thinking it was a one-eyed log, it slid backwards into the water with hardly a splash and was gone. Seeing the caiman – who had seemed so personable – allayed my dream-fears and that night I slept soundly.

Breakfast was flour and water flattened into pancakes, fried in oil and thinly spread with Bovril. Two mugs of coffee and we were ready to face the day. First we would domesticate the camp. Martin went to collect firewood while I organised the tent. Behind me I sensed a movement. Emerging from a pile of clothes was a spider, its body the size and colour of a walnut, with stout furry legs. As I backed away it ran at great speed into a corner – why do spiders never stroll? We regarded each other, like boxers waiting for the bell. I had read that large hairy spiders are always called tarantulas, but true tarantulas come from Italy. This creature was too full of energy to have made such a journey. It was a trap-door spider, capable of inflicting a nasty, but seldom fatal bite, and then only in dire circumstances. Trapped in the corner, towered over by a giant, it must surely feel justified in defending itself. Seconds out. The longest objects I could find were a plastic bottle and a large spoon and, thus armed, I herded it through the door and out of the camp.

I cleared an area around the tent with my machete, then with a branch, swept the jungle floor clean of leaves and debris, hoping that snakes and spiders would now think twice about crossing this no-man's-land. A rope between two trees made a washing line and the sleeping bags hung up to air. A thin sapling, felled with thirty-seven badly directed chops, made a trestle above the fire for cooking pots.

At the river, holding a branch to lower myself down the bank left my hand covered with itchy bumps and blisters. The tree looked exactly the same as the harmless one I'd tied the washing line to. The water looked like diluted Coca-Cola in our plastic containers. Coffee bubbled in the kettle. A mountainous bundle of firewood broke through the bushes, settled on the ground and Martin emerged from the middle of it, looking pleased with himself. 'This should keep us going for a while' he said.

The camp was like home, a place where we could relax and write letters that would not be posted for months.

Somewhere in the Aonda Canyon.

Dear Graham and Ginny,

Tanis will have filled you in on the details so I'll give you an idea of what it's like here. The canyon goes about seven miles into the mountain and is two to three miles wide. It's not marked on any maps, an oil company made an aerial survey of the whole north of the mountain a couple of years ago, but they missed out this canyon because it was covered in cloud when they took the pictures.

The jungle in the valley is of a low type, around fifty feet high with occasional big trees; it's nothing like the lowland forests. The vegetation is incredibly varied, like all jungles, and there are lots of flowers (which is unusual) and orchids everywhere. We've made a permanent camp twenty yards from the river and we leave our stuff and go out from here.

This place has a lot of cats, especially jaguar. Rudy thinks that it may be a breeding ground, or that they go to the top of the mountain from somewhere in the canyon to breed. Their tracks are everywhere, some much wider than my foot. Also, black jaguar which are rare in most places are found here. We haven't seen any jaguars yet, though we've seen a margay and an ocelot. It's very exciting to see a cat in the wild. It confirmed my belief that the skins look a lot better on the animals than they do on the backs of wealthy women. We've noticed that there are more humming birds here than we've seen anywhere else and today I found a place not far from our camp where they come to feed. It's fairly open country with lots of flowering bushes and there were humming birds everywhere, flying right up to us and hovering in front of our faces like insects. I found a nest, three feet off the ground, on the end of a branch. The nest was about two inches across and had a single tiny egg.

We've seen two other things of quite astonishing size: some bats which looked as big as vultures, and a spider (which fortunately Tanis didn't see, she'd probably be on her way home now if she had), it had a bright blue abdomen and about a seven inch leg span, it would have covered most of this page. This evening there was another rockfall, so now Auyantepui is a little bit smaller. I wonder how many millions of years that sound has been echoing over the jungles here?

It's very early in the morning and we've just had breakfast. It's cool and fresh like an early morning in Spain. Through the trees I can see the river, reflecting the jungle on the opposite bank like a mirror. Behind that rises the sheer face of the mountain, pink in the sunlight. Every so often, parrots and toucans fly across the river, making as much noise as they possibly can, for no apparent reason. There's nothing menacing about the jungle in the mornings and evenings, it's like being in a particularly lovely forest anywhere. Like that forest around Loch Marie in Scotland, on a hot summer day.

The canyon is much deeper than we thought. From our camp it takes about four hours to get halfway along it, through the jungle and across the rivers. The scenery is stunning. The river runs over wide, flat rock beds and everywhere are colossal boulders, fifty feet high and more, often with jungle growing on top of them. The canyon cliffs rise sheer on either side. I can't imagine more spectacular scenery could exist anywhere.

From our camp we go first through tall spindly trees, very close together. You have to cut your way through. This goes into big tree country higher up, with dangling lianas and epiphytes growing everywhere. This is fairly open ground but quite dark, with the canopy overhead; this is the kind of forest I like best. Higher still, it's much more open, with bushes and trees like oaks, lots of flowers and humming birds. The smells are lovely. In contrast, as you go down again, you get into damp, gloomy jungle, rotting logs everywhere and boggy ground, no sunlight getting through. Most of the trees are palms and ferns and many are covered in thorns and spines – a very ancient sort of jungle it seems, dank and oppressive, you could well imagine dinosaurs walking about in it.

Yesterday, near our camp was a troupe of big monkeys; they shook the branches and broke sticks and threw them at us. There was a young one which was so fascinated by us that he wouldn't go away, just kept jumping up and down and squeaking, until an adult came back and dragged him away.

It's strange living in the jungle. Most nights we just hear the usual rustles and noises, but a couple of nights ago it was terrifying. There was a dreadful crashing just a few yards from the tent, then more *crashing and a great splash in the river. Perhaps it was a jaguar killing a tapir? It was unnerving, we feared that something was going to come charging onto the tent.*

We think we might try to climb the mountain. It should be possible, the vegetation seems to go right to the top in places, it can't be more than four thousand feet high. We'll have to take provisions with us and sleep out. When you consider that this part of the world is largely unexplored, it's not hard to see why when you're trying to get into it. Much love to all.

Martin.

The incentive for Martin and me to explore the canyon came from a suggestion by Rudy about the possible existence of waterfalls even higher than Angel Falls. Cloud cover, air turbulence and jagged rock pinnacles hundreds of feet high, discouraged close investigation of the deepest parts of the canyons from low-flying aircraft.

So enthusiastic were we to make this discovery that we'd already named it and could visualize the entry in the *Guinness Book of Records*: '. . . the highest waterfall in the world is Jordan Falls, with a total drop of . . . discovered by . . .'

Weighed down with cameras, machetes, gun, antivenin, compasses, sleeping bags, food and the boat cover, we set off. By midday we had reached the end of our trail, a high point from which we could see eight waterfalls, all over a thousand feet high and one pouring from a hole in the canyon wall. From here on, the terrain got steadily worse. Where the valley sloped down from the cliffs, twisted trees grew on boulders the size of houses, separated by yawning chasms and spanned by bridges of matted tree roots and debris. Everything was so overgrown that we had to fight our way through. Often we couldn't tell logs from rocks until we sank to our waists in rotting wood. So tightly packed was the foliage that trees stood where they died, with no room to fall. Using machetes simply brought masses of debris down on our heads. In places we crawled through gaps between boulders, emerging covered in green slime. Everywhere was slippery and dangerous.

The upper canyon was a frightening place, cold, misty and

wet. Between the rocks we couldn't see the ground, only inky blackness with the hollow sound of water rushing far below The further we went, the bigger the jumbled heap of rocks became. Laboriously we continued, like two ants journeying across a bomb site. Martin dropped a rock into a crevasse and an echoing splash came back three seconds later. I stood on an ants' nest and hundreds of the red devils ran up my legs, biting and stinging. As I frantically brushed them off, the camera bag slipped from my shoulder, rolled over and over and fell down a crevasse. Flat on our stomachs we peered over the edge; the bag was balanced on a ledge four feet below.

'Right,' said Martin confidently, 'we can get it. I'll hold your legs and lower you down a bit, it's only just out of reach.'

'Oh no, *I'm* not going down there, no Martin. I'll hold *your* legs and you get it.'

'Don't be silly, you couldn't hold me. Anyway, you dropped it. Come on, I won't let you go.'

I edged forward. 'Don't just hold my trousers, hold my legs.' I had visions of slipping straight out of my loose trousers, head first down the hole. By the time we'd got the bag it was too late to continue.

The danger of rolling into a crevasse in our sleep seemed very real and we made our way down to the river. Here, the water was channelled through gulleys and plunged over ledges, beside gigantic boulders honeycombed with caves. Some smelled strongly of cats and in places the rocks were dark and shiny up to three feet from the ground, where jaguars or mountain lions had rubbed against them. A possible refuge for the night was an overhanging rock, one side of which had been worn away, leaving a shallow cave ten feet deep by twenty wide. Trees grew on top of this, their thick roots wound around its side and went deep into the soil below. The floor of this natural shelter was soft, white sand, marked only by a few lizard tracks. Remembering the rockfalls we heard regularly, all that weight above us seemed perilous to me, but it was late and we didn't have much choice.

In minutes we'd made camp. It was just a case of laying the sleeping bags on the ground and lighting a fire. As we ate tonight's special, vegetable curry with rice, with a sprinkling of over-adventurous mosquitoes on top for spice, there came a clicking and whistling in the darkness. Bats. They swooped around us, invisible except when the fire flared, to reveal that the air was full of them. Bats, in general, are well mannered creatures, but one kind in particular has a sinister habit. Complete with natural anaesthetic in its saliva, it creeps up on its prey, painlessly inflicts a wound by scraping away skin with its teeth and then proceeds to lap the flowing blood. The saliva of this mouse-sized, mobile operating theatre also contains an anti-coagulant which causes the victim to bleed excessively, out of all proportion to the size of the wound. A vampire bat's sleeping victim might wake to find face or feet glued to the bedding by dried blood. Taking a glowing log, Martin made a second fire, hoping to keep away curious animals and snakes. The expansive boat cover enveloped us completely, propped up in each corner by sticks and touching us nowhere. That should keep the bats at a distance.

It was a long night. At the slightest movement the stiff material crackled in our ears. The sticks had fallen at the first turn and the great effort required to keep it from touching our faces drove us mad. It was like sleeping in a massive paper bag. At midnight both fires gave a final flicker and plunged us into blackness. Explicitly stating his feelings about jungle camps, Martin rose and re-lit them. But further sleep was impossible and at four-thirty, sore-eyed from wood smoke and lack of sleep, but unbitten by anything larger than a mosquito, we rose, made coffee and waited for sunrise. During the sleepless hours we'd reviewed our position. It would take a week to reach the end of the canyon. If one of us fell between the boulders how would we get out? Food and rope. It would be foolhardy to continue without both. We returned to the tent, gathered the items and were on our way again by sunset.

Next day we continued the trail.

Chop, chop, chop. 'Martin, you're deviating to the left.'

Chop, chop, chop. 'Martin, you're still deviating.'

Chop, chop, 'Aaaaaagh!' He bounded into the air, hurling down his machete and tearing off his shirt. Oh my God, he's been bitten by a snake. He should be keeping calm, not jumping about in a frenzy. 'Get back,' he yelled, 'don't come, *slap*, *slap*, near, fire ants . . . everywhere.' Slap.

'Little red ones?' I said, gleefully, 'like the ones that ran up my legs when I dropped the cameras?'

He was on the floor now, pulling off his trousers. 'Christ, it's like red hot needles.' His performance would have inspired Houdini as he stripped to his pants to beat the last ants off. 'It's not funny, Tan, where's my machete?'

'I don't know, Mart. You dropped it.'

Later, as we returned to the cave, Martin stopped abruptly and pointed into the bushes. I caught a flash of red. 'It's a "Cock of the Rock" I think,' he whispered. We stole nearer. It was a splendid bird, the most intensely vivid red I'd ever seen, with a semi-circular crest. It strutted around the forest floor, took flight and settled on a low branch. 'Get the camera,' he murmured. As I unzipped the bag the bird skittered and flew across to a bush. We crept forward but alerted now it flew high into a tree, out of sight.

'Damn it,' I exclaimed.

'Never mind, at least we saw it.'

It was also our folly. When we turned back to the trail we couldn't find it. For a moment we panicked and dashed this way and that until Martin commanded, 'Stop! We're going about this all wrong, we'll end up in a mess if we're not careful.'

'Martin, we're already in a mess, we're lost!'

'We can find the trail if we're careful, now don't get excited.'

'I'm not excited, I just said that we . . .'

'Don't let's have an argument, Tan.'

'Argument? I'm not arguing, you said I was excited, you always say that. It's really annoying.'

'Well, you annoy me sometimes.'

'And you annoy me lots of times,' I countered, frustrated at not being able to flounce away.

'*Me*? What do *I* do to annoy *you*?'

'You ask where something is and don't listen properly when I tell you, then moan because you can't find it.'

'OK. Now we know we annoy each other, let's get out of here. You stay still and I'll search in different directions, but whatever you do keep talking, so I know where you are.'

Our initial alarm was tempered somewhat by a more reasoned appraisal of our situation. We were in a canyon and even if we'd lost the trail completely, we could make our way down to the river and follow it back to our camp – that's one good thing about being in a canyon.

I talked to the trees, they listened attentively. Three quarters of an hour later I heard a shout and led by Martin's voice, joined him back on the trail. The fright had given us extra adrenalin and we sped along. 'We mustn't do that again, Tan.'

'Blimey, not likely,' I puffed. 'Mart?'

'What?'

'You don't really annoy me a lot.'

'You don't annoy me either.'

Several days later, we were making our way around the end of the canyon. On the few occasions when the cloud lifted, we were granted a magnificent view down into the valley, while behind us soared a vertical wall of crumbling sandstone, thousands of feet high. A hundred feet above us was an overhanging ledge and on this grew the continuous line of trees, sloping gently upwards. Days before, viewed from a distance, it had appeared an easy prospect to walk up this ledge to the summit of Devil Mountain. There was nowhere we could climb it.

It was like a holiday to be back at our camp. The tent seemed like a four star hotel and we sunbathed, swam, read books and generally relaxed for days, before packing up and moving on up the Carrao River. If Jordan Falls exists, it awaits discovery by someone else; someone perhaps, with a more romantic name.

CHAPTER TEN

The first miners we saw, roared past our camp in a canoe with a powerful motor. There were four men. 'Shoot them, Martin!'

Minutes later they roared past in the opposite direction, eyes everywhere. I stopped laughing and loaded the gun. I needed to ask myself a question here. If there was no other choice, would I be prepared to shoot somebody; to blast a fellow human being apart with our sixteen bore shotgun? The answer was yes. It was like knowing we had a really good insurance policy. I sat on the bank, shotgun prominently displayed across my knees. I was nervous. I'd never shot anything, not even a rabbit. Perhaps it would have been better if I'd shot a few rabbits, by way of practise for my first goldminer. When they came by for the third pass they didn't stop and left me feeling like an actor in a western.

The exhilaration of being under way, out of the confines of the canyon, on a wide open river again, was like champagne. The weeks ahead were full of promise as we continued up the Carrao, though no longer were we in uninhabited country. Sometimes we'd pass huts on river banks, where lived Indians who had deserted the various Catholic and Fundamentalist missions, to return to a life of hunting, fishing and planting.

It seemed that these people deliberately kept as far apart from each other as possible, not wanting neighbours. It was unusual to find a dwelling within two miles of the next. The occupants, on the rare occasions we saw one, would watch unsmiling and without evident curiosity as we chugged past. A wave from us would produce minimal response; movement of a hand, nod of a head, no change of expression. But oddly there was no impression of animosity or even unfriendliness, just the profound impassiveness of those who had chosen solitude. These people, mostly Waika (Yanomamo) Indians, no longer enamoured of the missionary and his gods, did not return to the large tribal groups living to the south and west but stayed, as if in some cultural limbo, between the two.

The engine spluttered, coughed, then belched to a stop. No encouraging words could persuade it to start; we paddled to the bank. 'Perhaps it's hot,' said Tanis, sounding like a qualified mechanic. Around the bend, set back from the river, was a dwelling and we wandered over to it. The hut was twelve feet square, a palm-thatched roof, three walls of rough planks, the fourth side open. The occupant was away and we stood on the threshold looking into his home. A hammock hung diagonally across the room. Trousers, shirt and straw hat hooked over a nail on the wall. In a corner, a kettle, saucepan and some enamel-ware. The place was clean and there wasn't enough in it to be anything but tidy. He would have his other possessions with him: canoe, a dog perhaps, day clothes, fishing tackle, machete, and possibly a shotgun. We felt chastened. A yellowed newspaper clipping was pinned up, about an Indian from a mission who'd got an important job and lived in Caracas. The photograph gave nothing away, a blurred snapshot, an indistinguishable smiling face that could have been man, woman or child. We wondered if he was a friend or relative of the man who lived here. Or was it just a dream of aspiration? A reminder that it was possible for the outside world to embrace an Indian.

The engine still refused to start. Lifting the cover I studied the mass of machinery, fervently wishing I'd paid more attention to Graham.

'Graham always said "clean the spark plugs". Where's the wire brush?' said Tanis.

In my mind appeared a picture of the last time I'd seen it. 'I left it on the kitchen table at home.' The only thing we were capable of doing to this engine was to clean the spark plugs and we didn't have a wire brush. With a safety pin and a nail file we scraped the carbon-encrusted plugs clean and the engine purred smoothly back to life.

Even the sparse population along the Carrao was sufficient to make animals scarce, driving them away or making them shy and seminocturnal in habit. Near the mountain we'd regularly seen otters and monkeys, occasionally deer and peccaries and on a few occasions, cats big and small. Now sightings were rare events, though one creature was here in abundance, the river turtle. Along the miles of clean sand, exposed as the dry season progresses and water level drops, female turtles emerge from the water, crawl up the beaches, laboriously dig holes and lay scores of ping pong ball eggs into them. Frequently we'd see scavengers at work, eggshells scattered all over, nosed out in the first instance by an industrious mammal, then taken over by a posse of vultures, excitable and belligerent, gobbling down eggs (and sometimes young turtles) until bloated, they'd be unable to fly and would lumber off across the sands, like overfattened turkeys, in futile attempts to take off. Then they'd stand, panting and puffing, burping and farting, red-faced, angry-eyed and looking vulnerable and rather silly. There's something likeable about vultures that's difficult to account for. The Carrao River was more populated and less interesting than we had hoped and we yearned for the quiet solitude of the mountain. Next day we would head down-stream to the Churrun canyon.

By the second mug of coffee, as the dawn mist began to lift, our tranquillity was disturbed by voices. Around the bend, fifty yards away, came a canoe paddled by two wild looking men. 'Get the gun,' I ordered softly.

'It's in the boat somewhere.'

This is ridiculous, I thought. Our casualness with the firearm is appalling. 'Then get in the boat and find it,' trying to look ready for anything while speaking through clenched teeth like a ventriloquist. Nonchalantly I picked up a machete, as if I always greeted guests with a two foot long knife in my hand.

The canoe scraped on the sand. They were young and unshaven and wore scrappy tee shirts and stained jeans. Wide-brimmed straw hats hid their eyes. The silence was broken by the lap of the wake. They (the unknown) fidgeted nervously when Tanis snapped the loaded gun shut. 'Hi,' said the one in front, 'I'm John, this is Ed.' American law students, they had purchased a dugout at the Camarata Indian Mission on the Acanan River, paddled it down the Carrao, and now were planning to travel up to Angel Falls. Like us, they weren't living off the land and were worried that their remaining tins of meat and sardines would not be enough.

We'd met in mutual mistrust and fifteen minutes later, parted as friends, each having gained from the meeting: three dried dinners swapped for one fresh pineapple.

The Churrun river surged out of the mouth of the canyon. Facing us, the first of seventy-nine rapids. There is no right way to get up a rapid; each one is different and each a case of trial and error. The right hand side of this one was black and fast with polished boulders but on the left it was shallower, rocky patches strewn with deadwood and angry whitewater bursting through everywhere. We could wade through the shallows, floating the boat in the deeper water.

Near the top there was no choice but to get out into deeper water where the river channeled around a large flat-topped rock. The water was rib-deep as I inched my way round the rock. Every time I forced a leg forward, the current dragged it back and only with enormous effort did I make any headway. A glance behind revealed the top of Tanis's head as she held the boat firm, her back to the fast current, legs propped against submerged rocks and fallen trees. It was impossible for me to pull the boat up until I gained the shallower stretch above the boulder. Nearly there, I stepped forward and my leg dropped a foot down a hole. As if waiting for just such an opportunity, the current yanked me free. Hoping my leg still had a foot on the end of it, I was zipped past Tanis and accidentally tugged the painter, sending the boat spinning crazily. I just had time to remember to face the way I was going before I was horizontally running at high speed, feet bouncing from boulder to boulder. Good, both feet were still there.

I waded back up river and found Tanis with the boat. It was a sobering experience for us both, to see how in a moment things can go very wrong. Now we had it all to do again. 'I hope I can remember where that bloody hole is,' I said.

'Next time I'll have the camera ready, your face was a picture.'

Between rapids lay stretches of quiet water, sometimes with no detectable current, tranquil and dreamlike as a John Constable mill pond. Shaded by jungle, the water's surface was littered with a fine debris of dead leaves, twigs and dust. It created the illusion of sliding across the solid surface of a dusty mirror; that you could take a broom, sweep up the dust and make the water shiny again. Irridescent humming birds hovered among the flowers of rhododendron-like bushes along the bank. Kingfishers crowded into these quiet places; around one pool we counted fourteen, of three different species, taking turns to catch the fish disturbed by our passage.

We covered about two miles and fifteen sets of rapids that day, none as severe as the first and some merely tedious stretches of pebbly shallows.

Night, and a splendid campsite under a roof of corrugated iron, bolted onto scaffold poles, constructed by Rudy as a shelter for his expeditions. 'Tan, wake up.' Martin shook my foot.

'Ummmm,' I stretched sensually, 'come back to bed.'

'No time for that, there's a bloody great tear in the boat.'

It lay upside-down on the shingle beach, looking like an elephant's rump. Dozens of scratches, scraps of torn grey rubber; the bottom of the boat looked as though it had been lacerated by a giant cheese grater. 'Where's the tear?' I asked peering contact lens-less at the devastation. It was five inches long and would take an hour to mend but a day for the glue to dry.

The enforced lay up was a bonus. Travelling every day meant make-do and muddle. Tidy by nature, I had been longing for an opportunity to rearrange kit bags, clean the tent, scrub the boat, scour utensils, wash sleeping bags, shoes and clothes, and thoroughly scrub, scour and de-louse. The latter involved examining each other to remove the jungle ticks that dived with glee into our hair and down our backs for a soupçon of blood.

Porridge bubbled on the fire, little eddies of blue wood-smoke curling over the lip of the saucepan to add flavour to our breakfast. My toes hurt. 'You've stubbed them on rocks, that's all,' was Martin's flippant diagnosis.

'Pay attention. Have a proper look, they really hurt,' I complained. With a sigh he grabbed my foot, studied it in silence for a long time, then ripped off his plimsoll and looked at his toes.

'We've got maggots in our feet!'

Out came our little red book *Preservation of Health in Tropical Climates*. It called them 'jiggers', sand fleas picked up from damp shaded sandy places.

> After fertilisation the female flea penetrates the skin of man, usually through the foot; there it swells to the size of a pea and the eggs are discharged through a tiny hole in the swelling. Itching is considerable and ulceration of the skin can occur. The flea will die in the swelling but should be removed with a clean pin before inflammation sets in.

With disgusting enthusiasm Martin set to work and was soon hoiking them out like winkles from shells, twenty-five out of my left foot and nineteen from the right, removing two toenails in the process. But he suffered for sitting naked on the sand.

Keeping count of the rapids proved difficult; Rudy travelled in the rainy season when the river in spate would look vastly different. We stopped counting. Campsites developed person-alities. There was a place beside a creek which had a clean sandy beach, a perfect spot in the jungle for the tent and plenty of wood for the fire, but the place felt wrong. A vulture landed on a tree opposite, much closer to us than is usual. It spread its wings to the evening sunshine so that its shadow fell across the tent, then sat still as a piece of sculpture, unblinking yellow eyes scrutinising us. We capitulated and went to bed, to sleep fitfully, wondering if it knew something we didn't. Conversely we could feel happy camped in mucky, grotty jungle among clinging vines and ferns and dank vegetation. Our moods dictated by nature's moods, we felt able to sense when the jungle was jogging along happily and could perceive the tension that transmits itself through the forest before an event, such as a thunderstorm or a kill.

The scenery was on a grand scale. Massive cliffs visible on only one side, with higher waterfalls than we had yet seen, some cascading over the plateau rim and others issuing from fissures in the cliffs. The river progressed in a series of loops, like a child's illustration of Mr Earthworm. It was confusing; first the canyon wall was on our left, then round a bend it appeared on our right. Moss-covered islands dissected the river into narrow streams. In the distance a silver column of water, a river falling from the sky, glimpsed for a few moments until a veil of cloud drifted over the Angel Falls.

But we weren't there yet. Fast and wide, the rapid stretched for a quarter of a mile. Halfway up on the left, the river fell vertically seven feet, then continued without undue haste. The middle was an urgent tumult, rushing down to join the Orinoco as swiftly as possible, backflipping against rocks and churning through gulleys. There was just a chance on the right. Keeping close to the edge, we pushed and shoved till we were in a hollow where the river had undermined the bank. In front of us was a ten foot high bank, which jutted out like a breakwater. On top grew a substantial tree, its roots dangling over the edge. If Martin climbed the bank and I stayed in the boat we could pull and drag our way round.

The noise of rushing water was deafening. Inch by inch we progressed. Halfway, the boat turned sideways, waves broke over the stern and within seconds it filled to the top. Sliding back into the hollow I bailed out, mopping up the last puddles with our shirts. Up on the bank, Martin surveyed the scene. One choice was to start the engine and at full throttle motor diagonally across. The current would drag us back, but with luck not over the big drop. 'I'm not sure we should try it, Tan. If the sheer-pin went or the engine failed we'd go straight over the edge. Let's go back and start again . . .'

Clunk. A stone hit me on the head.

Crash. Earth and twigs fell in the boat. I looked up, what was he playing at?

Chunks the size of plates fell on me. 'Martin, the bank's collapsing!' A great clod of earth landed on my shoulder.

As he clambered into the boat I started the motor and pulled up and out into the surge. Instantly we stopped moving forward as our six horse power engine struggled valiantly against gravity. Automatically I leant forward, and Martin paddled like a maniac trying to force the boat to move. 'Come on, you can do it!' we shouted at the engine.

The drop behind us drew nearer. Then, imperceptibly we were creeping forward. Minutes later the tree that had been parallel was slightly behind us. The bank came closer, we moved faster, and faster. Now we were travelling at walking pace. 'We did it!' I shouted, over the roar.

'You're reckless, Tan,' Martin laughed. 'Do you realise how near we were to that drop, we almost went over it?'

'But we didn't have any choice.' I felt elated.

'Maybe we didn't, but for Christ sake next time give me a bit of warning first.'

Angel Falls. The great body of water that fell from the clouds seemed to be moving too slowly. As it descended, the stream broke up, tumbling over and over, turning and spiralling like an upside-down plume of smoke. No sound reached us. The water took fifteen seconds to fall. It was eerie, like watching a silent film in slow motion.

With the river between us and the Falls we established a camp. Nearby, a stone hut built by Rudy and Gerti was the only sign of civilization. Next morning, on the opposite bank, we found a steep forest trail. After about an hour we emerged onto an open rock ledge, drenched by fine spray, a hundred yards from where Angel Falls burst onto a boulder-strewn slope to form a fierce rocky river. The scene changed minute by minute; sometimes the Falls were obscured by mist, then later only the turreted cliff top would be visible, showing darkly through.

A butterfly, the biggest we'd ever seen, flapped along slowly and with great labour, buffeted by wind and spray. Its wings were larger than a man's hand. Accompanying it was a tiny butterfly, which fluttered erratically around its huge companion as if encouraging it, sometimes overtaking, sometimes dropping behind. It seemed appropriate that we should see our largest butterfly against the backdrop of the tallest waterfall in the world.

Time passed and we began to feel as if the entire canyon with its forests and orchids, cliffs and animals was our own private property; and certainly, Angel Falls belonged to us. But we were not entirely undisturbed. Swarms of harmless but maddening sweat-bees settled on us, hopelessly entangling themselves in our hair, crawling in our ears, eyes and up our noses. In the mornings, big black ants that looked like wingless hornets, wandered aimlessly over the tent. They fitted the description of the notorious 'ant twenty-four'. A sting from one of these inch-long insects is said to induce a twenty-four hour fever, but they are supposed to be loners. Why, then, were they converging on our tent in gangs?

And there were serpents in our Garden of Eden. Strolling along the riverbank behind Martin, trying to remember what it felt like to sit in a restaurant facing a plate of fresh salad and a glass of chilled wine, Martin stepped forward, gave a peculiar grunt then skipped impressively into the air, attaining a height that would have been the envy of a professional ballet dancer. He'd very nearly plonked his foot on top of a large bush-master, that dreaded rattlesnake-with-a-silent-rattle, the creature most feared from Mexico to Argentina. It reared up before us, lashing the ground with its tail but making no attempt to strike. Carefully we backed away, admiring it for the splendid creature it was and at the same time giving thanks that it had thoughtfully decided against giving Martin a lethal fang-dose of venom. Indeed, we'd been warned that bush-masters, and another pit viper, the fer-de-lance, were common around the mountain, but although we'd come across many snakes, including beautiful tree boas and deadly but mild-mannered coral snakes, this was the first pit viper we'd seen since leaving Ucaima.

Next day we were crossing a stream, eyes searching the far bank for hidden bushmasters, when Martin grabbed my arm and pointed. Not more than forty feet from us sat a fully grown black jaguar, the rosette patterns in its fur clearly visible as a deeper shade of glossy black. Standing knee-deep in water, feeling a delirious joy – after all, jaguars aren't aggressive – that soon gave way to anxiety, – who really *knows* they aren't aggressive? – then to something approaching terror, as we fully appreciated how large and close it was. It could be on us in a bound and, unarmed, we'd be helpless – Martin is very strong but it wouldn't do much good to punch a twenty stone jaguar on the nose. After a minute that lasted an hour, the big cat rose, stretched leisurely, yawned, then padded off into the forest to melt away among the shadows. The sight of that magnificent animal gave us a feeling of completeness, the fear adding to the intensity of the moment, increasing its value.

We were always hungry, obsessed with dreams of fresh foods. Martin craved sweet things. A morning bowl of porridge and a dried dinner and rice was fine when we were travelling, but in a permanent camp we had lots of time and little willpower. A fancy took hold; became a desire, a craving, a necessity. On the river we'd forgo lunch but now, we'd fill ourselves with pancakes made with the last of our flour mixed with water and sprinkled with sugar. Our appetites increased, our stores diminished. I introduced rationing, not a popular move. Food was kept in the tent safe from animals. One night I woke. Martin was stealing spoonfuls of sugar. 'A hundred years ago you'd have been shot for that.'

But there were more serious thieves than Martin. In the forest my attention was taken by an unusual sight. I watched fascinated as a seemingly endless column of insects made its way among the leaves and twigs. Brown ants, each one carrying on its shoulder what looked like a grain of rice. I picked one up to examine it. It *was* a grain of rice. I walked to the camp, fifty yards away, heart sinking with every step, for I was following the route of the brown ants. Sure enough, the column of rice-laden insects was pouring out from a tiny tear in the wall of the tent. Beside it, another column of eager porters was pouring inside, each tiny brain focused on the task of gathering up a rice grain and transporting it to some secret larder deep in the jungle. They must have been at it for days, for there wasn't much rice left.

'The jungle's wilting,' observed Tanis.

It hadn't rained for two weeks and was so hot that we longed to be cool again – for some nice fluffy clouds to cover up the sun, and a breeze, and a shower of rain. The Churrun river shrank and shrank until reduced to a shallow stream, flanked by puddles around which armies of discontented amphibians would gather each evening to croak their protests about the ever diminishing water supply. Early morning parrots on the way to their feeding grounds squawked wearily. On their way back in the late afternoon they'd be strangely silent, all effort concentrated on the more serious business of flapping through the hot sky.

Angel Falls was looking distinctly sad, so meagre the flow that the lower part had almost dissipated, leaving little more than a vapourised veil of mist. I remembered Rudy's words, 'In the rainy season it's the greatest sight in this Goddam world. In the dry season my dog can do better.'

'I wonder if it's ever dried up completely?' Tanis said. 'If it doesn't rain soon that's what will happen.'

By late afternoon those words seemed to have conjured up the rains. High in the blue sky, nasty little dark clouds appeared, scudding along at tremendous speed. Behind them came a solid mass of black cloud, like a suffocating blanket being drawn across the sky. Something serious was happening up there and it reached us in the form of a wind that threatened to lift the tent and send it sailing away over the treetops, all alone on a long journey to Ucaima. Then rain came, so intense that visibility was reduced to a few yards and breathing became a problem; with water sucked into nostrils and throats by inhalation, we felt as if we were partially drowning.

Even among tropical storms we recognised this as a special demonstration of natural force and though we'd much rather have been *inside* the tent, we were outside, frantically, desperately active, anchoring tent to ground to prevent it leaving us in the wind like a gigantic kite, then fighting to hold it up, to prevent the deluge flattening it into the mud. And there was the boat to be covered before it filled right to the top. At last, huddled inside the tent, gasping from exertion, soaked, cold and with no hope of lighting a fire until the rain ceased, we reassured one another.

'It's just a freak storm.'

'Of course.'

'It'll pass within the hour.'

'Oh, I know that.'

'Fucking hell!' Our damp darkness was blindingly illuminated. We saw each other in brilliant green light – two monsters out of a horror film. Open-mouthed in wonder, we lacked the presence of mind to cover our ears against a thunderclap which left us half deafened. How we longed for the languid heat of the distant afternoon that had ended, so cruelly, half an hour before. Already it seemed like a dream.

We woke to the sound of heavy rain drumming on the tent. The day passed and the next night too, and still the rain poured down. Our cigarettes began to swell and fall apart. Beads of moisture formed inside the camera lens. Our skins became soft and clammy. We developed sore throats and croaked at each other. 'We're turning into frogs,' said Tanis.

For days we had been considering moving out of the canyon but had eked out our meagre rations to stay just another day . . . I'd even stopped stealing sugar. Now it looked as though we might have been caught out by the early arrival of the rainy season. Angel Falls, on the rare occasion when we saw it through the cloud, was issuing many times its former volume of water and roared like distant thunder. Even more alarming was the change in the Churrun river. That formerly tranquil stream had risen by an astonishing thirteen feet and was transformed into an unrecognisable raging torrent, transporting mighty tree trunks past our camp at frightening speed. We'd expected the onset of the rainy season to be gradual. Noah would have felt at home in this situation. Our rubber boat now looked absurdly inadequate and the prospect of setting off in that deluge was something we didn't want to think about. If this was the rainy season it could only get worse. In the hope that it was a freak, we waited it out.

I decided to try to fish with some tackle Rudy had given me. There was a steel hook, so big it looked more suitable for hanging a carcass in a butchers than for catching a fish. Attached to this was steel wire, in turn attached to sixty yards of nylon cord, tied to a wooden baton that could be held with two hands. 'Good grief, Martin. What are you after, the Loch Ness monster?' Tanis said. 'If it's that big it'll take you water skiing with that lot.'

At dawn I threw out the hook baited with dough and waited in the rain. Within minutes it was twitching and jerking. Laboriously I wound it in and an extremely big fish appeared. It was an aimara, a creature with teeth more fearsome than those of the piranha. I held it up by the line. This must weigh twenty pounds, I thought. I took it up to the tent and called Tanis, she looked out sleepily and gasped. I began to feel quite proud. I laid the aimara on the ground. Somehow it managed to slip the hook, then it turned round and began writhing from side to side, like a fat snake, heading unerringly towards the river.

'Quick, Tanis, it's escaping!' I shouted stupidly. I grabbed it with both hands but it slithered through my fingers and the grizzly head bounced against my thigh, teeth clacking like castanets. I came dangerously close to losing a chunk of flesh from my leg. Or worse! I danced impotently around it, filled with conflicting emotions. The practical thing to do was to club it to death, but I was reluctant, I felt sympathy with its commendable escape bid. Thirty seconds later it reached the water, splashed in and was gone.

'There's enough food for four days, five at a pinch,' said Tanis as we ate our last treat; custard powder mixed with water.

Clearly we had to leave while we still could, but it would be on a river very different in character to the one we'd ascended. The boat was empty when we made a trial run. With the engine ticking over, we pushed tentatively away from the bank and were immediately taken by floodwater. I was alarmed by my inability to control the boat. I turned and headed back upriver keeping close to the bank. 'There's the camp,' said Tanis.

'Grab a branch!' I said nosing the boat under the over-hanging trees. She clutched at twigs and leaves then with both hands grasped a thick branch and hung on. I cut the engine and turned to tilt it out of the water. 'Martin, come back!' she shrieked.

The boat swung into the current and she was whipped out and left hanging, feet dangling in the water. Slowly the branch descended under her weight until, when she was in the water up to her chest, she let go.

We took the first rapid with a speed and dexterity that amazed us both. Most of the boulders were beneath the water and we were rushed along at a tremendous pace. 'I've a feeling there's a big drop around this bend,' I said, 'listen to that roar.'

The whole river ahead was a mass of writhing white water and to avoid being carried down it I headed for the safety of the bank. 'Get ready to jump onto the rocks, Tan,' I shouted. The current fought the motor, we were four feet away . . . three feet.

'Jump!'

'It's too far!' She hesitated, balanced on the tube, painter in hand.

'No it's not.' From where I sat it was just a step, the boat began to sway, 'Quick, Tan, don't mess about.' I swung the boat nearer. She jumped. It was further than I thought; her head disappeared under water. Spluttering to the surface, eyes squeezed shut over contact lenses, she scrabbled for a hold on the rocks. 'You're facing the wrong way.'

'And you're a rotten sod,' she said as she hoisted herself out, 'why is it always me who has to jump in?'

By the end of the day we were at the mouth of the river. The Mayupa rapids were no longer seven, just an unbroken raging torrent a mile long. Gone were the rocks we'd struggled up, buried under tons of surging water. From where we stood there was no pattern to the rapid, no vee to follow. A dugout canoe, manned by two Indians approached. 'Follow us,' they said, 'you won't make it otherwise.' We hesitated, they looked hurt. 'We know the way,' they insisted, 'come, follow.'

The first wave swamped us. The bow lifted until the boat was almost vertical. Tanis threw herself forward to stop us flipping right over. The boat was never flat enough for us even to see the Indians, let alone follow them. And then we stopped moving. We were balanced on the rim of a huge spinning crater of water. In the middle was a cavernous hole and at the bottom, a sickening view of the riverbed. Waves broke over us and pounded us downwards till the boat scraped the riverbed, then it surged upward out of the whirlpool, burst above the water like a whale and crashed wildly down the rapid, bouncing across the rocks like a beach ball. And then we were out in calm water. 'We do have some fun, Mart, don't we?' said Tanis. 'Perhaps we could try it in a barrel next time.' The Indians were smiling happily, having enjoyed the spectacle.

Now, we headed toward Ucaima. No dry land was visible, water had flooded into the forest and trees appeared to grow straight out of the river. Flocks of waterfowl had flown in with the rains completing the impression of lakeland and swamp.

Phut, phut, splut. We ran out of petrol. Drifting along, we watched a long-legged hawk swoop down from the sky and pluck a green snake from a tree. It flew to a branch overhanging the water with the dead snake held in its talons. As we floated past, it took fright and the snake fell into the river and sank. We felt like apologising to the hawk for the loss of its meal.

Rudy was waiting at Ucaima. 'I heard an engine an hour or so back, and I knew,' he said to the group of tourists, 'it's those crazy Jordans.'

Our first drink made us light-headed and silly. Martin looked like a suntanned tramp and I couldn't have looked much better. People had gathered to stare at us. In a hushed voice somebody said, 'Those two are explorers. They've been on the river for months in that little boat,' and somebody gasped, whether in admiration or horror hardly mattered. Like Alice in Wonderland I felt myself growing taller and taller. Martin was looking pretty pleased with himself too.

CHAPTER ELEVEN

Surinam.

Dear Mum and Dad,

Just a line to let you know all is well. I sent you a massive tome from Venezuela, a tourist posted it for me, I hope you received it. Since then we have had a change of plan.

You know about the flood, when Rudy said he'd never seen the river so high and thought it would flood Ucaima? Well, two days after we got back, it stopped raining, the sun came out and within a few days the river dropped. It was as if someone had pulled out the plug. We were back in the dry season again. He said he'd never known that happen before, either. And now the weather was back to normal, would we do a little job for him?

Do you remember the corrugated iron shelter I mentioned in the jungle? Rudy asked if we'd take a group of Indian workers back up there (in one of his dugout canoes) with bags of cement, etc. and build a house. We agreed. I must admit I was a bit disappointed at first, I was longing to get back to Caracas to read our mail. And, to eat lots of delicious food. It was great fun but hard work, and Rudy has been so kind we couldn't say no. We built it from stones from the river. It took three weeks and it looks pretty good. I wouldn't mind living there permanently!

Rudy suggested we give up our trip to Surinam and work for him instead. As we'd arranged to meet Martin's brother, Dominic, in Paramaribo, and have planned a river trip with him, we had to say no.

So now we are in Surinam. I still haven't got your letters as John Forbes sent them down to Ucaima and we left before they arrived. With luck they are now on their way here. I drive the people at Poste Restante mad, I call in three times a day!

We've planned a trip up the Coppename River with Dom. As there won't be room in our boat, we've borrowed a fibreglass canoe from STINASU, the Foundation for Nature Preservation. In return, we're going to the coast for a few weeks – a place called Bigisante – to work on a marine turtle conservation project. Leatherback turtles are as big as double beds.

Could you ask Dom to bring out some dried dinners, I can't buy dried food here and can't face any more tinned corned beef! I yearn for a piece of Christmas cake covered with thick cream. Also a jar of Nivea cream, I'm using cooking oil. Martin's nose suffers in the sun, it goes pink, then red, then peels and then the process starts again, takes about a week.

In Caracas, we didn't stop eating for a week. After the river trip we'll leave for Trinidad to pick up the Monster Rat, if it hasn't sunk! Dom is coming to Trinidad with us and will fly home from there.

It feels as if we've been away for ever, can't wait to see everyone again. How are the guinea pigs?

Happy Father's Day, Dad.

Lots of love,
T & M

CHAPTER TWELVE

Home again. Everything was comfortingly as we'd left it. I met a casual acquaintance who worked in a local factory, a man who was eternally unhappy with his lot. We chatted for a while. 'I hear you and Tanis are off on another expedition. When do you leave?'

'We've already been. Got back last week.'

'But we met quite recently, didn't we?'

'Not for nearly a year. We left in January.'

'My, how time flies!' he said.

I understood his surprise. I once worked in that same factory for six months and retain little recollection of it, so dull had it been. Single days from our travels occupy larger spaces in my memory than that entire episode. It was one more reason to make another trip as soon as possible: before we started saying things like 'my, how time flies' and meaning it.

The first inspiration came with the first glass of wine. 'Let's use a canoe on the next trip,' said Tanis. In Surinam, with my brother Dominic, we had used a fibreglass canoe to travel on the Coppename river and we'd liked it; it handled well, cut through water at speed and, with our now considerable experience of rapids and tricky rivers, we no longer felt reliant on the additional stability afforded by an inflatable boat.

With the second glass of wine came another inspiration. 'Let's not use an engine,' I said, 'let's paddle it. We'd see more wildlife.'

'And we wouldn't have to carry five hundred gallons of petrol. It would be more . . . er . . . natural.'

We were enjoying being home and were well into plans for the next trip when tragedy struck. Tanis's father was seriously injured in an accident and died three months later, without recovering consciousness. I knew what Tanis was going through during this deeply dispiriting period: my parents died within a year of each other when I was a teenager and it still hurt to remember. Slowly we emerged from sadness to find that we needed to travel again even more than we had before. It would be cathartic. It would help rid us of gloom. 'Go on, you go, loveys. We'll look after your mum,' said Tanis's Aunt Julia, who always encouraged and enjoyed our travels.

Our idea was to paddle a canoe up the Marowijne and Lawa rivers in Surinam, on towards Brazil and into the Tumucumaque mountains, to the lands of the Wayana, Tirio and Akurio Indians. Because we knew Surinam well, and had many friends in the country, there was no need to make elaborate plans for the expedition. We were impatient to be off. Already we could smell the scent of night flowers on a tropical breeze and hear the whirr of cicadas in forest glades. The magic was working again.

WHITE RUM AND RED DOGS

CHAPTER THIRTEEN

Nearby a cockerel crowed. Far, far away in the forest, barely audible but unmistakable, howler monkeys roared at the moon. 'That cockerel can't tell the time,' said Martin.

Two o'clock in the morning outside the forestry post at Albina, and Martin and I were hurrying back and forth to load our canoe, which sat in the Marowijne river ready to catch the early tide that for a few hours would carry us upstream against the river current. In eerie silence we glided away from the bank into the blackness of the tropical night; it was like being swallowed into a warm velvet cavern. There was barely room in the canoe for the mountain of equipment, provisions and us as well, and we sat hunched up with chins on knees. The river smelt of the ocean.

With the tide carrying us forward and a nicely synchronised slap, slap of paddle strokes, we fairly sped along. But, unable to see more than a few yards ahead, I feared we'd crash into something in the darkness. Dawn revealed a river half a mile wide, brown, smooth and vast. The bank fifty yards to our right was all crab-covered mud and mangroves along this tidal stretch – dreadful places for campsites. We increased our pace, hoping to reach rocks and sandy beaches before the day ended. We were feeling great and stopped only briefly to eat boiled eggs and crackers while the tide carried us upriver.

Soon, inevitably, the tide turned. With both tide and current against us, every stroke of the paddle was an effort. The canoe jerked forward a foot and slid back six inches. Tired, aching and sunboiled, we lost rhythm. 'Martin, you're paddling too hard.'

'No, Tan, you're not paddling hard enough.'

SPLASH, SPLASH, SPLASH, SPLASH.

'Now you're overdoing it, we're turning left.'

'Let's change sides, my arm aches.'

'It's no good, I can't paddle that side, my knee is in the way, and there's nowhere else to put it.'

The jungle bank was still inhospitable, swampy and edged with mangroves as we searched for somewhere to stop. In the distance was a break in the bank and a speck of yellow. A beach? The place was deserted; jungle grew over two derelict huts, both full of cobwebs, cockroaches and we knew not what else. Our shelter was two eight-feet square pieces of water-proof material, united with Velcro. Tied to trees they formed a canopy, beneath which we slung our hammocks, one above the other, mine so high, I needed a leg-up to get into it.

It was weeks into the dry season but in the late afternoon the sky darkened and a great wind got up. It huffed and it puffed and it blew our house up. Whipping and flapping, the shelter broke loose; we clung to it doggedly. Lightning and thunder exploded simultaneously over our heads and rain bucketed down. Within minutes the sandy jungle floor became a paddling pool and kit bags sat in two inches of water.

That first night in the jungle was a testing time. Somehow we hadn't quite got the hang of our new hammocks and gradually, as the ropes eased and the material gave, we sank. Martin lay with his bum on the ground and I lay with my feet on his head. One side of my hammock was taut as a bow, the other hung like a sack. Our mosquito nets drooped on our faces threatening to smother us. First too hot, sleeping bags out; then chilly, sleeping bags in. It was dark when the smell of coffee woke me and stretching my arms up I touched something with a hard shell, inside the mosquito net. Through my mind flashed a story I'd heard years ago, about a man who woke with a deadly snake asleep in his hammock. Hardly daring to breathe, let alone rouse his companions, he had lain there too terrified even to shake with fear. He and the snake both emerged intact due to a quick-thinking friend, who lit a fire and smoked the snake out of the hammock. I wasn't prepared to wait that long and fled screaming from my bed, just as a three-inch long cockroach dropped into my sleeping bag.

Deprived of my usual lie in, we were away by six-thirty. A boat appeared out of the morning vapour – a Bushnegro family paddling downriver in a dugout canoe. Miraculously they understood our rusty Taki Taki and on learning we were bound for Stoelmanseiland, the father threw up his hands in horror. 'No, no, you cannot go there, the water too high now. Big, big, rapids, you will fall out of your canoe and die!'

We pressed on past miles of forest, broken occasionally by riverside villages. Daily our muscles tightened and our skins turned brown. We felt fit and exuberant, ate well, and, now we slung our hammocks side by side, slept well too.

The first rapids were no more than sandy shallows. We nipped up them easily. Gradually the river narrowed and rapids increased in height, length and frequency. Tugging, hauling, pushing and paddling we climbed towards the mountains, still a hundred and fifty miles away. For a day we paddled up fast water and could hear a roar that indicated something ominous, hidden round the bend.

'Should we wear clothes today?' Tanis said as we loaded the boat.

'Let's be on the safe side and tie everything in as well,' I suggested.

'Listening to that rapid wasn't conducive to a good night's sleep; at three o'clock this morning it sounded like Niagara.'

I was uneasy. Try as I might, I couldn't conjure up the lighthearted mood of the previous days. Through binoculars I studied the rapid. Deep fast water, a barrier of rock visible just on the bend, beyond that I couldn't see. We'd paddle nearer to it, moor in the bank and walk through the jungle to check it out. Perhaps it was time for lifejackets. To my surprise, Tanis didn't demur: 'It feels different today somehow,' strapping her jacket on, 'or am I imagining it? Sort of, more serious.'

Below the rapid I reconnoitred. Above the first rock barrier the river widened, then narrowed before widening again like a figure eight. Along the bank under the trees the water ran swiftly, but no worse than we'd coped with before. If we hugged the bank we should be able to paddle round. Manoeuvring the canoe between two rocks we were up over the first barrier. 'The inflatable would never have squeezed through there,' said Tanis cheerfully. 'Mind you, I'll be glad when we've got rid of some of the food, this canoe weighs a ton. Perhaps we should eat more. Imagine if we had a load of petrol as well!'

For half an hour our paddles fought the water round the fat bit of the figure eight. As the river narrowed, the current increased. Tanis dropped her paddle. The water carried it away, relinquishing it against a rock. 'Sorry,' she mouthed over the noise. Clutching the straggle of branches, she pulled the canoe against the bank. 'We'll have to go back, MAR. . . !'

The river closed over my head. I was caught in an undertow and carried, bouncing, along the river bed. I was drowning. Directly above me, six feet up on the surface, floated our canoe: upside down. Red and yellow kit bags, suspended from it by ropes, dangled strangely in the watery space around me like living things. I must be in a nightmare with this colourful, surreal, flying octopus hovering above me!

The sequence of events had a dream-like quality. The accident had occurred so suddenly that I felt divorced from what was actually happening. In my plight there was no room for fear or concern about Tanis's fate. The single overwhelming need was to get my head out of the water and breathe again. Surfacing briefly I managed it, seeing at the same time that I was a long way from the bank, travelling at speed towards more white water. Back in the depths, brilliant blue lights flashed in my head before I surfaced again, this time to discover that my lifejacket, torn from my body, was now so tightly wrapped around my neck and face that I could see nothing.

I woke up. I was floating in quiet water near the bank with the lifejacket straps still strangling me, but with head now pillowed against the inflated tubes. I felt alert but my limbs were paralysed, and for a while would not respond to messages from my brain. When the information filtered from nerves to muscles, I made for the bank, hauled myself ashore and stood up, wobbly and trembling. From where I'd landed on the inner sweep of a bend, my view of the river was very restricted. I'd no idea how far I'd been carried and couldn't see the canoe or Tanis. Had she drowned? Stupidly, I wondered what I'd do with her belongings if she was dead. She had such tiny feet I could think of no one who would want the shoes she had at home. I was in a state of considerable shock.

For the worst half hour of my life, I struggled through riverside jungle, shouting for Tanis but expecting to find her body – until, with inexpressible relief, I heard a reply over the roaring waters. She was out in the river anchored precariously on some underwater perch thirty feet from the bank. Waves broke over her shoulders, her face was covered with blood. In one hand she clutched a yellow kit bag. 'What are you holding on to?' I called.

'Legs . . . round . . . tree . . .'

'Let go of the kit bag, hold on with both hands.'

'No, got . . . gun . . .' shout terminated mid-sentence as she swallowed a mouthful of water.'

'Let go of the bloody bag!' Terrified that she was risking her life for the sake of a bag of saturated rice and beans.

'No!'

I almost danced with frustration. She'd made up her mind to keep hold of the bag and that was the end of the matter. It was impossible to swim across that narrow stretch of surging water, but inspired by urgency I broke down a long slender sapling with my hands. Holding the thick end, I waded out as far as I could and pushed the leafy part into the water upstream. It swept round in a wide arc, the branches rushing over her head as she grabbed it, launched herself forward and swung into the bank downstream. In the process she lost the kit bag but saved the gun.

The euphoria of finding each other alive soon gave way to an agonising appreciation of our predicament – forlorn, on a remote riverbank in the Surinam jungle, with nothing but the few clothes we wore. While pulling myself from the water I'd collected a cluster of needle-like thorns, deeply embedded in the palm of my hand. I'd hardly noticed at the time, but now my hand was swollen and throbbing. And I was barefoot.

Tanis's nose had stopped bleeding but as she bent to wash away the blood, a big red hornet swooped down and for no reason, stung her on the head. I swatted it frantically so I could stamp it into the ground and vent some of the shocked rage I felt at the events of the last hour. But the hornet escaped.

For five hours we struggled through the jungle to a village we'd passed the previous day. Stepping from the relatively cool forest into the blazing heat of a sizeable clearing we saw five huts, all but one dilapidated and on the verge of collapse. There were three people. An old woman, naked to the waist, busy with a log fire; a little boy who stood nearby, idly poking the ground with a stick, and an elderly man in a loincloth and football jersey sitting on a stool gazing vacantly out over the river. Clearly in view was our lurid green fibreglass canoe, unnaturally conspicuous, its nose buried in a sandbank a hundred yards away. Evidently none of them had noticed it. 'Hello,' I called.

The man sprang to his feet with youthful agility born of shock. The child ran to the woman for safety. They stared at us in open-mouthed amazement. I walked forward and they backed nervously away. Reaching the man before he fled, I grabbed his hand and shook it. Discovering that I was of the flesh, and not an apparition from the spirit world, calmed him. The woman smiled, exposing a set of teeth so white and perfect that in a city-dweller of her age, they could only have been artificial, but she refused to shake hands. Three fingers on her right hand were missing along with many of her toes. I explained what had happened.

Collecting his machete the man beckoned us to follow him. Through old plantations and overgrown tracks we came to a place where a dugout canoe was moored and with a pole, he punted us across to the boat. Tanis's face was a matching shade of green at being on the river again.

The two rucksacks were still tied to our canoe, along with sleeping bags and a cardboard box full of swelling rice and beans. As Martin and I righted the boat and piled the gear back in, the old man pointed upriver. In the bank, trapped by branches were two yellow kit bags. We towed the canoe to the village and went to retrieve the other things.

With one end of a rope round his waist and the other tied to a tree, Martin waded into the river. They were stuck fast. 'There's something on the bottom they're tied to.' He reached deep under the water, 'I think it's the camera box!' With a bubbling glug it came free and we fumbled to open it: something would be salvaged, it was guaranteed waterproof. The camera equipment was floating in water.

In the village the woman brought us hot coffee and boiled rice that we fought to swallow; food was not the sustenance we needed. On a flat grey rock we unpacked the sopping bags. Cameras and lenses were full, water poured from the antivenin boxes. Soggy packets of rice, flour and custard powder were dissolving among books, tobacco and clothes, and everything was covered with wet tea leaves. In one kit bag our hammocks were quite dry. A double pack of playing cards in a leather wallet that Dad had given us to take to Morocco, and that had been on every trip since, were stuck together face to back; Martin tried to separate them but they tore and fell apart. He threw them in the river. We tried to smoke wet tobacco rolled in damp pages of airmail paper and wondered when we'd wake up.

We'd lost all our porridge, sugar, beans and milk, our machetes, fishing gear, both paddles, pacamacs, a towel, water carrier and lamp; my wallet which contained travel permit, gun permit, insurance, English money, travellers' cheques, some Surinam guilders and a photo of my dad taken not long before he died. Safe in our money belts were passports, the bulk of our money, and pinned in each, our tiny St Christophers.

Our hosts gave us the least tatty hut to sleep in. As Martin opened the door it came off in his hand, disturbing a colony of bats which fluttered past us like a gale of autumn leaves. In our nervous, depressed state, the shock almost made us throw up.

We started calling each other Flotsam and Jetsam in a feeble attempt at cheerfulness. Martin was Jetsam because he'd been washed up on the shore.

Over the next two days we debated what to do. The boat was split down the middle but repairable. We had enough dried dinners and rice to live meagrely for several weeks. It would be possible to continue but not to go where we'd planned. We couldn't face going on, nor could we face going back. Our fighting spirits were floating way above the trees mocking our gloom and indecision. Our egos were at the bottom of the river.

The man's eldest son, Daniel, arrived in a long motor-powered dugout. He was going to Stoelmanseiland and offered us a lift. If we said yes, we'd be committing ourselves to do something, though we didn't know what. 'No' meant giving up. We decided to go. It was a harrowing journey. Five times the canoe was stuck on rapids and we had to jump out and help. Martin was still in shock, but glad to be moving. I'd lost my nerve completely. I hated being on the water and was terrified of rapids.

At Stoelmanseiland, Daniel took us to his relatives, telling them the story of our disaster, acting it through by lying on the ground flailing his arms and legs and glug-glugging for breath to demonstrate how we swam for our lives. We expected them to laugh at our misfortune, but they commiserated, two men shook our hands, indicating that they too had fallen out of canoes in their time. They fed us sardines and rice.

Stoelmanseiland now had a police post manned by three young Indonesian men. There we stayed for five melancholy days, waiting for our deep depression to lift and a glimmer of enthusiasm to return. I started a letter home but didn't know what to say; 'Dear Mum, a few days ago we nearly killed ourselves. Now we're trying to pluck up the courage to do it again!'

'Tan, come down and see who's here,' Martin called from the jetty. A massive forty foot long dugout canoe, flying the Surinam flag on its blue and red wooden canopy, had pulled in. It was crammed with cargo as if for a long trip and several men milled around, stretching their legs. Martin and a man in khaki trousers and shirt were shaking hands and thumping each other on the shoulders.

'So, Tarnis, how are you?' The face was only vaguely familiar but the mis-pronunciation of my name was instantly recognisable.

'Rainier?'

'Yes. I tell you you come back. You drink the river here.'

The amount we'd drunk the other day, we'd be here for ever. 'You still work with the Anti-Malaria Campaign?'

'No, Tarnis. That finish now. I work in the town, for the Government. This the first time I come to this river since when I see you here six years ago. In the village they tell me about two white people here, but I not know it my friends.'

We were flabbergasted by the coincidence, but Rainier didn't appear in the least surprised. He was a member of a Government expedition bound for the far south, near Brazil, to gather information about Indian tribes and visit remote Bushnegro settlements on the way, exactly where we had planned to go. The party was staying overnight in a long wooden hut behind the police post. Rainier sprung the invitation on us that night. 'I talk with the boss. You can come with us if you like to, you must pay him with three bottles of rum.'

Something was needed to shake us out of our morbid introspection. We agreed, the team would take us and our canoe up to Cottica and from there we would paddle upriver alone for a few weeks, then paddle ourselves back to Albina. We bought the rum.

At six in the morning the powerful engine roared into life and we were off. It was somebody's birthday and a bottle of rum was opened, a plastic beaker of the fiery liquid was passed to each of us to drink his health. A rosy glow of intoxication spread through us. For the first time since the accident, the tepid brown water rushing past the hull looked friendly.

At Cottica, the group sat arguing on the jetty. The boss called us down. 'The boatmen like you, they don't want that you die. They don't wish that you go back in the little canoe.'

Now the whole group got involved. The little boat would break in pieces on the first rapid. Certainly it would break at the rapid by the big bend. No, the rapid where the tree lies in the water. Or the rapid of two rocks. Please, leave the little boat here and come with us. We were loathe to sacrifice our only means of independence, too preoccupied with our feelings to appreciate the kindness of their offer. It would mean a final end to all our plans. We had the night to decide.

'What shall we do Mart, do you want to go?'

'No, it's not what we came here for. We didn't plan to stay in villages, we came to be on our own, to get away from people.'

'Well, we can't stay here, we don't want to go back, the trip we planned is out of the question now, so we don't have much choice. It's better than nothing.'

'I think I'd rather do nothing.' He was in a sour mood.

'It's crazy you know, this is a chance most people would give their eye-teeth for, and we're grumbling about it. At least we can salvage something of the trip if we go.'

'It's a compromise. It won't be a proper trip, will it?'

'Look, try and be a bit positive, what else do you suggest we do?'

'Right, Tan! If that's what you want we'll go, let's go to sleep now, I don't want to discuss it anymore.'

'Oh no, hold on a minute Martin, don't pass it on to me, every time you're fed up you'll blame me.'

'No I won't, we'll go and that's that. Goodnight.'

'What do you mean "that's that", you've decided for us have you? Suppose I don't want to go?'

'You do though, you said it was a great chance. You said be positive. I'm being positive. OK?'

'You don't sound very happy.'

'I'm very happy, I'm deliriously happy. Now let's leave it and go to sleep.'

'We don't have to go, Mart, we could do something else.'

'What?'

'I don't know but there must be something, if you really don't want to go.'

'Tan, we're going! Now GOODNIGHT.'

I turned my back on him. Sometimes he was really horrible.

I turned my back on her. Sometimes she was really irritating.

CHAPTER FOURTEEN

'U weki-oo.' 'U weki-jee.'

People were rising, calling morning greetings to each other. I knew Martin was awake but kept my eyes shut. I wasn't going to speak first. I was still cross. Someone entered the hut. It was Rainer, who blew gently on our faces to wake us. 'U weki-oo, Tarnis, Martin, we go soon.' He left.

We dressed in silence.

'Don't let's argue, Tan, it's silly.'

'I know, let's forget it.'

'I love you, Tan.'

'I love you, too.'

'Happy, Flotsam?'

'I'm very happy. In fact Jetsam, I'm deliriously happy!'

Cottica, Lawa River.

Dear Mum,

By now you should have received my letter telling you that our plans have changed. I have no idea when I will be able to post this, so I will write it as a diary. Slowly, we're adjusting to being part of a team.

Our day starts early with a wash in the river. Breakfast is rice and tinned herrings. We gave the boss all the food we had left, to be shared among us all. About nine o'clock, work begins.

The head of a tribe is called a Granman. We haven't met a Granman yet. Head of the village is the Captain, then comes the second Captain then the male Basha then the female Basha (Basha may not be the correct spelling, but it's what it sounds like). The Basha speaks for the Captains and if they are out of the village, he acts for them. If he too is out, the female Basha is the hostess. Her job is to see to the village, making sure it's clean, etc., and she attends to the dead. That reminds me, when we arrive at a village our group are given a large open-sided hut to hang our hammocks in. The boss then looks around for an empty hut for us. He likes us to have our own place. In one village there was a small hut with a thick odd-looking canoe inside. Seeing us eyeing it he said, 'That is the dede oso (dead house), they put you in there when you dead.' When a Bushnegro dies, his body is placed in a canoe for a few days until it begins to decompose and juices have run out, then the nearest relative bathes in the juices, (that's what he said, but it sounds ghastly! I wonder sometimes if it gets muddled during translation?) The body is then wrapped in his hammock with all his possessions and when buried, planks are laid on so earth doesn't touch them.

Back to work!

We begin with a formal meeting which the whole village attends. The Captain speaks through the Basha, the boss replies through Rainier. It's quite easy to follow, it's acted out almost like a play. Rainer explains what we have come to do, i.e. gather information on all children under eighteen, so the mothers can be given a child allowance (so we are told). The Basha intersperses Rainer's speech with lots of na so, da so and da letti so (roughly translated means, that's so, it's so, it's certainly so). When all the speeches have been made, the Captain fetches a bottle of rum. Chanting, he splashes rum onto the ground as an offering to the gods, asking that our work should go well, half the bottle can go at this stage if the Captain gets carried away by religious fervour. The boss looks very anxious, fearful that the whole bottle might be tipped out before he gets a drink. Then we all have a drink. At that time of the morning a shot of neat alcohol almost takes the top of your head off.

Most little boys are naked, but wear a cord around their waists in preparation for loincloths. Men wear cord or knotted string around the top of their calves, just under the knee and around wrists or necks. Women wear skirts wrapped around their waists, called pangas. Bare breasted but not bare bottomed. Some women have scar patterns on breasts, back and faces. Anyone who owns an elastic band wears it round his or her wrist, including our crew. I'll describe them.

The boss: he's in charge of the expedition and his brother is a Government minister. He's forty-two, part Creole, part Chinese, heavily built, well-educated, easy going and altogether a likeable person, but with one fault, he frequently gets so drunk that he doesn't know what he's doing or saying! Rum is freely available at every village and drink is taken as early as six in the morning.

Brewster: expedition cook, a quiet, even-tempered unexcitable man. He, more than the others, has become a friend. Chief tea maker, he calls us in the morning for tea, then insists on boiling it again or waiting for it to cool for another hour, leaving us gasping.

Naro: tall, thin and rather dissipated. He rarely speaks when sober and never stops when drunk. Naro never has any tobacco but is a heavy smoker and sidles up to us, puts his tongue in the corner of his mouth, rolls his fingers and says 'em, pst, mumble, pst, mumble'. That means 'give me a cigarette'. We have a lot of rolling tobacco, or rather we did! He becomes very loud and argumentative when under the influence of rum, (called 'soapy' or 'tafia') but doesn't give a damn about it the next day. He will also share his rum with us to the degree of over-generosity.

Rainier: our good friend from before. He is subject to moods which we found were completely baffling until the penny dropped. If food is short or plain, like only rice for dinner, he won't talk to us. If there is an argument among the others, he won't talk to us. He wants everything to be perfect for us and when it isn't, he is upset and won't speak to us until he can say things are better.

Matte: quiet, refined, well educated, very nice guy, same age as Martin but looks a lot older because he's small, plump and bald. He's a bit out of it because he's a Hindu, the only Asian in the group (the others are black). He's normally vegetarian and will only eat meat when he absolutely has to. He has a pot of super-concentrated shrimp paste which he puts onto his rice while the rest are tucking into monkey steaks. The paste is so strong that half a teaspoon is all that's needed to flavour a plate of rice. Matte likes town life, dressing up, going dancing, reading, working in an office – he hates being in the bush. He's drinking a lot, not eating properly and is obviously unhappy, we feel sorry for him and worry about his health.

The three boatmen.

Camissie: in charge of the boat, twenty or twenty-one, he's not sure. Plump, jovial but sulky too (though not with us). Superbly skillful driver, considered to be the best on the river, desperately wants to buy our gun, he uses it all the time. Married with four children, but a bit of a ladykiller.

Esto: only twenty-eight, but has had two wives die on him already, which meant he had to spend four months at Granbori, the seat of the Granman, being purified in case he had a curse on him. Because of this he lost his job with the Government and had to become a boatman again. He often drinks too much and insists that he 'carry' our torch, hairbrush or anything else until we go 'fo to' (to town) which means we'll never see it again as he'll give it to one of many girlfriends. Like a sailor, Esto has a girl in each village. The other night, drunk and full of smiles, he flung open the door of the hut he shared with us, almost throwing me out of my hammock, and blew on my face until I woke up to say goodnight to him.

Adeng or Denny: seventeen, loud, flashy talker, but shy with us. Getting chattier as the trip progresses, but not like the other boatmen.

At night, you'd think we were in the Arctic the way they carry on, banging their arms and pulling on sweaters, complaining about how cold it is. Martin and I feel nicely comfortable.

The boss has told us that among Bushnegroes the father doesn't take responsibility for his children. Any scolding or reprimanding is done by the wife's brother. If anything should happen to the wife, her family take the children and the father has no say in the matter. Likewise the husband must 'look to' his sister's children. The family line runs through the sister. For example, a Granman or Captain's child can never become a Granman or Captain, because, they reason, the wife could deceive him and produce another man's child to become Granman. But the sister will have the same blood, no matter which man she has. Our boatman, Esto, has six children but his wife's brother has them since she died.

Our diet is now supplemented by fish and hunted game and we're eating all sorts of exotic dishes. It seems such a shame when we came here to see wildlife to end up eating it. The Bushnegroes and Indians naturally live off the land, but it shouldn't be necessary for our expedition, they could easily have brought enough food with them from town. But the boatmen think they will die without fresh meat. If hunting is bad and we only have tinned meat or fish, they moan and wail about how weak they feel. But it's no use for us to protest; we've mentioned the subject tentatively and they don't understand our views about conservation. Why should they? They'd just think we were complaining about the food they are so kindly sharing with us. Everybody hunts here, it's as normal as it is for us to go to the supermarket.

More later.

Breakfast was tortoise and rice.

Tanis was acting as chief assistant to the boss who had a hangover and wanted to get the work done and be away. But he was having problems. Surrounded by women and children all speaking at once, rivulets of sweat trickled down his face and arms onto his notepad, while he valiantly endeavoured to establish which children belonged to which women and their various ages. The latter could be answered by an intelligent guess but it was the former that presented the difficulty.

At birth the child's name is written in a family book, but shortly after, the mother changes the name once or twice. The boss was given the family book but when he called the name of the child there were blank looks all round. If there are a lot of children in a house, one or two will go to live with grand-mothers or aunts who have fewer offspring, gaining yet another, different name. Incredible as it seemed, several of the women were in dispute about which particular members of the crowd of children they had given birth to.

'Eksi is *my* son.'

'He is *not* your son he is mine. So well I remember his birth,' (clutching her belly, swaying from side to side), 'eeya, Eksi he my fifth.'

Bushnegro people must be among the most skilled workers of wood in South America and the most outstanding demon-strations of their abilities are seen in canoes. The idea that a dugout canoe is nothing more than a crudely hollowed-out log is totally wrong, for above all Bushnegroes are river people and the elegant, tapering craft they produce reflects this. The construction of a boat is a tough and lovingly undertaken process using simple tools. First the finding and felling of a suitable tree, then the carving of the shell, which, in the final nerve-wracking stages, has to be burned and stretched to open it out into a boat – one badly judged move here and the shell splits and months of work are wasted. The end product is invariably a craft so sleek and perfectly symmetrical that it looks as if it could have come off a plastic mould in a factory assembly line.

This pride in craftsmanship can be seen in everything from eating utensils to giant log-drums. All are splendidly carved and decorated with uniquely distinctive patterns of circles, rectangles and triangles, interwoven by snaking spirals and curves, elaborate, abstract designs with a strongly three-dimensional aspect. Huts have triangular front and back walls with a roof of palm thatch that almost reaches the ground. The wooden fronts are frequently so lavishly decorated with a combination of carved and brightly painted panels, that a stroll around a village is as visually exciting as a stroll around an art gallery.

At one village, spare huts were in short supply and we were well-meaningly given the Captain's equivalent of the English-man's garden shed. Either side of the doorway were tethered two emaciated and insanely ferocious hunting dogs, on ropes exactly the right length to allow us to squeeze past, risking only the hairs on our legs to their broken, yellow fangs. These crazed, drooling brutes almost strangled themselves to get to us. Inside the hut we were visible to all eyes through gaps in the plank walls. Groups of children assembled outside, talking to us in our cage. When we grew tired and fell silent, they poked us with sticks to encourage sound from us.

But dogs and lack of privacy were nothing compared to sharing the hut with a colony of rats. At dusk, out they came, hundreds of them, lurking in shadows where the flickering candelight hardly penetrated. As we lay in our hammocks they climbed the walls, ran round the floor and searched through our belongings. We lay listening to them gnawing. Each time we dozed off, the hammock ropes would vibrate as they ran along them. In the morning all our soap, candles and a tin of milk had been eaten.

It became apparent that there was bad feeling between the boss and Naro. While there was plenty of rum available, there was a daily drinking session of two or three hours' duration, which might occur at any time. On these occasions, heated arguments invariably ensued between the two of them, with the rest of us acting as peacemakers.

Very early one morning, with mist still on the river and

green parrots commuting to their feeding grounds, we sat round a portable table drinking rum and playing cards, a routine for the daily booze-up. Garrulous Naro was cheating blatantly as he always did, the boss became angry as he always did. Finally Naro swept the cards from the table and walked away (as he sometimes did). The game was over. The sun was above the trees and it was now swelteringly hot.

The boss and Naro were angry and drunk. Brewster, Matte and Rainier ran round like mother-hens trying to calm them. Believing that trouble was now over for another day, we all trooped down for a pre-breakfast swim. Naro couldn't find his toothbrush. He walked to the water's edge, looked down upon the boss, wallowing up to his chin, and loudly accused him of stealing it. Even the jungle went silent as the magnitude of this insult was absorbed. With a roar, the boss leapt up, dragged his colleague into the river and for the next few minutes they were lost from view as they thrashed about in the foam, endeavouring to drown one another.

Dozens of children leapt up and down, hysterical with excitement, while cheering, clapping, jubilant villagers rushed from their huts to witness the unexpected entertainment provided by these ambassadors of the civilized world, from the great city downriver. After this frantically violent fight, the two men stood facing each other, gasping and retching, quite incapable of making another aggressive move, then, aware of the audience, walked out of the river, heads held high, dignified.

Passing the last Bushnegro settlement, we travelled on into the far south of Surinam, where the rivers are narrow and boulder-strewn, rapids fierce and frequent. The country is hilly, the nights colder. The land of Wayana Indians. Annapaike, a large village of some forty dwellings, stood in a forest clearing, reached by a steep path from the river. The huts had no walls, just conical, palm-thatched roofs on poles and were set well apart. It looked nothing like a Bushnegro village.

A woman appeared from among the trees, brown skinned, naked but for an apron of bright red cloth, which hung from a cord around her hips. She had a shining mane of almost blue-black hair, with a short fringe cut at the widow's peak. Red feathers adorned her earlobes and her arms were stained as red as her apron. Our first impression was of redness. Men wore red loincloths, with elaborately patterned belts two inches wide made from thousands of tiny red, white and blue beads. Adults and children wore strands of beads around necks, arms and calves.

At the edge of the clearing stood five bamboo cages on stilts, each containing a lean, mad-eyed, hunting dog. The fur of these creatures was stained red with vegetable dye to keep them parasite free. 'The little houses keep them safe from snakes,' explained the boss as we stared, goggle-eyed at the bizarre sight of red dogs in parrots cages. To complete the impression of redness a small child handed us bananas, their skins a deep maroon.

The village was clean, quiet and calm, its people soft spoken and shy. On pole rafters, beneath the roofs of huts, lay bows and bundles of arrows, some seven feet long, tipped with wood, bone or barbed metal. People swung gently in hammocks. Beneath a shelter we sat on upturned canoes, with eleven elders of the village. Chief Annapaike and two chiefs from nearby villages lay in hammocks. Naro, twitchy and deprived, demanded I roll him a cigarette. Observing this with great interest, the man next to me indicated I make one for him. When I'd rolled and lit it for him, the next man wanted one too. Then the third man, and so it went on until I'd made fourteen cigarettes, by which time the first man had finished his and wanted another. I wondered how long our dwindling supply of tobacco would last at this rate.

A man in a loincloth, so long that it nearly touched the ground front and back, dipped a saucepan-sized calabash into a vat full of liquid and handed it to Chief Annapaike, who slowly drank it down. It was re-filled and passed around the group, each draining it dry. This was cassiri, made from fermented cassava, the women adding to its potency by chewing certain ingredients and spitting them into the must. It was pale beige in colour, full of lumps of various sizes, and tasted like diluted beer without the bitterness. Pleasant, but unexciting.

After a couple of hours we'd each consumed about five pints of fluid, but, apart from feeling uncomfortably bloated, nothing interesting happened. I felt no sense of intoxication and doubted if it had even one fifth the alcohol content of mild beer. The Indians, though, were becoming tipsy and were noticeably unsteady on their legs. One man was telling a story, his deep voice wonderful to hear, unlike anything we'd heard before, full of glottal-stops and grunts, short, sharp explosions of sounds, words like IK EPOC GU EK delivered with a flow and confidence that was slightly hypnotic. Everyone paid rapt attention. He stopped mid-sentence, gripped his nose between thumb and forefinger, turned his head to one side and vomited. It came out like a jet of water from a hosepipe and continued for several seconds, landing accurately outside the shelter. Then he continued the story as if nothing had happened. Projectile vomiting is a habit regarded as casually among the Indians as spitting is in many communities. It's merely a convenient way to make room for more cassiri.

With a hut to ourselves and a few days to spare, we unloaded the camera box to gaze with renewed dismay at the wreckage. When we'd rescued it from the river, our Pentax camera and assorted lenses were full of water and we'd taken everything apart and hung the bits in the sun to dry. The rolls of film in their individual sealed canisters were all right and consequently there remained a faint possibility that we could reassemble the assortment of screws, clips, pieces of glass and plastic, into a machine that would once again make photographs. It promised to be a monumental, and I thought futile, task and left to me to decide, I probably would not have bothered. But Tanis, ever optimistic, encouraged me to get on with it. Soon we had a camera that appeared to be functioning normally and with little hope on my part and total conviction on Tanis's, we started taking pictures again.

The Wayana people were generous, and as prepared to give as to receive, their communal spirit such that we were expected to enter any dwelling and help ourselves to food. They would come to our hut, help themselves to tobacco from our pouch, remove items from our kitbags and examine them. At first we worried about our camera equipment and sheath knives, but our personal possessions were never taken, even when we left them lying about. A lifetime's conditioning made it impossible for us simply to take without asking, but our requests seemed so unusual to the Wayanas that sometimes they misunderstood. A woman placed a bowl of fish stew near to me. I pointed to the bowl and then to my mouth seeking permission to help myself, but she took it that I required to be fed, picked up a lump of fish and placed it delicately in my mouth, no doubt thinking what a helpless, over-indulged creature I was.

Some of the men had a few words of English from missionaries and a few spoke Taki Taki, acquired through contact with the Bushnegroes, but most knew only their own language of which we understood nothing. But the absence of a common language proved to be a surprisingly minor disadvantage. Our time was spent in the company of delightful people who watched us, smiled at us, showed us things, gave us food and generally made us feel welcome without words being necessary.

There was a fundamentalist Christian mission in the village and the religious programme was all-inclusive and pretty time-consuming. Two services on Sunday plus Sunday school; Monday morning, a service for everyone, with a sermon; Tuesday, ladies meet six-thirty in the morning, a sermon; Wednesday, nothing; Thursday, men meet six-thirty in the morning, a sermon, then a prayer meeting at night; Friday, morning service for everyone, afternoon meeting for younger girls, Saturday, afternoon meeting for older girls; then Bible study for all. We were invited to church. The Indians conduct their own services we were told, and indeed the three that attended, 'all that are left after disciplining the others for sin in their lives', the missionary said, read passages from the Bible. The mission frowned on the Indians' culture and banned all of their traditional pastimes.

The missionary had some fascinating written reports of recent contacts made with Akuriyo Indians, a nomadic people who travel in small groups through the forests of Southern Surinam and neighbouring Brazil, hunting and gathering what grows naturally as they go. One report concerned a woman with an estimated age of twenty-five and a child of about ten, who had been wandering in the jungle for several years without contact with others of their tribe. They were naked and had no possessions except lighted sticks which were never allowed to go out. They had no means of making fire. The missionary who found them was led by Tirio Indians, one of whom spoke a little of the Akuriyo language. The woman told how they travelled through the woods keeping clear of big rivers and eating whatever they could find. On one occasion they'd seen a group of men with machetes. They hid till the men passed, then examined the gashes they'd made on the tree with their knives and were amazed. When asked 'What makes you happy?' the woman replied, 'When I have food I am happy.'

In the early 1970s many Akuriyos were contacted and went to live in Tirio Indian villages where they could be taught Christianity. Within two years a quarter of them had died from chicken pox, dysentery, and psychological problems associated with adjustment to a new life. In this part of South America lie tracts of virtually uninhabited forests as large as some European countries. Certainly there is no shortage of stories about lost tribes.

CHAPTER FIFTEEN

Camissie stood in the stern, hand on the throttle of the outboard motor. Gently he eased the craft through a narrow, winding channel between smooth, bare boulders, scoured by weather and water, rising fifteen feet above us. Under his capable control the canoe was like a long wooden antenna with which he probed the river ahead. As we glided past some driftwood a pile of crumpled leaves took flight, as if suddenly wind-scattered; scores of tiny bats. Even Martin didn't take much notice, we'd been travelling for six hours up the Tapanahoni river and the heat, coupled with the glare from the water, had stupefied our senses. Nothing less dramatic than an attack by caimans would have jerked our minds back to alertness.

Our arrival at the first Bushnegro village, Tabbetja, was cause for celebration. Martin and I were taken to a tall, highly decorated hut which the boss explained was a sanctuary, similar to a church. Anyone threatened could stay there in safety, a hefty fine being imposed on anyone who made trouble within.

Late afternoon, the rum and the drums were brought out; drums the size of buckets, drums as big as barrels and shoulder-high drums whose deep mellow thudding could be heard over a great distance. Just before dark, boats arrived from up, down and across the river, summoned by the drums. Esto, Camissie and Denny went off to get spruced up, returning with their hair braided into tiny plaits and wearing their best clothes. The women danced in a circle, shuffling first in one direction then another, chanting and smiling as the men appraised them. When the dancing ceased, each woman approached the drummers and placed her hands on their shoulders. The drummers responded by placing their hands on the women's waists for a second. Then the men began. After an hour in which the pace hotted up by the minute, dancing became frenzied. Men threw themselves onto the ground in convulsions and were picked up and dragged away. Some rushed blindly down the steep, dangerous path to the river and hurled themselves into the water. Impervious to pain, a man in a trancelike state held his foot in the fire for so long that the Captain and Basha tried to pull him away, but he shook them off like irritating insects.

Drumming continued till dawn and in the early hours we lay in our hammocks, drifting between wakefulness and sleep. South America had receded and we were in Equatorial Africa in the nineteenth century.

Slowly we travelled upriver, stopping daily at villages with names like *Sang be Soemie* – What has happened to me?, *Moy Takki* – Nice Talk, *Man Lobbie* – Man Loves.

Rapids became fearsome. Esto and Denny would position themselves above the rapid with the rope, while Rainier stood in the bow. At a given signal Camissie gunned the motor and the boat shot forward, with Rainier pushing it off the rocks with a long pole. Always, after a successful ascent of a notoriously bad rapid, the boatmen swam in the river, it was good obeah. Bad obeah was to reveal the name of a rapid before we were safely past it; the boatmen would suddenly be struck deaf and dumb if we asked. Many stages in the long journey upriver involved portaging. Often the route was a well-used path among the trees, but unless all of us pulled together with every bit of our strength, the canoe, which weighed half a ton, would stay as if concreted into the ground. Little by little we would tug it up to a mile into calm water above rapids. Dugout canoes are unresponsive creatures out of water.

The boatmen were playing up. The boss was eager to continue but Camissie and Esto declared that we must take their photos on the rapids. It infuriated the boss that they often asserted their independence in such minor ways, but there was nothing he could do. Off we trouped across the rocks, hopping from boulder to boulder, crushing purple flowers on long stems, so prolific that this part of the river resembled a meadow of blossom with channels of foaming, booming water surging through it. Camissie posed holding a banknote, Esto a gold chain. When we returned to the canoe, Camissie had lost the banknote. For hours we searched while the boss seethed. By the time we found it, most of the day had gone.

Next morning, with the boat loaded and everybody on board ready to leave, Esto announced that his family lived nearby and he was off to visit them; Denny was going with him. The boss ranted, then sulked with impotent rage. Unable to move without boatmen, the expedition was held up for another day. In South America you learn to wait; for hours, days, weeks. The only way is to wait patiently, giving up that period of your life, allowing it to slip by without caring. Temporarily, the boss had forgotten how to wait patiently and was looking very stressed indeed.

Granhola Soela, a waterfall that stretches half a mile around the river, is crossed using modern technology plus muscle. A four wheeled trolley waits at the bottom of a railway track, partially submerged. Camissie drove the boat onto it and then, by means of chains attached, we heaved and pulled the boat to the top of the hill, then heaved and pulled backwards to restrain it from hurtling down the other side. Where the railway meets the water, the river is sixty feet wide. The canoe was forty feet long and Camissie sat in it. The instant it touched the water, he started the engine and threw it into reverse, to prevent it crashing into the opposite bank.

We arrived at Drietabbetje, a large settlement boasting an airstrip, electric generator, school house and a clinic; the modern world meeting the ancient one, like a cat meeting an injured mouse. It was an unhappy place, full of old folk, women and children. Most of the young men had gone to work in the coastal towns. An American couple from the Summer Institute of Linguistics lived in the village with their two children and were engaged in language studies, with the ultimate aim of translating the bible into Taki Taki. They had been there two years trying to integrate with the Bushnegroes and being manifestly unsuccessful. They had had built a square, two-storey house, a copy of their place back home, which looked totally incongruous among the palm-thatched huts. 'We never use the upstairs,' the husband said. 'It's like an oven.' The wife spent much of her day at the riverside washing clothes, cleaning pots, peeling cassava (which they didn't use) and generally pursuing all the activities of a Bushnegro housewife. She even adopted native dress, except (God forbid) for bare breasts.

The villagers, though not openly hostile, didn't accept them. They were *bakrahs* (white people) whose presence among Bushnegroes was both incomprehensible and suspicious. Their pretty daughter had not mastered the language, had no friends among the children and was subjected to much tormenting by them. Her education, undertaken by her university graduate father was, he freely admitted, getting nowhere. Her behaviour was erratic, typified by wild tantrums, long sulks and bouts of uncontrollable excitability. To us it seemed they were all on their way to cracking up under the strain.

It was the hottest part of the day when the wailing began. Faint at first, it carried across the village like an animal in distress, a tortured cry no one could possibly ignore. We sat up in our hammocks, Sunday afternoon nap forgotten, and peered from the doorway; the village was eerily empty. Slowly first from one hut, then another, the wailing was picked up until it filled the air. A woman emerged from a doorway, shrieking and screaming, flinging her arms wide and beating her chest, then turned and pointing in our direction, let forth what could have only been a hail of abuse. From neighbouring huts came men and women to calm her. A man who could have been her husband tried to console her, but she pounded him with her fists. A very old woman began to shout at her, skirting around the flailing arms. Soon a dozen or more men and women were shouting and wailing, gesticulating wildly in our direction.

We couldn't begin to guess what was happening, but fervently hoped it was nothing we'd done inadvertently; it appeared very serious. 'I hope it's not because of the football,' Martin muttered.

I'd got off to a bad start when we'd arrived. Some children were playing football and kicked the ball to me. I gave it a hefty swipe and it flew from my foot and smacked the Basha on the back of his thighs. He didn't laugh but everyone else did. 'Surely that's a bit trivial, I think something awful has happened.'

All afternoon we stayed inside while the wailing continued intermittently. At last the boss came and explained. A girl of six had died and no one knew why. The family believed that a 'winti' had taken her, placed by the woman in the hut next to ours. 'Winti is very bad spirit,' he said. 'If a winti on you, then you die. The family will find who put the winti on the girl and will put a curse on that person, who will then die slowly, in fear and terror of the winti. There was no reason for the child to die, the nurse treat her for a bad throat but that get better. Winti very strong, very powerful obeah.'

Next day we heard from the nurse what had happened. A week before, the child had fallen out of a tree and some days later was taken to the nurse, complaining of a sore throat. The nurse wasn't told of the fall and the child refused to be examined and so was given antiseptic lozenges for a sore throat. But the child couldn't sleep. The nurse wanted to send her to Stoelmanseiland to see the doctor, but the girl kicked up such a fuss, her mother said she needn't go. Sunday morning, while playing a game with other children, she fell over and her neck snapped, killing her instantly. Almost certainly she had fractured it days before, when she fell from the tree.

Serious trouble was brewing in the village. Rainier told us that murder would follow this tragedy. After a four day stay, we were glad when the engine roared into life and we departed from that sad place.

I remember the opening of the last tin of sardines. Brewster ate one when he thought no one was looking and choked on it for five minutes. 'Serves him right for being greedy,' said Tanis unsympathetically. The rest were divided equally among us, served with rice. A tin of sardines with one missing doesn't make very generous helpings for nine hungry people.

Sadly we were no longer ten. Poor Matte, whose health had been steadily deteriorating, became so ill at Drietabbetje that we'd had to leave him there, yellow and feeble but cheerful at the prospect of returning to Paramaribo, even though it would mean going straight into hospital. We wondered if we could help him with something from our medical kit and asked about his symptoms. 'When I piss, only blood. When I shit, only blood,' he said gloomily. It sounded too serious for us to play at being doctors.

Food was becoming scarce and increasingly the boatmen hunted and fished to supplement our meals. The bland, inadequate diet of rice and occasional cassava bread had the effect of concentrating our thoughts on food. Occasionally, the women of a village would prepare their speciality, a favourite of the boss. From a thick dough of cassava flour, they take tiny pieces, roll them into pea-size balls and drop them into a big vat in which meat or fish is boiling. The end result is a bitter tasting, glutinous soup, resembling boiled frogspawn.

As the weeks passed, we dined on numerous creatures whose passing we mourned but whose flesh we craved: green parrots, toucans, red and green macaws, gold and blue macaws and many others joined the colourful procession into our cooking pot. Regularly featured on the menu were reptiles such as iguanas and tortoises, countless different sorts of fish, mammals such as peccary, deer, tapir and a variety of rodents like agouti and capybara. Most frequent of all were monkeys; we ate so many individuals from so many different species that we felt qualified to write a 'good-food guide', comparing such things as 'capuchin cutlets' to 'black saki stew'.

The preparation of red howler monkeys was horrifying. The carcass would be submerged in boiling water for a minute or two, then the fur scraped off with a knife to expose pinkish-white skin beneath. The body shaved clean resembled a human child. Tanis was always a little upset when Brewster, in a gesture of generosity, placed upon her plate of fluffy white rice a delicate little hand or foot, or luckier still, the head with the brain to be sucked out.

We never came to terms with living off the land. Even with an abundance of tinned food our boatmen would have hunted anyway, it was their way of life. And it cannot be denied that once things were skinned, cut-up and simmering in the pot, our feelings of guilt gave way to anticipation of a tasty, nutritious meal. Perhaps we were being hypocritical. Here we were, feeling guilty about hunting while hungrily devouring everything offered us. It was time for me to adopt a more positive attitude and make a contribution to the kitchen. I loaded the gun and set off into the forest.

Within minutes a large bird settled on a branch above me and without hesitation I shot it. It was a guan, a common bird the size of a small chicken. The feathers were beautiful, blue-black with a wonderfully lustrous sheen. I carried it to the river, cut off its head and began plucking it, hoping to get it bald and pink and looking less like a magnificent wild creature and more like food, before Tanis saw it. But she'd heard the shot and found me while I was still busy, glossy plumage floating away on the water. 'What lovely feathers,' she said sadly. That evening the guan was added to the communal meal and our companions were pleased, while I was haunted by the thought of a nest of chicks somewhere, starving.

Some animals remained in a happily unsimmered condition because of superstitious beliefs among the crew. No one would kill snakes, birds of prey or cats. Neither Esto nor Camissie would eat land tortoise, nor remain in the presence of those dining on it, though they happily ate river turtles. Meat could not be kept for long and following the kill of a 'biggi meat' we gorged ourselves and gave the excess to the villagers. Even with hunting and fishing, days passed when all we had was rice, in small, carefully rationed quantities, spiced with raw chilli peppers. While this is certainly not starvation and may not even sound like hardship to a Third World farmer when the rains don't come, by our standards these were hungry times.

We thought how overindulged we are at home, where people complain when they have to diet to lose weight.

Godoholo, Tapanahoni River.

Dear Mum,

We are at a village called Godoholo. It's nine in the morning and we've just had our first shot of rum! It must sound as if we spend our days drinking, but it's part of the ritual ceremonies and nobody seems to get drunk (except Esto). It does make sitting for hours amid mosquitoes, gnats and kabouri flies (big flies that sting) more pleasant.

The other day the Captain of a village brought out the traditional bottle of rum (made from sugar cane and exceedingly strong, it anaesthetises your mouth for about two hours). He prepared the usual tumbler for the libation, but only filled it half full. Pouring the liquid on the ground he chanted to the spirit of the river to let our boat go well and safely, to the spirit of the ground to let us walk well and not get bitten by animals or snakes, and that we should get plenty of fish and meat to eat. Feeling perhaps a little guilty at his economy (after all, there are nine of us) he half filled the tumbler again and bent down to pour it on the ground But his hand began to shake and his resolution wavered; just as the first drop was about to fall he changed his mind, was beaten by temptation and drank the lot.

This morning we were woken at five by the Basha walking around the village shouting a piece of news. I don't know how, but I immediately guessed someone had died. I was right, a few minutes later all the women started wailing. We were very worried as this is the fourth village we've stayed in where someone has died, and wondered if they might think we were 'winti' (bad spirits). Martin went to see what he could find out. He learned that a young man from Godoholo working in Paramaribo had been killed by a tractor. He had died three weeks ago and it had taken that long for the news to reach the village. Half an hour later, the village returned to normal.

Tobacco is used by the villagers, a lot of the men roll cigarettes but some of them and most of the old women mix tobacco with a tiny drop of water, pound it to a juice with wood ash and keep it in a small pot. This they sniff up their noses (the tobacco not the pot) although sometimes they're so vigorous I think the pot's going up as well.

This is a quiet work session for a change; sometimes it's like

Billingsgate market, with everyone talking, kids shrieking and women arguing, but the Captain is quite strict here.

The boss insists I write everthing down. Last night he told us the story of Bonni. The people on the Marowijne and Lawa rivers are all the Bonni tribe. Bonni was the best fighter in the uprising against the Dutch and in the intertribal warfare. Baron, of the Okansi tribe, sent a woman to seduce and betray Bonni. Because his weakness was women, the ruse worked. Bonni was killed and the body taken by canoe downriver, but at a certain point the severed head jumped into the river and was never found.

The people are extremely kind and welcoming towards us, in some villages we are highly honoured and called *moy* (nice). In one village we were unknowingly set up for a joke. A man spoke to us for half an hour in jibberish. We hmm'd and nodded and politely pretended to understand him. It turned out that he had told all the people watching this little comedy that he spoke perfect English, and had taken bets that he could prove it. He won!

One problem in the villages is going to the toilet! The river is the usual place but somehow, we're never alone in the river. Either I creep off into the jungle, or stride nonchalantly away from the village. Whichever, the children follow me, they know damn well what I'm up to! It's a little off-putting to have twenty giggling children watching your every move. Sometimes I really think I've beaten them and squat down in comfort when there's a snort from among the trees and that day's action is curtailed.

The young girls have a fashion for wearing 'washee dukus' (towels) around their waists instead of pangas and my brightly coloured towel gets some envious looks. The sign of a sloppy housewife is to get her panga wet when washing dishes or clothes in the river. To wash, they bend double, backbreaking work they all agree, but it's tradition. The women have gardens or plantations located some distance from the villages (an ancient precaution in case of attack when villages could be burned, but the food supply saved) where they grow cassava and bananas. They go to tend them early in the morning when it's cool, and hoe them with short-handled hoes, bending double again because it's tradition. It's a good thing for a wife to be fat, as this proves her husband is taking care of her.

At one village we stopped and took on a teenage boy whose name is Adodey but everyone calls him Carat. He does the chores. He has a stupendous appetite, I've known him eat four dinners then finish my rice for me. Likes to say 'jess' and 'dangue' to us, but his favourite

156

*saying is 'sweetie mumma'. Twice he's had a high fever and been ill.
He's treated with especial kindness by all and is regarded by the
Bushnegroes as a 'special person' as he is slightly retarded. There is no
stigma to affliction or handicap in this society. He's never been to
town, never seen the sea, never seen a car, never seen white people. At
first, on the canoe, he sat staring unblinkingly into our faces from a
distance of three feet, hour after hour. The boss says this is probably
the only time he will ever leave his village. He spends the work time
sitting next to me helping me to write, before falling asleep on me –
which he's just done, so I must stop! More later.*

In one respect Carat was the envy of every man he met: he
possessed a huge penis. It was always conspicuous, even when
tucked away inside his baggy trousers and when he stripped to
his underpants to swim in the river, it was as unmanageable as
ten inches of rubber hosepipe and the men would tease him
mercilessly, making him squirm and giggle. He sometimes
wore shorts which reached halfway down his thighs and the
penis always made an appearance below them, down one leg or
another. Because of this, the boss made him wear long trousers
in villages, so that he wouldn't offend anybody. Although
Bushnegroes dress scantily, in much the same way as they have
always done, the idea that a bit of nakedness does not matter
could not be more wrong. The Bushnegro definition of
'indecency' is about the same as in our society and public
display of genitalia is regarded as obscene.

Not only the crew teased Carat, village people did too,
especially women. One afternoon Tanis and I lay swinging in
our hammocks, drifting pleasantly in and out of sleep. From
nearby came screams of laughter and hand-clapping; a group
of girls were tormenting Carat who sat in the doorway of a hut,
hunched over with both hands in his lap, covering his bulging
embarrassment. The taunts continued with more women
joining the group. Carat began to cry. The boss was annoyed
and with a grunt, heaved himself from the hammock, to put a
stop to it. But he was too late, the gentle, inoffensive Carat had
been pushed to the point of retaliation. He was on his feet and
to yells of alarm, opened his trousers to expose himself, then

chased the crowd of screaming women through the village, while people rushed from huts to stand transfixed, paralysed by shock. When the women had scattered into the jungle, Carat returned looking mightily pleased with himself.

The incident was treated seriously. Carat was sent to a hut and told not to leave it, in effect he was under arrest. Captain and elders assembled and discussed the matter till sunset, then Carat was set free, excused because he was 'special'. Instead, the boss had to stand, meek and submissive, while the Captain gave him a good telling-off.

Bushnegro people seem to have no need for privacy. Always you find them in noisy, cheerful groups, revelling in the company of others, usually as many others as possible. A consequence of this gregarious instinct of theirs was that we were seldom left alone. As people who, when at home, turn down all invitations to social events for weeks at a time, merely to enjoy the luxury of uninterrupted evenings sitting alone in our kitchen, reading and listening to the radio, the constant attention, though kindly meant, was burdensome. At every opportunity we'd head for the forest and solitude among the trees. On hunting expeditions our companions discharged shotguns at anything that moved, but alone we could simply observe.

The notion that large animals like deer and tapir glide silently through the woods like shadows is untrue; they make quite a lot of noise as they tramp around. They do, however, stand as unmoving as statues at the slightest sound and this makes them difficult to spot. When the animal charges away, crashing through the bushes, it's lost to sight in seconds. Deer can be lulled into a trance-like state by a human voice and providing we were careful, we could edge slowly towards a lone animal, crooning quietly, until we were within thirty feet of it.

The most dangerous forest mammals are not mountain lions or jaguars but peccaries, the small wild pigs who snuffle through the undergrowth in herds. Although the danger they present is exaggerated – usually they scatter at the approach of people – their response is determined by the action of the leader and if he decides to attack, as he sometimes does, the rest will follow fearlessly. A frenzied peccary is capable of biting off a human hand or foot and herds sometimes contain two hundred individuals. Tanis's passion for pigs stops short at peccaries.

We were far from the village, enjoying a morning of privacy, when Tanis stopped still. 'What's that noise?' From all around came a grunting and rustling. We'd walked unannounced into a herd of peccaries. An alarm call went out, immediately followed by a braying, honking racket and a stampede of bodies, then we could hear them re-grouping among the trees behind us. 'Christ, there must be *hundreds* of them!' said Tanis, looking oddly pale in the forest gloom. 'Let's get out of here.'

For the next half hour the peccaries circled us. Not once did we see them, but heard them first from one side, then the other, then behind us, and so on. It seemed that we were in their territory and were being escorted out. It was frightening. We hadn't brought the gun and the thought of standing back to back, like two of the Musketeers, slashing it out with machetes against a herd of ferocious pigs, was not a bit appealing. 'Climb a tree' say some advisers. Around us the trees were either slender as ropes, or mighty and smooth, with not a branch to be seen below sixty feet from the ground. It was a great relief to get out of peccary-land.

On the upper river we were objects of considerable interest. Arriving at a village we'd step from the boat and women, piles of washing balanced on their heads, would stare in astonishment, drop their bundles and run full pelt up the trail. One evening at dusk, Indians came to the village where we were staying. Two canoes, four men in each, slid silently into the bank. Something momentous had occurred; the village became so quiet that we could hear the breeze rustling the leaves and even the children stopped yelling and stood still. Silence is exceedingly rare in a Bushnegro village, even in the middle of the night there is always somebody chattering, laughing, crying or banging around.

They were Tirio tribesmen from upriver and they'd come to

trade, bringing armfuls of hunting dogs. Only the Indians know how to make the potions that enable the dogs to sniff out particular animals. Villagers began to whisper to each other and watched cautiously as the men walked up to the Captain's hut, leisurely and erect, looking neither right nor left, as though the villagers didn't exist. Naked but for red loincloths, seed necklaces and feather decorations, their features were sharp and delicate, eyebrows plucked away, skin fair in the fading light.

We looked at their canoes. Piles of jungle fruits and leaves, wooden paddles, bows and arrows and a dead squirrel monkey bound with vines. No guns, knives or anything made of plastic, metal or glass. Nothing about this group suggested that the twentieth century had arrived. The villagers' reaction to these people was very different from their reaction to us. Trade between the two peoples was fairly regular and they had all seen Indians before, but it was impossible to avoid the impression that they were in awe of the Indians.

We were heading toward Granbori, the seat of the Granman. After several sets of rapids, we came to what the boatmen would only call 'the big one'. Leaving the boat, we cut our way through the jungle carrying as much as we could to ease the weight for them. An hour and a half later, we saw not one, but seven boats come round the bend. They had met up with two going to Granbori and four, manned by Indians, escorting the new Indian Chief, Puloewima. He was returning to Apetina for some hearty celebrations after three months in Paramaribo for his inauguration. Chief Apetina had died some months before and the village was to be renamed Puloewima.

Granbori was like an island fortress, with steep bush-clad slopes and a flat summit. Canoes were moored in an inlet, where a path led up a rocky bank to the village, sixty feet above the river. This was the residence of Granman Garcon, king of a tribe spread throughout ten or more villages. To signify that it was a place of powerful magic, a freshly killed vulture had been strung to the top of a tall pole, positioned so everyone entering had to pass beneath it.

Drenched in sweat from the exertion, we arrived at the top where all vegetation had been cleared, except for a single ubiquitous kan-kan tree. Two neat rows of huts faced each other like soldiers on parade; between them a cleanly swept path led to a two storey hut, lavishly decorated with paintings and carvings, the Granman's house. An audience was to take place next morning and promptly at dawn our party assembled in readiness for the meeting.

The boss, anxious that neither Tanis nor I should do anything to offend this important man (who, we were assured, was quite capable of imprisoning anyone who upset him), gave us a few tips on how to behave in his presence. 'The Granman is the most important man on the river. When you are in his house or garden,' he instructed solemnly, 'you must not run, shout, fire your gun, or do a number two!'

At the house, the butler, an elderly gentleman in a fancy loincloth, opened the door and beckoned us to enter. With the boss's instructions fresh in our minds, we resisted the natural urge of the English abroad to rush yelling inside, shit on the floor and blast holes in walls and ceiling with our shotgun. Instead, we walked in quietly with the others. The door was closed behind us. It was so dark inside that I was rendered temporarily blind and found myself shaking hands with someone I couldn't see, before being ushered to a seat. When my eyes had adapted to the gloom, I saw that our host was a handsome man dressed in smart shirt and shorts, seated in a rocking chair facing our party, which was lined up on a long wooden bench. I'd expected to meet somebody like an old West African witchdoctor. This man was young, sophisticated, well-educated, spoke English and was well travelled; he'd recently returned from Nigeria where he'd met African leaders. He was charming and friendly.

The room in which we sat seemed out of keeping with the Granman's appearance and manner. It was as full of things as a shop. On the walls, covering every substantial space, were knives, shotguns, bows and arrows, bunches of dried leaves and herbs, old photographs, ancient pictures from magazines, canoe paddles, bicycle pumps, oil lamps, animal skins and feathers. The floor was piled high with woodcarvings, jars, bowls and bottles. A dog was chained in one corner and in another stood a cot, containing a baby. Hammocks were draped over the rafters.

A bottle of rum was produced. It was six-thirty in the morning and we'd not eaten yet, but we'd got used to this early morning drinking, which seemed to be the preferred time of day for Bushnegroes to consume alcohol. The Granman opened the bottle and commenced the chant and splash routine. Then he poured a generous measure into a plastic beaker, handed it to the boss who swallowed it in one gulp and passed it back to be refilled. In this way, rum was consumed by each of us in turn. For anyone not in the habit of chucking down half a cupful of neat, white rum before breakfast, it brings a ruddy glow to the cheeks and puts a sparkle in the eye!

The Granman was courteous and friendly and questioned us about our journey, in a way that was polite rather than probing. He was very generous with the rum and every five minutes or so, conversation would stop for the formality of another beakerful, but he drank nothing himself. 'He's going to get us all pissed,' I said.

'Sshhh!' said Tanis.

Obviously we weren't going to get out of the Granman's house sober. This man was as generous with rum as Redmond O'Hanlon with a bottle of Jack Daniels.

While we could all still walk, we stepped outside into the glaring sunlight, which temporarily blinded us as effectively as the initial darkness of the hut had done. Mustering all our reserves we climbed on wobbly legs down the steep bank to the waiting canoe. With Chief Puloewima's boat in front and the other four fanned out in convoy, we set off for Apetina.

CHAPTER SIXTEEN

Martin thought these Indians might be wary of cameras. We'd heard that a French expedition had visited Apetina some time before and taken loads of photographs. These were published in a French magazine, which depicted the men as homosexuals because they held hands and put their arms around each other, and later in a pornographic magazine, which portrayed them all as loose living perverts.

In most Bushnegro villages, once I had obtained permission from the Captain, young and old alike acquiesced to the camera, and I had a list of names and villages where copies were to be sent the minute we got home. Only once, when I had photographed a sacred shrine had things gone badly wrong. The female Basha had stormed from her abode and almost attacked me, screaming viciously and summoning the whole village to witness my indiscretion.

Just below the village of Apetina all five boats pulled up beside a deafeningly noisy rapid and we joined forces to manoeuvre them, one by one, to the top. Chief Puloewima and the boss huddled in discussion before beckoning me from my hauling place at the first canoe. 'You are to take photographs,' the boss informed me. 'Go up onto those rocks and take many pictures. Go now, quickly!', shooing me away.

Scrambling over the rocks, I aimed the camera at the first boat. It had a devastating effect. Far from being wary, even if at a crucial point in the operation, as soon as anyone spied the camera pointed in his direction, he immediately let go of the boat (which promptly slid backwards) and stood up straight for the picture, until everyone else shouted at him. Three hours and films later, we regrouped and motored to the village.

Guns were fired into the air to welcome the new chief. Hands reached to help us from the canoe and carry our equipment. A young man named Roni asked if we would like to sleep in his house. He moved his hammock, knives and beaded belts into his mother's house opposite, but left bows and arrows and fishing spears. Very soon his sister Domili arrived with bananas and cassava bread for us. Roni's grandmother lay in a string hammock in their hut, looking over every few minutes to smile a greeting. In a basket by her side was a great fluffy mound of cotton, which she skilfully spun into thread. When the supply grew short, she signalled to a group of children to gather more from the bushes around the village. A baby lay at her side and she talked to it as she worked. Water boiled on a log fire. Industry and domestic bliss in the open air with a roof over the top.

Near the grandmother's house was a cashew tree. The nut, familiar to us as a shelled and salted delicacy which comes in plastic bags, grows in a hard case on the end of a pear-like, yellowish pink fruit, full of clear juice that gushes out when you bite into it, drying up the saliva and leaving black stains wherever it touches clothes. Papaya trees bordered the forest and beneath them lay piles of rotting fruit. Picking the freshest, we asked Roni if we could eat it. He laughed, surprised. They only used the fruit for fishing bait. By the river grew a tree laden with a fruit we'd never seen before, pastel pink and heart shaped, the soft flesh held the fragrance of roses. Roni called them apples. We looked forward to the days ahead, eating as much fresh fruit as we wanted.

The Wayana way of life seemed entirely without ritual or routine. All necessary work was done, but it was done when it needed doing, by whoever felt the need to do it. A man would lie in his hammock for a week, getting up only to drink and chat with his friends. Then, one morning he'd become active, taking up bow and arrows for a hunting or fishing expedition which might last days. It was difficult to avoid an impression that they lived an enviable life of plenty with the forest full of game, rivers full of fish and trees loaded with fruit. But this was the dry season when the living is easy. For at least half the year rivers are swollen, fishing and hunting difficult, cultivation impossible and not much wild plant food available.

A feast was planned. At dawn a group of young men, skins stained red with achiote, went off to hunt accompanied by our three boatmen, while we joined another group on a fishing trip. For half an hour we followed a forest trail to a rocky stream and walked along its bank, until we arrived at a section that had been dammed with slabs of mud and stone. People had been busy the previous night. The dam had caused it to overflow and form a large pool, in a natural low-lying depression among the trees. It was teeming with fish, their escape route upstream cut off by a palisade across the water, draped with nets. Occasionally a fish would break the surface with a splash. Standing close, I could see dark shapes, zipping around in confusion beneath the muddy water.

An old man arrived with two bundles of thin, woody vines and for the next hour, children sat on the rocks methodically pounding away at these until they had been reduced to a mass of milky, fibrous pulp. This was thrown into the water and we beat the surface with sticks to mix in the sap. The fish were being poisoned and soon began to appear, to shouts of excitement, swimming feebly or floating belly up, to be speared with pointed sticks or clubbed to death. The catch was impressive in quantity, variety and the size of some individuals; there were a dozen fat catfish over three feet long with even longer tapering barbels. The poison they'd used was a neurotoxin that interferes with oxygen uptake, partially suffocating the fish but with no danger of the eater suffering the same fate. Conveniently, the fish will recover fully if kept in fresh water and can be saved for another mealtime. A neurotoxin similar to this, just one of a hundred or so known to South American Indians, is used today in open heart surgery.

In town, the views expressed to us about indigenous forest people were generally that they were primitive and unsophisticated. Yet they are so supremely well adapted to their environment that they possess the knowledge to utilize more than two thousand plant products for food, tools, clothing, housing and transportation. Their jungle medicine chest, which gave us quinine among other valuable drugs, boasts a number of oral contraceptives which were probably in use when our comparatively unsophisticated ancestors were bashing each others heads in with stone axes.

The hunting party returned with four saki monkeys, a capuchin monkey and a deer, but no spider monkey, which were extremely common near the village. Once long ago, a Wayana man turned into a black spider monkey and now, to kill a male, might mean killing a relative. Our diet changed dramatically from rice and rice and yet more rice to as much as we could eat of fruit, vegetables, fish, animal meat and cassava bread. The Indians travel great distances to hunt, fish and gather fruits, practising their own form of wildlife conservation. They don't destroy the forest, nor hunt until there's nothing left, and their reward is an ample food supply. We were with people who live in harmony with their environment.

When I woke from a nightmare in the early hours, I didn't immediately realize where I was, cold and damp, hanging in a bag surrounded by swirling white mist from which strange, gnarled tree-shapes appeared then disappeared as the fog obscured them. For a few moments I wondered if I had died and this was my introduction to the afterlife – if only I'd given all my money to the poor! Then I saw Tanis turning over in her hammock.

Nights are relatively cool up country, particularly during the pre-dawn hours. Stealthily, silently, men left their hammocks and built little fires to huddle around for warmth, chatting softly in hushed voices, playing mysteriously enchanting melodies on reed pipes. Drowsily I gazed at the sight of dozens of fires scattered around the clearing, a family squatting in the dancing yellow light of each, and drifted back to sleep to dream of childhood bonfires and Christmas tree lights.

Daybreak revealed a scene that could have come straight from an illustration in a child's book of fairy tales. Semitransparent mist trailed wispily from the riverside bushes and hung suspended in a layer just above the water's surface. Trees were draped in this insubstantial vapour, serving to emphasise their fantastic shapes. Only the occasional plop and splash of fish jumping disturbed the stillness. But this time of gentle light and tranquillity passed too quickly. The mist vanished as the first rays of the sun hit the river and within minutes it was as hot as the hottest summer day in England, with the temperature rising by the minute. Work was forgotten as the feasting continued throughout the next few days. Twice a day, the hunting dogs were removed from their cages and taken by the women to the river for a bath. These ferocious creatures, that lunged at the bars of their cages, hackles raised, snarling malevolently if they so much as caught sight of us, became as playful as puppies when the women washed them. This done, the soppy, docile beasts were rubbed from nose to tail with a block of material made from the pounded seeds of achiote. Resplendent in their bright red fur coats, they would be led back to their cages, there to become vicious monsters again the moment Tanis or I stepped into their line of vision.

Near our hut I found an exceptionally large scorpion, picked it up on the end of a stick, set it on a rock and was just preparing to photograph it when somebody tapped me on the arm. It was the oldest-looking human being I had ever seen. A bald, shrunken, emaciated man wearing a tattered loincloth, that hung from a string of shiny beads around his waist. He looked like a small, brown, mobile skeleton. Shuffling closer on stick-like legs, he peered up at me from eyes barely visible behind slitted, wrinkled lids. A fragile, withered hand was thrust toward me. Recovering from my initial shock, I looked around; just about everybody in the village had gathered to watch the pair of us. Obviously he was an important person.

Leaning against me for support, he guided us wordlessly and very, very slowly, towards the riverbank. He wanted me to assist him down to the water, but unfortunately he'd led us to where the bank was particularly steep, twenty feet high and treacherously slippery. I considered the possibility of picking him up and carrying him down, he couldn't have weighed more than a hundred pounds, but I wasn't sure if that would be socially acceptable; if I were escorting a frail old lady across a busy road, I would hardly hoist her over my shoulder for expedience. I did my utmost to make this potentially disastrous operation a success, steadying and supporting him while performing a balancing act myself. We sweated our way down towards the water, watched silently by the crowd, with no offer of help from anybody – a thing in itself most unusual. What would be the response of the tribe if we were both to go tumbling down into the river? I nearly giggled at this idea, then sobered as I realised that there was much I didn't know about these people and such an event could produce a response that for me might be far from funny. It took us ten minutes to get to the water's edge, where he lowered himself to the ground and completely ignored me. Discreetly I left him.

Later Rainier told me that I had been greatly honoured to be chosen. Good fortune would be mine from now on. 'He a powerful Shaman, Martin, but he old, he looking for some place to die.'

Next morning I returned to the rock, the scorpion was still in the same position. I poked it with a stick and it scuttled away.

Rainier came to us one evening and in a conspiratorial whisper told us that upriver was a mountain, a place of pilgrimage for local people. The following morning a party would be going there and we were invited along, but first we needed some instruction, because it is a sacred mountain. Though we would see the mountain from the river, we must not stare at it or it would disappear. On no account were we to mention that we could see it. We must ask no questions and mustn't say where we were going, even to the people we were going with, not even to him. If we mentioned it, it would disappear! In short, we were to behave as though it did not exist until we actually set foot on it – then we had to climb it barefoot.

With the first glow of dawn in the eastern sky we were

motoring upstream. Within twenty minutes the sacred mountain came dramatically into view, a dome-shaped granite hill, swathed in mist, no more than a thousand feet high, but an impressive sight nonetheless, not least because it looked so incongruously bald, sticking up out of that riotous forest. I quite expected to see the Wizard of Oz perched on the top. Obediently ignoring one of the most conspicuous objects that's ever entered our field of view, we gazed solemnly at the river ahead.

The canoe was beached at a well-trodden spot, where a tell-tale gap in the greenery showed a jungle trail. Off we went. Two barefooted Indians led the way. At a cracking pace they sped along the trail, Tanis had to run to keep up with them. For a while we climbed through forest then burst out into the sunshine at the foot of the dome. From below it did appear truly gigantic and very, very steep. Shoes removed, we began the ascent. While we puffed our way up sometimes on all fours, the Indians ran. Prickly bramble-like plants grew in patches over the rock and here and there, clumps of bushes, but otherwise it was naked. Halfway up, we came to a Bushnegro shrine with a ragged white sheet on a propped up pole, like some ghostly scarecrow. Beneath it stood gifts of bottled beer, woodcarvings, coins and even banknotes, weighted down with stones. None of our companions gave these items so much as a second glance.

The view from the summit was splendid. Stretching to the horizon in every direction lay unbroken forest. We were looking across what must have been extremely remote and even totally unexplored country. In the distance were many other rocky outcrops, similar to the one on which we sat. As we came down, on our behinds most of the way, Rainier broke his silence. 'This mountain, it have a door. One time the Indian people they came here and two of the little children, they find the door and go in. But the mountain close the door and swallow them. Now sometime, you hear them, knock, knock to come out.'

In the still air, we listened for the sound.

Apetina, Tapanahoni River.

Dear. Mum,

Tomorrow we leave the Wayana village, we'll be very sorry to go. The people are extraordinarily kind. They load us with fruit, and Roni's grandmother presses sticks of sugar cane on Martin since she found he has a sweet tooth. The village is quiet and peaceful, very different from the noisy, boisterous Bushnegro villages.

The threat to forest Indians from the outside world is almost unimaginable here; all around are miles of seemingly endless forest. But we greedy lot are chomping away at it, swiping vast areas for cattle ranches. All the beef goes to fast food chains for hamburgers and once grazed, the land is finished, so they chop down more. All those replacement doors and windows they're forever advertising are usually made from tropical hardwood, chop, chop, chop. The building of roads is lethal. Streams of settlers arrive to farm, coaxing a living from what proves to be highly unsuitable land, chop, chop, chop. Multinational companies looking for oil and minerals cause untold devastation. You can imagine who benefits. I feel very angry and depressed about it all.

While I can't deny that the mission here protects the Indians and is helping them toward self-sufficiency in a modern world, they've banned smoking, singing and dancing, shamanism, festivals and the making of cassiri. The Wayanas appear to drink about a gallon of the brew most days, but become no more than happily intoxicated, but with the import of hard liquor, often brought by the Bushnegroes, all inhibitions vanish and they become totally unpredictable, (hard drink affects a lot of people this way, but for some reason the effects upon Indians, perhaps for physiological reasons, are stronger). The missionaries told us that in this village, two murders followed rum-drinking sessions.

The missionaries themselves are very pleasant, but we personally don't like their fundamentalist religion, it seems a form of blackmail, protection in exchange for your soul. The Wayanas are required to relinquish everything that makes them Wayana Indians: tradition, culture, and the technology that enabled them to survive and thrive.

Since we've been here, one by one the people have complained to the boss about these prohibitions. Yesterday, he assembled them all outside the mission house. This, he told them, is a Wayana village and not the missionaries' village. They have a chief and it is he they should listen to and if they don't like the missionaries, they should send them back to their own country. Strong stuff eh? Actually, it's a bit unfair as the Government doesn't have a policy towards the Indians and has happily left them to the missions' care. Since all Indian groups are fast losing their territories, big change is just a matter of time. Who apart from missionaries are willing – for good or bad – to devote their lives to the welfare of these people? I don't think that turning them into Born Again Christians is the answer though.

Yesterday I cut the boss's hair, he was very pleased. Today it looks as though I'll have to cut everyone else's! I had an upset stomach and was given a potion, followed by as much smoked deer and cassiri as I could take! The medicine worked though. Carat has a bad foot which I bathe with antiseptic, Esto has eye drops from the doctor but only I administer them properly, Camissie has decided he, too, needs eye drops but Esto won't share them.

More later.

Our contact with the Wayanas and their missionaries had left us with a kaleidoscope of impressions and half-formed opinions. We left the village enriched by our experience but ashamed that we were part of the greedy Western world that one way or another would eventually lead to the destruction of these people.

Downriver, just below the big rapid, now allowed to be named as Poun Soela, was a village of six huts. This was Apala Campo, formed by a breakaway group of Wayanas who disliked the mission and all it represented. Their Chief, Samé, was a constantly cheerful young man who spoke Taki Taki and a little English.

In the shade of an empty open-sided hut, Samé welcomed us to his village and invited us to stay as long as we wished. 'Where is the old Chief?' the boss asked.

'He died, he is there,' said Samé pointing at Martin's feet. We looked down; he was standing on a newly covered grave.

While rest of the group slung their hammocks above the old Chief, Samé insisted that Martin and I share his hut. A

Wayana's hut does not serve quite the same purpose in family life as a European's house. The hut is a place to store things and to sleep. Samé, his wife and two children, slept together in one hammock with a blanket over the top. They obviously found the arrangement comfortable, but I can imagine few situations less conducive to a good night's sleep than sharing a hammock with three other people. On the few occasions Martin and I have been forced to share one, usually because one of ours has collapsed in the night, any change of sleeping position was impossible unless we were both awake for a carefully co-ordinated action. 'I'm going to turn over, so move your knees back and lift your head so I can get my arm out . . .'

Occasionally, when the children were asleep, Samé and his wife would leave the hammock and make love on the ground.

The boss lay in a hammock, drinking cassiri with three older men. When we entered he politely offered the hammock to me. I had just settled into it when snap, something bit me. Startled, I shot to the floor, clutching my behind. 'There's something in there!' I said, nervously, backing away. The Indian whose hammock it was, looked afronted and scowled as he peered inside. His look changed to one of perplexity, then amusement as he reached in and brought out the boss's false teeth.

We were summoned to eat, seated on stools around a low table of bound bamboo poles. The people had prepared a delicious looking meal for us. Flat pancakes of freshly baked cassava bread, piles of turtles' eggs, still steaming from the boiling water, bunches of tiny sweet bananas, a selection of wild fruits and a dish full of smoke-blackened meat and fish. The boatmen had contributed a dish of 'bitter wiwiri', the leaves of a jungle bush. Boiled, they look and taste like spinach and according to the boss, have a similar effect on the man who eats them as spinach does on Popeye, though the organ that expands is not the biceps! 'Give you big strong!' he said with the lewdest gesture imaginable.

Martin began the feast with a chunk of meat, I selected something which looked like a tomato, but hesitated as a

warning from the jungle survival handbook of our very first
trip imprinted itself on my mind: 'NEVER eat any fruit which
resembles a tomato'. Ah well, after all the things we'd eaten, it
couldn't hurt.

'Taste that Tan,' Martin placed a piece of meat on my plate,
'I've no idea what animal it is but it's very good.' As I looked at
the meat it moved. Slowly it worked its way across my plate. I
began to wonder if that tomato had had hallucinogenic
properties but no, the meat was definitely moving. Arresting
its progress with my fork, I turned it over. Dozens of small
white maggots wriggled away from the light, disappearing
amongst the fibres. I looked desperately around. Several
women smiled shyly at me, nodding encouragement. I cut a
piece and raised it to my mouth. A maggot wriggled frantically
down the fork and fell in my lap. I remembered a dinner party
I'd given, where all the guests had bravely eaten a dessert called
'Pitch Lake Pudding' that looked truly awful and how gratified
I'd felt. I ate the meat. It was delicious.

I had with me a bright red tee-shirt. Tanis was sorting our
belongings when Samé spotted it and his eyes positively
glazed. We gave it to him. Later he came to tell us that he was
going to make fishing arrows and a bow for us and he required
specifications. The bows and arrows used by the men were up
to six feet long and transporting them would be difficult. I'd
seen children using sets of weapons half that size and asked
Samé to make some like that. Next day he presented us with
the finished product, a beautiful bow and three perfect arrows.

Samé was proud of his village; the people were content and
healthy, the forest full of game and the rivers teemed with fish.
They lived at peace with nature, rather than at war with it. I
was sitting by the river when Samé joined me, looking serious.
'Soon you will leave,' he said. 'In your country do you live in a
big village?'

I nodded, 'A very big village.'

'Does it stand beside a wide river with many fish?'

'There is a river, but the water is dirty and few fish live in it.'

'But there are many animals in the forest where your village is?' he prompted.

I thought of London with its frantic pace, thousands of commuters jammed into tube trains, the sparsity of Epping forest and the sprawling concrete suburbs. 'Years ago,' I tried to explain, 'men chopped down the trees, killed the animals and now there is little left.'

Samé gazed at the abundant, generous forest that stretched for hundreds of miles in every direction. 'That is very sad. It could not happen here.'

CHAPTER SEVENTEEN

During the final weeks of our travels, I developed a rash in my groin. By the time we arrived home, it had spread alarmingly and occupied virtually the entire area covered by a pair of swimming trunks and itched appallingly, especially in the nooks and crannies. Tanis was constantly telling me to stop scratching in public.

I stood in the doctor's surgery, trousers round my knees. 'A Dhobie Itch,' said Dr Brace with delight, as if he'd suddenly recognised a dear old friend, 'haven't seen one of those for years. I'll give you some cream. Might sting a bit, but it'll soon clear it up.'

At home with my tube of cream, I remembered the doctor's words: 'might sting a bit' probably meant it would sting a lot, so I applied a small amount and waited. A mild tingling sensation, not at all unpleasant. I applied some more. Minutes passed and still a tingling. I squeezed out a load and massaged it in everywhere. It was five minutes before the burning sensation started. I turned on the TV and tried to concentrate on what was happening there, as the pain intensified. A hip bath in boiling oil would have been mild by comparison. Desperate now, I rushed to the bathroom, wedged myself under the cold tap and tried to wash the dreadful stuff off, but it was too late; like a mouthful of red-hot chilli peppers, accidentally chewed up with a chicken vindaloo, it had penetrated the tissues.

When Tanis came home half an hour later, I was standing in the centre of the room, legs apart, a newspaper in each hand, fanning myself front and back.

The Dhobie Itch had gone, but more serious disease was diagnosed. Tests carried out at the London Hospital for Tropical Diseases revealed parasitic infestations. Worms and amoebas were living inside us, particularly surprising as neither of us had any symptoms. Tanis could be treated as an outpatient, but my illness necessitated being whisked, bewildered, into hospital. I'd never felt more fit and healthy in my life.

When I arrived, the man at the desk gave me a briefing. 'There's a lot of emphasis on stools in here,' he said mysteriously. I soon understood what he'd meant, for in the hospital nothing is allowed to escape unchecked into the sewer. Everything has to be inspected first. Each patient had a plastic pot with his or her name on it. On the toilet walls were notices: 'Please inform a nurse when you have passed a stool.'

I walked up and down corridors and stood outside wards holding my plastic pot. Eventually a nurse appeared. 'I've just done this,' I said, feeling excruciatingly embarrassed.

'Congratulations,' she said, 'but you don't have to tell me. Just put it in the cubby hole that has your name on it.'

Doctors from all over the world come to the hospital to learn their profession. They assemble in serious, whispering groups that travel swiftly from bed to bed, seeking answers to their questions. I lay on my bed and eleven faces looked down on me. Then eleven pairs of eyes peered up my backside. Nobody commented and when I was allowed to turn over, they all looked as glum and serious as they had before. 'Thank you Mr Jordan,' said the doctor in charge, and they went to the next bed where I heard the patient say, 'Ever since I returned from Zaire, I've needed to sleep for eighteen hours a day.' In the middle of the examination came a startled voice. 'Good God, the man's gone to sleep!'

Tanis had avoided all this, but her turn was to come.

While Martin was in hospital, I was treated as an outpatient for amoebic dysentery. Travelling up on the tube, my daily offering sealed in a yogurt pot, safe in my bag, I wondered what the doctor would make of my new symptoms. It was winter but I was exceptionally brown and people stared at me. Had they known what lay underneath, I would have had the carriage to myself.

'It started with this little patch on my hand.' I showed the doctor. Two Chinese students stood eagerly by his side.

'We'll test that,' he said, scraping the surface into a dish with a scalpel.

'And then, well, it sort of spread to my trunk.'

'Let's have a look. In there, clothes off.'

In the cubicle I stripped off. The doctor halted so abruptly that his students bumped into him. 'Goodness!' he exclaimed, 'you look like a Dalmation in reverse. Look at that,' he said to the students, who were gaping at me, delicate hands over delicate, laughing mouths.

'What is it?' I asked, alarmed.

'What is it? Yes. What is it?' he demanded, turning to the students. They tried to look inscrutable, but a brown body covered with pure white, thumbnail-sized blotches, was too much. 'Our students are taking their exams tomorrow,' said the doctor. 'I'd be very grateful, very grateful indeed if you'd let them have a look at this.'

'But what is it?' I pleaded.

'Ah. Hmm. Perhaps we'll wait till the students have seen it, to be perfectly frank, I've never seen anything like it before!'

The hall was crammed with a hundred noisy medical students. The doctor beckoned me in. 'This patient has spent some months in South America. She has, as you will see, rather unusual symptoms, you may ask questions. Take off your top, my dear.'

I looked at a sea of blank, puzzled faces. Nobody knew what it was.

This time it was woodsmoke that did it.

Our neighbour lit a bonfire of branches and leaves and on that bright autumn afternoon, smoke drifted through open windows to pervade every room in the house. There is a theory that part of the brain, once used to analyse smell, now deals with emotions; hence, the theory goes, the close association between familiar smells and emotional nostalgia. With intense poignancy, our neighbour's bonfire reminded us of campfires in faraway jungles.

In a wildlife magazine we read about a region of southeast Peru at the foot of the Andes. The description was intriguing; tens of thousands of square miles of pristine wilderness. No roads, no towns. Part of the region, the Manu Valley, had been designated a National Park, an area as big as Northern Ireland. The author claimed that this part of Peru is the least known and least disturbed of the Amazonian ecosystem, probably containing the greatest diversity of flora and fauna in the world; more than a dozen species of monkeys, six hundred of birds, a thousand of butterflies and so the list went on. It sounded extravagantly wonderful.

Indians live in Manu and neighbouring valleys, so off we went to Survival International, the ultimate information source about the world's tribal people. 'There are three tribal groups known to be living there,' we were told, 'Yaminaguas, Amahuacas and Machigenguas, though our definition of groups by name is pretty arbitrary because we know so little about them. Certainly there are many hunter-gatherers who have had no contact with contemporary society. They could number thousands. The Manu Valley is largely unexplored.'

Trembling with excitement, we studied maps. 'What's known about this river here?'

'Very little. A few years ago a party travelled along it for three days. They saw a group of men who ran off into the forest.'

We waited, expecting more information. 'Is that it?'

'That's it.'

'What about this river?'

'That's where Bob Nichols and two companions were killed by Machiguengas in 1971.'

'Bob Nichols?'

'An English journalist who worked for the *Lima Times*.'

Trembling now with emotions other than excitement, I

moved my finger across the map, a long way from the previous area. 'Is anything known about this river? The one with no name.'

'No. Nothing.'

Uncontacted tribes, rivers without names, teeming wildlife; a lost world nestling in the foothills of the Andes. But how to get there? 'Very difficult' we were told by everyone we asked. From a wide range of sources, we gathered that our journey to the Park would involve a truck ride across the Andes and a long canoe journey, merely to get to our starting point. Barring landslides in the mountains or flooding in the valleys, it could take a week or two and promised to be a mini-expedition itself.

All we needed to do was to persuade the Peruvian authorities that they should allow us to go there. We were confident we'd be able to manage that, even if it took a year. It took eighteen months.

During the weeks before we left, as the last of the thorns acquired in the canoe crash worked their way out of my hand, we remembered something important. There had been one period that for sheer joy remained unsurpassed; the months we'd spent in Venezuela at Auyantepui. It wasn't only the region that had made it so wonderful, for if it was that, we could simply have returned. It was something deeper; our first experience of being on our own in the wilderness, of having stepped out of time as well as place. Even though it was only five years before, it seemed that we were very young then, experiencing everything with childlike appreciation.

And so, while we anticipated the unknown jungles of Peru, we recalled the magic of that earlier time and hoped our journey would recapture the spirit of it. Days were spent in feverish preparation for Peru, nights were spent dreaming memories of Venezuela; endless forest, amber rivers, shining waterfalls and Auyantepui, the Devil Mountain.

We were Devil Mountain dreamers with tickets to Peru.

GREEN MAGIC

CHAPTER EIGHTEEN

'It was the prawn omelette that did it,' I groaned to Martin, as we climbed the fourteen flights of stairs to the Ministry of Agriculture in Lima. I was suffering from a malady which had rendered me evil at both ends and was known affectionately by gringos as 'The Inca Quickstep'.

Today, we were to collect our authorization to travel alone in the Manu Park. Our plans hinged on that single document. We were early and the Minister hadn't arrived. His secretary directed us to seats, brought coffee and placed a stack of newspapers on the table. On top was the English language weekly, the *Lima Times*. From the front page a headline jumped out and smacked us in the eyes: JUNGLE EX-PEDITION IS AMBUSHED BY INDIANS.

'It's Manu isn't it? I know it is,' said Martin, 'I can't bear it!' With a feeling of inevitability, we read on. It was Manu all right.

An expedition travelling in the southeastern jungles of Peru was attacked by Indians early this week but managed to escape, according to radio reports, by sinking the canoes of the attackers. . . . The expedition had applied for a permit to visit the Manu Park but had already gone out of radio range by the time the answer came back. The permit was refused – precisely on the grounds that Indian groups in that part of the Park are an unknown quantity and are especially restive at this time of year. . . . This area is known as one of the most inaccessible and potentially dangerous areas in the Peruvian jungle.

'Shove it under those magazines,' hissed Martin.

Our nervousness about the forthcoming interview was magnified to something near terror that our carefully laid plans might be thwarted at the last minute by somebody else's irresponsibility. But our interviewer was friendly and obliging and we left his office with a permit that promoted us to doctors, with permission to travel in our boat throughout the Manu Park, but feeling that we should flee hotfoot from Lima before he read his morning newspaper and revoked it.

Next day we were aboard a plane, flying inland from the Pacific coast, bound for the thin air of Cuzco, ten and a half thousand feet high in the mountains of the Andes.

Dear Mum,

At last we are in Manu, but the fun and games we had getting here, I'm beginning to wonder if I dreamt it!

There was an air strike in Lima the day we left and all regular flights were cancelled. Everyone left, but we must have looked so dejected that an airline official approached us and said that if we waited, he would arrange for us to 'hitch' a lift on a military plane to Cuzco (for a price!). He took us to the runway and soon an old propeller-driven war plane thundered towards us, sounding like the end of the world arriving. They loaded up cargo, tar and cement, money changed hands and we climbed on board. It was an old American plane, inside were signs saying 'ensure all paratroopers are secure before firing', there were no seats and loose wires crackled and flashed. We clung to the sides as it took off, then sat on bags of cement. It wasn't properly pressurized and over the Andes it got colder and colder. We wanted to smoke so Martin located the crew, there were no inside doors, just two men at the top of a flight of stairs. He tapped the nearest on the leg and the man slumped forward and dropped a half empty bottle of whisky. He was the navigator. 'May we smoke?' 'No, it is too dangerous'. It took five hours but we got there in the end!

At Cuzco we stocked up and made friends with the man in the Ministry office. He's charming and extremely helpful, even though he spoke so quickly and quietly that we couldn't understand a word he said to us. He arranged for their van to collect and deliver us to the truck depot at eight in the morning.

Quite unbelievably the van arrived, only two hours late, we loaded up and he took us to fill our ten five-gallon cans with gasoline (petrol). Gas is as precious as gold in the jungle.

Off we drove to the place where the big trucks gather. Unfortunately the one for Shintuya had gone. The driver, who'd made us late in the first place, was very worried and rushed off to find another. Including the gas we have thirty items of luggage.

Our vehicle was like a big cattle truck with no roof and open slats you could see through. A price was agreed of two pounds each. For two hours he drove around Cuzco collecting cargo, sacks of rice, maize, soya flour, dried milk, etc. bearing the words 'Furnished by the people of the USA.' Also we had on board assorted sacks of pasta, a spare wheel and tyres, and an assortment of passengers. There were no seats, just bare boards. We had been told that the trip would take six hours.

Soon we were on a dirt road, being thrown dangerously about. Each jolt bounced us a foot into the air and everyone had to cling to the sides of the truck or to a long pole down the middle – to let go was to risk injury. Beside us were sheer drops of thousands of feet, the road a narrow ledge that twists and curves around the mountain – it made us giddy just looking at it.

The driver was drunk, we'd watched him drinking with his mates in Cuzco and he shot along at forty miles an hour, taking bends without slowing at all. He had a bottle of Pisco in his cab and we could see him taking swigs out of it to keep his alcohol level topped up. There are no barriers on these mountain roads and dotted along the edges are wooden crosses, often with photographs of people and bunches of flowers pinned to them, where vehicles have gone over the edge.

Way down in the valleys we could see burned out trucks, looking like Dinky toys among the boulders. We reckoned getting on this lorry was the craziest thing we'd ever done.

By four o'clock the snow-covered peaks looked quite close and it was icy cold. I couldn't smoke because of the gas; we'd made pinholes in the tops of the cans for the pressure to escape if it got hot and due to the jolting, it was flowing out. We weren't too popular with the other passengers when we stopped them casually scattering burning ash and matches around; if we hadn't, there was a real possibility that we'd all have been dramatically cremated – another cluster of crosses to decorate the roadside!

We caught up with another truck and to indicate that he wanted to overtake, our driver placed his hand on the horn and left it there for five minutes, all the time banging into the bumper of the truck in front, presumably trying to push it over the edge. My heart nearly flew out of my mouth when the truck in front pulled in and we shot past on the outside of a bend, with our outer wheels over the edge of the precipice. The road is single track and trucks operate a one way system on alternate days.

At seven, we stopped to squeeze in more passengers and it began to dawn upon us that we might not reach our destination quite as soon as we thought.

Even in the dark, the driver didn't slow down until at the top of a mountain we skidded to a stop, cargo shifting dramatically from one end to the other. This was Tres Cruces (three crosses), the highest point, from here we would descend to the jungle. We were up in the clouds, it was cold, and the mist very wet. A tarpaulin was dragged over the back of the truck and we carried on.

Next we stopped to eat. Earlier, we'd shared our three days' ration of bread, cheese and olives with the rest of the passengers, mostly Quechua Indians, descendants of the Incas, poor and gentle farmers and herdsmen of the Andes. Up here in this stark, high-altitude land of terraced hills and snowy heights, they keep herds of llamas and alpacas. They play hauntingly beautiful music on harps, flutes and pan pipes. It's a land of lost cities and buried treasure and giant condors soaring in the sky; the mystery of the mountains has already affected us.

The Quechua women wear masses of petticoats under brightly coloured flared skirts, waistcoats and bowler hats, a costume decreed by a Spanish ruler centuries ago to make him feel at home in a distant land. Many of them chewed coca leaves (cocaine is made from these), it probably helps relieve the monotony and discomfort of the journey. The driver's mate came round and told us we should eat as much as we could because soon we would reach the jungle where '. . . There's nothing but trees and animals, not even bread!'

We asked what time we'd reach Shintuya. 'Tomorrow morning ten o'clock. Tonight we sleep.' So we slept on sacks in the truck, bodies wrapped in blankets everywhere. Martin had flu and felt lousy. Fortunately I'd kept the torch handy so at least we could take out our contact lenses. It rained all night and the tarpaulin leaked. Some of the sacks had bust open and every time anyone moved we were all covered with a film of flour and dried milk.

At noon we reached a place called Salvación. By this time we were the only passengers left and the driver decided he wouldn't go on to Shintuya. The road was bad, the bridges down, 'You'd better get another truck,' he said. Furious, we unloaded all our gear in the mud and rain and humped it into the police post, to wait for another truck. This could mean two or three days, so we weren't in the best of spirits, tired, hungry and cold. The jungle looked dismal and wet. We tried to keep cheerful by remembering that we were nearly there; soon we'd have a camp with a big fire, lots of coffee, our boat and engine ready to take us upriver, comfortable hammocks and all would be well.

Only hours later a truck arrived and agreed to take us, but charged extra for our gasoline as it was dangerous!

After an hour we stopped. Opening the back, the driver said he was sorry, he couldn't go on, the bridge was damaged and underwater. The bridge, made from massive logs, was partly submerged in a fast, narrow river, about twenty-five feet wide. You could see that if the truck tried to cross and one of the logs was loose, it would just turn over. Locked in the back we'd probably drown! We'd have to wait a few days for the rain to stop; (rivers here go up and down dramatically). While we sat glumly in the back, wondering where they'd dump us, he started the motor and with a heave and a lurch drove straight onto the bridge. Honestly, these drivers take some believing!

Shintuya, at the end of the road has a mission station, established to save the local Machigengua Indians from hellfire and damnation, a cluster of huts and a clinic. Here we negotiated a price with a boatman (a Machiguenga Indian) and arranged to leave next morning for Manu. That night we slung our hammocks in a small wooden government building, occupied by two workers, a parrot, two green parakeets, a prosperous colony of bats that live on the birds' bananas and a sick Indian boy and his father, who had overflowed from the hospital next door. All night the poor child screamed and cried in pain. There was nothing we could do. We rose next morning shattered, after a second sleepless night.

Our boatman arrived late and immediately demanded we supply him with gas; no gas, no trip. We refused. Then, a strange light came into his eye, he began hurriedly loading our equipment onto his canoe. Halfway through the trip, we realised he had positioned our gas behind us and was surreptitiously syphoning it from each can in turn.

At four o'clock, after a speedy journey down the fast-flowing Alto Madre de Dios River, we stopped at the police hut to show our papers, and were told we could sleep at the school house. The teacher gave us a meal of porridge-oat soup, followed by tapir meat with yucca. We settled on the floor and insect warfare began. Next day, after a third sleepless night, we set off upriver for the two day trip to the Park.

For anyone who imagines sitting in a canoe going along a jungle river is comfortable (me? when I'm home wallowing in nostalgia? Perhaps you should cut this bit out and stick it on the staff room wall, mum!), it isn't, it's absolutely back-aching. For the first few hours you feel OK, after that you try to get more comfortable and after eight hours it's hard to find a bit of bum to sit on that isn't already bruised. You can't change position, stand, or stretch your legs. But, and a big but, we saw some of the most unspoiled areas we've ever seen. Caimans and turtles sunbathed on beaches and logs, and birds were everywhere, it really is super here.

After ten and a half hours motoring, we stopped, lit a fire on a beach and ate fried bananas. What a night! Enough to say I got up five times, rebuilt the fire and stood in the smoke, to avoid the mosquitoes. Each time I went back to bed (on the ground, wrapped in shelter and blanket) millions of them descended, if I put the shelter over my head I nearly suffocated. By three-thirty I could stand no more, found the torch and went looking for more wood for the fire. There were caimans all over the beach, but at the time I couldn't have cared less. I piled the fire high and stayed in the smoke till dawn. Breakfast was a banana. Our fourth night with no sleep! We reached Pakitsa at noon and were given a mosquito-netted room in a mosquito-netted building. Heaven at last!

Love T & M

Pakitsa. Four wooden buildings in a clearing beside the Manu River, manned by guards whose job is to keep out gold prospectors, skin hunters, logging companies, fanatical fundamentalist missionaries and other undesirables whose energetic activities decimate wildlife, level forests and destroy ancient, tribal cultures in a remarkably short period of time.

A Park administrator, Dr Cee, was there on a visit. Despite presenting him with a sheaf of permits and documents, covered with official stamps and important signatures, he greeted with disbelief the news that Martin and I intended to sail off into the wilderness of Manu Park alone. 'Boat? You have a boat? But it is not allowed to bring a boat into the Park!' he said, looking perplexed. 'No one is allowed to bring a boat into the Park, it has just been decreed by the Minister.' Martin and I exchanged glances. Perhaps he'd read the *Lima Times*.

He pored over our documents, scrutinising the Minister's signature. 'It is true, you have permission, it is all in order,' he said.

Our elation turned to shock with his next remark. 'But I wish you to be safe, I will let a guard go with you. All you must do is provide him with food and pay his wages while he remains with you.' The guards looked equally shocked, the prospect of being squashed in a rubber boat and fed dehydrated food for three months didn't seem to appeal to them.

'Are you sure you can spare a guard for three months? If it's difficult, we really don't mind going alone,' suggested Martin tactfully.

'I must think about it, I have, how do you call it? A predicament.'

A man like Dr Cee was rare among bureaucrats, he genuinely wanted to help. What's more, he loved the jungle and understood our desire to spend our time alone. 'You understand the dangers?'

We listened as the guards relayed them:

'There are snakes, cats and other dangerous animals.'

'You might become ill, or get lost, or drown in the river.'

'There are Indian people living in and around the Park, with many there has been no contact. Now it is the dry season, they will come to the main river for food, to dig for turtles' eggs.'

'Some of these people are hostile, from Tayakome onwards the Yaminagua can become very hostile, they will turn you back with arrows. You must not go to Tayakome.'

Tayakome, high on the Manu was the former site of a Machiguenga village. It was near there that the expedition was attacked that we'd read about in the *Lima Times*. 'We planned to travel up the Pucacungayo River to its headwaters. As a couple, perhaps we'll present less of a threat than a boat-load of men,' I remarked.

'No one has ever been far up that river,' said a guard who'd been impressed by our boat, but now looked as if he'd rather get a bout of malaria than set foot in it.

During the next couple of days the atmosphere relaxed. The night before we left, we stood on the riverbank, looking down at our overloaded boat. 'I have decided,' said Dr Cee. 'I regret that you have not enough room in the boat for a guard. I am afraid that you must go alone.' I almost hugged him.

Just upriver were uncontacted Indians, they said. The group had simply appeared on the riverbank a week before, three women, about whom nothing was known, except that they had no fire, no boat, and no recognisable language. 'You must not stop when you reach them, go past quickly, others may be hiding in the forest, it is possible they will shoot at you if you stop.'

This warning was reinforced by Lucho, a Machiguenga Park guard. A year before, deep in the forest to the north of Manu, he'd met two Indians from an isolated and unknown group. The men were armed with bows and arrows, but were friendly and inquisitive on this, their first contact with outsiders. At dusk, they had made camp together, but dawn revealed that the two Indians had departed silently in the night, leaving behind a bow and several arrows, presumably as a gift. Lucho showed them to us proudly. The bow was seven feet long and the arrows the same length. The heads, tipped with hardwood and bone, were twice the length of a man's hand; arrows that looked like spears.

Responding to our interest, Lucho offered to demonstrate. He was a powerful man and his muscles swelled as he drew the finger-thick bow-string, aimed a horrendous arrow vertically into the sky and released it with a FFFZZZZZZZ. It soared into space and hung for what seemed like minutes before descending, to bury itself two feet into the earth. 'Bloody hell,' I said 'the ones that hit John Wayne never looked like that.' The reality of being struck by such an arrow was daunting. There'd be no gritting of teeth and bravely plucking it out, like they did in westerns. It would probably lift you out of the boat and impale you to a tree.

Half a day upstream we made our first camp. In a forest of thousands of trees we couldn't find three the right distance apart where both hammocks would be under the shelter. We slung them almost side by side.

The attack came suddenly.

One minute after the blackflies departed, the whine of the mosquito rush hour assaulted our ears. Relentlessly they came, so desperate for blood they punctured shirts, trousers and socks to get to our flesh. We ran to the haven of our mosquito nets. Within seconds the nets were black, thickly covered by the layer of mosquitoes, whose whining din was frightening as the belligerent insects fought to gain entry. I fell asleep smugly pleased with the mosquito nets I had made from net curtains.

'Tan, they're getting in my net somewhere, quick, turn the torch on.' A seam had come apart, leaving a gaping hole. Mosquitoes were queuing to get in. 'Move over!' I lay awake, not so pleased, squashed and uncomfortable with Martin's sandy, dirty socks under my nose.

On a sweeping bend, an Indian woman emerged from the forest. Crouching low she watched us approach. Stealthily, on all fours, a younger woman crept out beside her. The young one stood up and began signing to us to pull in. She wore nothing but a short skirt made from tree bark. The older woman rose to her feet and hesitantly clapped her hands, then became bolder and clapped wildly, shouting unintelligibly at us. Days before, the guards had left a shirt and mosquito net on a beach for the women and the older one wore the green net wrapped around her hips. She was less than five feet tall, plump, hair cut just below her ears and a small fringe. The girl was thinner but stocky, with long hair that hung past her shoulders and a thick heavy fringe.

As we drove past, less than thirty feet away, they started to run, clapping and calling to us. 'Martin, it seems so rude not to stop.'

'I know, but we promised not to, and don't forget, you've got a cold and I've had flu. That could kill these women, they'll have no resistance to our germs.'

On seeing that we weren't going to stop, the women turned and slipped into the forest. On the beach ahead stood a lone hut made from palm fronds, tall and pointed like a sentry box.

A girl, younger than the other two, wearing the man's shirt (left by the guards) that came to her knees, stood in front of it. She too, clapped, waved and called to us, less cautious than the others, she waded into the river as we drew alongside. She ran, keeping pace with us before stopping where the river looped.

For some reason I hadn't expected them to do more than let themselves be seen, and the desperate attempts to make us stop were unnerving. Ignoring their calls made me feel guilty and ill-mannered. 'They won't get a good impression of our society if we all sail by and ignore them,' I said, then got a catch in my throat which induced a coughing fit.

'You ought to stop smoking you know, Tan,' Martin said pompously, having given it up the day we left Cuzco.

'Don't moan at me, you're awful when you give up smoking.'

'Me? Awful? I thought I was quite good-natured. It doesn't bother me at all, I don't even miss it. I was just pointing out that you've got a bad cough. Did you know you've smoked five cigarettes already since you got up? I bet you don't even enjoy them. Why don't you give up now, throw them all in the river? Go on, you'd feel great.'

'*Martin*, I haven't got a bad cough, something caught in my throat.' He laughed derisively. 'Don't start on me, Mart, OK? You've given up, fine. Leave me alone.'

'I won't say another word.' Pause 'I won't even mention it when you start puffing and wheezing when we climb hills and I have to wait for you.'

'I don't puff and wheeze,' I said, mentally determined to run, without complaint, up the first hill we came to, 'and I don't ask you to wait for me, I don't want you to wait for me. You're so bloody superior sometimes.'

'At least I've got healthy lungs.'

'Oh, shut up. And how come you had flu but mine's just a cold?' I stared angrily at the river. It was stupid. 'You know, we're ridiculous, here we are in the middle of a river, we've just seen uncontacted Indians and we're having an argument about smoking.'

'You're right. I promise I won't mention it again. I'll enjoy healthy lungs alone.'

'You do that, Martin, and if, if you decide to start again, as you usually do, don't even think about asking me for a cigarette!'

'Oh, don't worry, I'll never smoke another one, I'm over it now, never will filthy tobacco smoke enter my lungs again.'

Inappropriate arguments are our displacement activity in times of stress, like two parrots in a cage who start squabbling and pecking each other when something outside upsets them. Twenty minutes later, when we'd rounded the bend, describing an enormous loop and ending up only a short distance (as the parrot flies) from where we'd left them, there were the women again. They'd simply cut through the forest. One of them was now holding up a turtle, imploring us to stop for supper. It seemed absurd to just keep on going and, but for the danger of infecting them, we would have stopped. For three quarters of an hour they followed us, until we left them behind and were once again alone with the warm ochre water, high green forest, and caimans, like carved rocks on the sandbanks, slipping into the river as we motored past.

In the lowland forests, the rivers flow in great meandering loops and curves. As years go by, the loops tend to migrate downstream as water cuts away the banks. Sometimes the loops join at the neck and the river flows across the shortest distance, leaving the loop itself behind, as a so-called oxbow lake. These abandoned meanders immediately begin to silt up and, like all lakes, eventually disappear. In Peru the oxbow lakes are called 'cochas' and there are scores of them along the Manu River.

Our first stop was 'Cocha Cashu', half a mile from the river, the site of Manu's Biological Research Station, used as a study centre for visiting scientists.

'This is really weird,' said Martin as we followed a well-trodden trail through high, virgin forest, 'one day we're in Pakitsa among people who live most of the year in Cuzco, next day we're being pursued along a riverbank by three Stone Age women – I mean, we might as well have come from Jupiter for all they would have known about a rubber boat with an engine on the back – and now here we are about to introduce ourselves to a bunch of European biologists. Talk about culture shocks, it's just weird.'

The Research Station was a well-made wooden house on the shore of a tranquil lake, a lovely, timeless place. 'Hello,' we called.

Young, blonde and serious, dressed in jungle fatigues, a girl appeared. 'Who are you please?' clearly surprised to see us.

Brigitte came from West Germany and was the scientist in residence, engaged in the study of giant otters. Her assistant was Michael, also from West Germany, a tall, dark-haired, serious-looking young man. A Park guard called Manolo completed the trio.

That evening with fireflies dancing in the darkness and caimans grunting in the lake only yards from our front door, we sat around a table, drinking a bottle of excellent brandy and all getting along surprisingly well for a first meeting. Brigitte explained that their work was not going well, for in order to study giant otters, it was necessary to have some giant otters to study, and the family of animals that lived on the cocha had mysteriously departed three weeks earlier and showed no signs of returning. Manolo, who knew the cocha and its inhabitants well, said they would certainly return, but it might not be for several months.

'We were thinking of making a journey up the Manu River. A little exploration for a couple of weeks,' said Brigitte. By an extraordinary coincidence, their outfit was almost identical to our own, a twelve foot Avon inflatable boat, powered by a Yamaha outboard engine. We decided to travel together, in the two boats, up the Manu River to the Pucacungayo.

CHAPTER NINETEEN

'You two go ahead and make a camp, we will join you tomorrow,' said Brigitte. 'Here is a tent for you to use, it is not necessary to sleep in the jungle.'

For five hours Tanis and I motored up the Manu River to the appointed spot on the map, just opposite an unnamed river. Brigitte, Michael and Manolo arrived the next day. From the inflatable, the men unloaded a great metal box; Brigitte's luggage. Inside was a complete change of clothes, a large, folding, canvas chair, a cassette player and a teapot. Michael had a guitar, Manolo a fishing rod. 'Surely fishing isn't allowed in the Park?' we queried.

'I thought not, but Manolo says it is allowed for the guards,' Brigitte said. 'He also wishes to dig for turtles' eggs, but this I do not allow.'

For bait, Manolo used mole crickets: strong, lively insects living in holes in wet sand just above the waterline. To catch them he would scrape out the hole very quickly with his machete, thrust an arm inside and grab the insect before it burrowed deeper. When I tried it, I found I needed to muster some nerve to reach into a hole and blindly grab a struggling, three-inch-long insect. With the unfortunate mole crickets on hooks, he caught small fish to use as larger bait, and at dusk would go midstream to hunt for catfish, bottom-dwelling scavengers whose varied colour, pattern, shape and size was wonderful. Some nine hundred species of catfish are known from the rivers of Amazonia. Manolo was extremely clever at fishing, knowing exactly where the lines should be cast. The largest fish would grunt and squeak alarmingly and often had small parasitic fish clinging to them, which would drop away as they were pulled clear of the water.

Michael and I were not so successful, until one evening when we hooked a giant catfish. Because it put up no struggle, we didn't appreciate just how big it was, until we began to haul it aboard. It was seven feet long and weighed at least a hundred and fifty pounds. Michael looked at me aghast as we struggled with the creature. It lay on its side unresisting, half out of the water, far too heavy to be dragged aboard by the line, gazing unblinkingly with one sad eye into the sky and the other into the boat, no doubt wondering what the hell was happening to it. I felt a surge of pity. Such a magnificent and successful creature might have been living unmolested in the river for over a century. 'Let's put it back,' I suggested, and Michael, who'd been thinking the same thing, carefully pushed the hook through its cheek, cut the line and it splashed back into the water and swam away.

Manolo stood on the beach as we paddled back to camp and he held up a catfish. 'He vill not believe our one that got away, Martin,' said Michael, pausing to pee into the river.

'No, no, Miguel,' Manolo cried urgently, '*Muy peligroso, pescas!*' Manolo mimed the actions of a fish swimming upwards, using the big fish to demonstrate.

'Vot does he mean with the fish?' asked Michael, stopping mid-flow.

'He's telling you that a fish may swim up your penis,' I explained. 'They're dangerous buggers, you don't know they're there until they open their barbs inside you, it takes surgery to remove them. Come to that, they'll swim up any orifice.'

Michael stared at Manolo, still waving the two foot long fish at him. 'Martin. I am to believe that such a fish vill swim up my orifice? I think that you make a joke with me. Vould I not feel such a fish.'

'No, not *that* fish Michael. A tiny fish called candiru, it lives in the gills of bigger fish.' Most Latin men would not swim naked in a jungle river for a guaranteed first prize in the National Lottery, nor will they urinate directly into a river, believing that the candiru can swim up the stream of urine like a salmon up a waterfall.

For days we followed narrow unnamed tributaries on foot. Flowing into the Manu from the north, they seemed to snake through the forest for ever, with the canopy meeting overhead in places. Most of the time we walked along sandy shores, exposed by the falling water level as the dry season advanced. When the beach ran out on one side, we would wade or swim across, and continue along the opposite shore.

We searched for giant otters, which grow to six feet long and weigh-in at half a hundredweight. Not surprisingly, such large animals leave ample evidence of their presence, most noticeably wide areas of riverbank stripped bare of vegetation and trampled flat, like muddy demolition sites. They eat fish and crabs and there was an abundance of both in these rivers-without-names. Everything seemed right for giant otters but we found none. Instead, we found frequent evidence of people. In the forest were trails marked by finger-snapped twigs and broken leaves; on the beaches, human footprints among those of other mammals and birds. One set told a story: clear and sharp-edged, the prints of an adult and child showed how they had wandered across the sand, searching for turtles' nests. Finding one, they had sat and eaten the eggs raw, leaving broken, sucked-out shells strewn all around. We wondered who they were, and for how long they would be safe within their jungle sanctuary.

Manolo knew a great deal about the jungle but essentially he was a *civilizado*, a man whose home was the city of Cuzco. Like so many city dwellers, he entertained a profound fear of 'wild' Indians. In contrast, we four, perhaps from a combination of ignorance and the magic of being on unexplored rivers, were sharing few of his anxieties. At any unexpected noise Manolo would leap up, all aquiver, spilling things, dropping things, knocking things over. His concern was not just for himself, but for all of us, and his worst time was first thing in the morning when everyone would wander away from camp, searching for somewhere secluded to shit. I think Manolo would have been happier then if he could have had us all tethered to long ropes, ready to yank us in at the first sign of danger.

Ting. Ting. Machete blades severed the vines and branches that barred our way. Ting. Ting. Ting. Leaves and twigs showered down as we cut a trail through the forest.

Martin looked cheerful to be off the river and among the trees again. Manolo tried to look cheerful but would rather we'd stayed on the river. Somewhere ahead of us was a cocha. It was shown on Brigitte's map to be shaped like a crescent moon and as the map was compiled from aerial photographs, we were certain the lake existed. Travelling north on a compass bearing, we deviated occasionally to avoid marching into swamps or climbing over piles of tree trunks where jungle giants had tumbled, bringing their companions down with them.

We came to a tree like a banyan, with dozens of slender trunks reaching up to horizontal boughs, forty feet above the ground. From the boughs, other trunks stretched vertically upwards into the greenery. It was like the timber frame of a strange building. 'Never did I know such trees are here in the Amazon,' said Brigitte. Manolo assured her they were quite common in Manu.

'Let us climb it. Perhaps ve vill spy the cocha,' suggested Michael, and up we went, like a troupe of European monkeys. But it wasn't helpful; we could get no more than fifty feet with ease and from that height we might as well have been on the ground, for all we could see through the wall of leaves.

We'd been trailcutting for four hours. Wearily we sat down to rest. A procession of fluffy little marmosets scurried along a branch, twittering and glancing nervously at us as they went. The solitary note of a bell-bird rang across our heavy breathing. '*Surely* we've covered a mile by now?' I said.

'More like two and a half, I reckon,' said Martin. We studied the map again. The cocha was no more than a mile from the river. It seemed hardly possible that we could have missed a body of water half a mile long. Our starting point must have been wrong, we decided, and the lake lay to the east. It was getting late, we'd continue the search next day.

Ting. Ting. Freshly-sharpened, early-morning machete blades sliced a path eastwards, bringing the leaves down around us again. Manolo was uneasy on this, our second day in the forest, because we'd camped for two nights, which might lead any Indians in the neighbourhood to assume that we intended to stay. Torn between anxieties and duty towards Brigitte, he would have preferred to leave the cocha undiscovered.

After an hour we came out from high forest into a field of heliconias: soft-stemmed, banana-like plants with leaves ten feet long and double rows of red, boat-shaped flowers. We'd found our cocha. It had dried up and the heliconias had colonised the lake bed. 'It vos a vaste of time,' said Michael. All of us were a bit disappointed except Manolo, relieved now that there was no reason to remain.

On the way back, Martin noticed what looked like avocado pear stones on the ground. Manolo examined one. Its surface was scarred by tooth marks where the flesh had been gnawed off. Eyeing us fiercely he announced 'Indios!' in a tone which said 'you wouldn't listen, now do you believe me?' To us, the marks looked too small for human teeth, but Manolo herded us down the trail at a jog trot.

Ten minutes later, at the river, Manolo cursed loudly. He'd left his machete at the spot where the seeds were found. Grimfaced, he went back into the forest, to reappear within five minutes, dripping sweat, fighting for breath, holding the machete aloft. He must have been up and down that trail like an Olympic sprinter going for gold.

As the distance from Cocha Cashu increased, so did Manolo's nervousness. Working our way through the log-strewn shallows of the Pucacungayo, his glance darted restlessly this way and that. In the evenings he told us about Indians. The Machiguengas steal women, Brigitte and Tanis must not wander far from camp alone or we might lose them. Never must we stay anywhere for more than one night, we could be considered too permanent and be driven out by force. If they didn't want us in their territory they might shoot arrows near us to scare us away, or, on the other hand, they might kill one of us to show they meant business. If they did attack us, it would be at dawn.

Our progress up the river was worrying him, too. Indians have been known to allow travellers to move freely, damming the river behind them with tree trunks so that on their return, when they are at their most vulnerable, wallowing in the water clearing a passage for the boat, they attack. Manolo's anxieties were not unfounded. The tradition of regarding forest Indians as dangerous wild animals, to be chased away with bullets, had been carried on here, as elsewhere in South America. Consequently, the only experience that some of the isolated groups living here had of outsiders was of aggression. Hardly surprising that they felt hostile.

The ghost-like, black-headed forms of four giant jabiru storks flapped eerily into the sky as we approached. On the beach was an improvised shelter made from broken sticks. In the remains of a fire were fish and animal bones and the skull of a howler monkey. Near it, the oblong resonator that amplifies the voice so powerfully. 'Machiguengas,' said Manolo.

But with all his fears, not once did Manolo refuse to continue. Always willing, always working, happiest when cooking fried fish steaks or talking of his home and family.

In the middle of the river their outboard began to splutter and smoke but rather than pull in again, Manolo attempted to change the plugs while drifting in deep water and dropped the plug-spanner overboard. Kneeling on the side of our boat Tanis reached across and passed him our spanner, but in the exchange it slipped from their fingers. 'Look out!' Tanis tried to grab it as it fell, overreached and splashed head first into the river.

'While you're in there, you might as well dive down and look for it,' I said as she surfaced, spluttering.

'Me? I didn't drop it, Manolo did. He should look,' she said.

'It doesn't matter who dropped it, anyway you're already wet.'

'Tanis, pay attention for the little bugger fish,' added Michael.

'Sod the bugger fish and sod the plug spanner!' Tanis raged, trying to climb into the boat and sliding back. Manolo didn't speak English but he understood. He tried to keep a straight face as Tanis bobbed between the two boats.

It had been a day when everything went wrong. It was raining when we got up, a fine persistent drizzle that depressed the spirit and looked as though it would continue forever. On the beach, half in the water, lay Brigitte's boat, the back end looking like a crumpled, grey sock. Something, probably a caiman, had bitten it during the night. This was very worrying indeed, an unexpected new hazard, wanton vandalism by the local reptiles.

While the others set about repairs I attempted to light a fire, with little success because everything was saturated. After a liberal application of petrol, the pile of sticks exploded with a great 'WHOOMPH' burning off one eyebrow and half a moustache. Tanis tried to be sympathetic, but kept turning away from me and I could see her body convulsing as she laughed silently and uncontrollably. When finally the fire was blazing merrily, I realised that I'd left my knife on a stone right next to it. The knife was all right, apart from being red hot, but the magnificent hand-tooled leather sheath was like a black-ened potato crisp which crumbled between my fingers.

The insects were terrible. The rain seemed to have encouraged them. There were blackflies *and* mosquitoes and a plague of half-inch long triangular flies that stung maddeningly. 'Pay attention to your left foot,' said Michael, 'something happens beneath the sock.' Somehow, half a dozen of the stinging black flies had got inside my sock and were dancing a jig in there. Michael was always calm. I imagined a situation where I'd hear his calm voice say, 'Martin, pay attention to your right ankle,' and I'd looked down to see an eight foot bushmaster poised to strike.

But it was Michael's turn for a mishap. Hurrying away with his delayed breakfast, he fell over Brigitte's chair, hurling his coffee and freshly made bowl of porridge into the sand. 'WHO PUT THAT FUCKING CHAIR THERE?' he roared in German, all calmness gone. He kicked the inanimate object into the air. Had there been a machete to hand, he would have chopped it to pieces. The chair had stood innocent and alone, with no other object within yards of it. Outraged by the insult to her chair, Brigitte rescued it, placed it by the fire and stirred the remaining porridge. In a shower of sparks the pile of blazing sticks collapsed, the big aluminium pot turned eagerly on its side and half a gallon of porridge poured out into the flames, to become ashes and steam. Violent Germanic oaths burst from Brigitte's lips. There was no pacifying her and I sympathised, but it made me feel better about my knife.

The only responses to such events on days like this are rage, or hysterical laughter. While each in turn had a rage, the others shared the laughter. But silently.

We saw more animals than ever we'd seen before: ocelot, tapir, deer and in just a few days, seven species of monkeys, but no giant otters. One afternoon, an exceptionally large flock of blue and yellow macaws settled on some riverside trees, right ahead of us. 'Count them!' yelled Brigitte excitedly, grabbing notebook and pencil, not neglecting for a moment the job of the scientist – to quantify observation.

'What?' we said together.

'Count them, Martin do that tree; Tanis that one; Michael over there; Manolo (rapid change to Spanish), sit still and stop waving that paddle about, you'll scare them away.'

There were sixty-three birds. A dazzling spectacle. When they took flight with the sun on their plumage they symbolisd everything that makes me glad to be in the jungle.

Calf deep in mud, we squelch-gerlumped along, dragging the boat through six inches of water, round the edge of a log-jam. Brigitte, Michael and Manolo wallowed in our wake and their bad-tempered cursing kept us in good humour: it often worked like that, when we were swearing and arguing they often looked happier. 'Why are we doing this?' Tanis mused.

'What?'

'Going up this river?'

She didn't expect an answer; it was a joke between us, the dreaded question from the public appearance. 'Now tell me,' the interviewer says, and we tense, sensing what's coming. 'Why do you make these expeditions?'

'Er . . . em . . . adventure . . . privilege of visiting wilderness . . . er . . . fun . . . excitement . . .' we mumble lamely, unable to respond easily to something so difficult to explain. Though sometimes the reasons seem obvious. Last evening, during an unusually insect-free interlude, I'd been standing at the forest edge, idly watching the others: Manolo, down on the beach on hands and knees, grunting with concentration as he poked a machete into the sand in his obsessive quest for mole-crickets; Brigitte in her chair, bathed in the last of the day's sunlight, oblivious to all as she studied a scientific paper about otters; Michael sitting on the sand next to her, playing a tune from southern Spain on his guitar; Tanis, brown-skinned, hair bleached yellow by the sun, winding a snake of rolled-out dough around a stick, for stick-bread. Five specks of humanity among an immensity of trees and rivers. In the unlikely event of an aeroplane flying over this forgotten part of Amazonia, anybody looking out would never notice us. The world could have been at war for all we knew, cut off from news.

Woodsmoke drifted and slanted shafts of sunlight probed the forest, lighting the rows of gothic columns which supported the green roof of our cathedral. At that moment, not for a million pounds would I have been anywhere else, doing anything else.

Manolo spotted a trail leading up a steep clay bank from the river to the forest. Narrow and well-trodden, it was unmistakably a trail made by people, not an animal track. Manolo looked quite grey, he had expected the worst from this foolish adventure and now he felt it was about to happen. As guard and guide, he would be known to posterity as having been brave and in control. This, he declared in an urgent whisper, was a job for men, the women would remain in the boat. I truly thought Tanis would explode she was so angry. Not one to suffer sexual chauvinism gladly, when Manolo asked for her machete I feared she'd lop his head off.

With Manolo in front, we crawled up the bank on our bellies. The tension and excitement made me grin nervously; we'd roared up to this place in two motor-powered boats and if there were any Indians up there who were still unaware of our presence, we certainly need not fear them for they must be both deaf and blind. At the top, deep among the trees was a village of six thatched huts, none higher than my shoulder. The poles that supported them had been made to appropriate lengths by scraping, pulverising and snapping by a people who evidently possessed no cutting tools. Sleeping mats made from palm fronds stood propped against the bushes to keep dry.

The mantle of leadership sat well on Manolo. His nervousness departed, he called the girls up and beamed at them, showing us around as if it were his village. Like a party of tourists in Trafalgar Square, we took photos of everything though we touched nothing. Leading into the forest behind the village was a wide and carefully cleared trail. Across it, at perfectly regular intervals of three feet, straight, clean sticks had been laid. First I thought of rollers for dragging canoes to the river, but these sticks were too small for that. On the verge of walking the trail to investigate, I drew back with a jolt as I thought of traps. Was it possible that those sticks were triggers for some kind of weapon?

In front of the huts a fresh, green, palm-frond had been stuck into the earth, its blades carefully bent back so that it was perfectly oval in shape. Manolo said this was a sign to other people that the place was still in use and that it was a Yaminagua village. We noticed a sleeping mat on the ground inside a hut. There were some fresh-looking berries beside it. Manolo's euphoria left as suddenly as it had arrived. He eyed the surrounding forest uneasily. Perhaps there *had* been someone at home when we motored up. Was it possible that from among the green shadows, at that very moment, bowstrings were drawn and arrows pointed in our direction? We left, brushing away our footprints with leafy branches as we did so.

That afternoon Manolo had a premonition that the giant otters were back at Cocha Cashu. So sure was he, that he even knew how many there were, describing their position near the house. Brigitte and Michael would have liked to continue upriver, but they needed to get back to Cocha Cashu for some serious work— as far as otter studies were concerned, the trip had been a waste of time.

Next morning as they loaded their boat to return downriver Brigitte asked, 'How long have you and Tanis been married?'

'Thirteen years.'

'Do you have any children?'

'No.'

I wondered if she was going to ask us not to continue upriver for the sake of the children. She turned away embarrassed. 'I'm sorry, I shouldn't have asked.'

'No, it's OK,' I hastened to reassure her. 'We've never wanted children.'

Her eyes were now full of sympathy, 'That is a very positive attitude. It would be good if all people ceased to want what they cannot have.'

'No, no, Brigitte, you don't understand . . .'

She interrupted me, holding up her hand for silence. 'It's all right Martin, I *do* understand and perhaps one day you will be lucky.'

It was useless. And she was being kind. We'd had this question before on trips, and often invented a couple of children.

Two hours after saying goodbye to our friends, we were drifting across a lagoon when, one after another, four furry heads popped up out of the water to observe us. The comical, bewhiskered, droopy-mouthed faces followed our progress for thirty seconds, then with a great splashing, thrashing and snorting they disappeared beneath the surface. Giant otters.

Alone on the Pucacungayo my wisdom was increasing. I now knew with certainty that a jungle expedition is not the best time to quit smoking. In Cuzco when I decided I could do without cigarettes on this journey, I'd refused to buy enough to last us both for the months we'd be away.

'Now listen,' said Tanis the day we were to leave, 'I don't mind what you do, but if I run out of cigarettes halfway through this trip because you've smoked them all, I'm coming home, wherever we are!'

During the argument in the boat, I'd irrevocably reasserted my superiority to the addicted and burned my boats, so to speak. But as weeks went by a disgusting craving for tobacco developed and jealously I'd watch Tanis smoking, too proud to admit my feelings. Eventually, after much grovelling, I scrounged a cigarette (just to see what it would be like), smoked it and was immediately re-hooked. Cadging became a daily occupation: I would break up each cigarette, roll the tobacco in airmail writing paper into three slender cigarettes. By this means I could get nine smokes a day when Tanis was in a generous mood

'It's a pity you bought cigarettes with filter tips,' I said.

'Why?'

'Well, if you'd bought ordinary ones, I could have rolled up the dogends.'

'That's a thought,' she said. 'If you feel like a drink there's a bottle of methylated spirit in the tool box.'

One afternoon the air became very hot with an oppressive stillness, that indefinable 'something' that can herald a violent change in the weather. On a beach, in the shade of trees, we lit a fire to brew coffee and for the first time in weeks there were no blackflies biting us. It was strange. 'There are no birds singing,' observed Tanis, 'and the light's getting dim.'

No breeze, no insects, no birds, one-thirty in the afternoon, sun shining from a cloudless sky, but its light cast an amber glow on the landscape as if it were sunset. Evening frogs started croaking. It was odd and a bit sinister. I shuddered, feeling my mouth go dry. *Had* a superpower 'pressed the button' and was something unimaginably catastrophic taking place in the upper atmosphere? Then we realised that a considerable chunk of the sun's disc was blacked out. A partial eclipse. With that realisation, what had been an alarmingly strange experience became mysteriously moving.

At dusk, I stood in the river, tying the sheet over the boat. Because we'd had a good day, I was 'tucking her in for the night'. The evening before, after a day plagued by minor mishaps, and in far less sentimental mood, I'd been 'covering the sodding thing up'. The torch began to flicker, yellow and feeble. The batteries were dying. 'Shit!' I said, wondering how I was going to find spares now, in the dim light, confronted by three kit bags, each crammed with stuff. I called to Tanis, fifty yards away on the beach.

'Where-are-the-torch-batteries batteries batteries. . . ?' My voice bounced off the forest and echoed across the water.

'Kit-bag-number-two, half-way-down, wrapped-in- yellow-shirt shirt shirt shirt. . . .'

I've never understood how she's able to remember where everything is.

Progress up the ever-shrinking Pucacungayo had become hopelessly slow. Never had we seen so much fallen timber; mighty tree-trunks lay scattered along the banks and piled into loose dams, blocking the river on every other bend. There were days of dull weather with not much wildlife to be seen and travelling any distance required hard physical labour from dawn till dusk. Our journey was losing its sparkle and becoming a slog. The aim in coming to Manu was to see as much wilderness as possible in the time available, not to trudge ever onwards to nowhere-in-particular. Impulsively we decided to turn back and venture up another of the Manu's tributaries.

CHAPTER TWENTY

'How do you feel, Mart?'

'Ill. Very ill in fact. I thought I'd die in the night.'

'Now don't be silly, you can't die here, it's probably something you've eaten.'

'I've eaten the same as you!'

That was true. We were holed up at the mouth of the Pucacungayo. Martin, laid low with fever, vomiting and diarrhoea for twenty-four hours, showed no signs of recovery. I studied the little red book. There were countless alarming diseases it could be.

'Fever, loss of appetite, nausea, malaise and abdominal discomfort . . .'

'That's it! What is it?'

'You didn't let me finish, "followed by jaundice. Tobacco smoking is avoided". You're not yellow and you're smoking, so its not infectious hepatitis.' I flipped over the page.

'Slow pulse, severe headache, no, I don't think you've got typhoid, we had jabs against that anyway.'

'I'm greatly relieved.'

'How about "fever and general ill health? If it becomes chronic, the heart and intestines are affected". Oh, no, visitors are seldom infected.'

'What was it?'

'Chagas's disease, widespread in South America.'

'Maybe it's dysentery, look it up.'

'Here we are, hmm, doesn't mention vomiting. Liquid stools? Listen, "people living in warm countries tend to become amoebic-dysentery conscious, and many are sure that they suffer from this disease without any good evidence".'

'I've had plenty of evidence, every ten minutes!'

'Nope, with amoebic, there's no fever but colic is acute, with bacillary, nausea is frequent but vomiting rare.'

'Tan, look up sandfly fever.'

'It's not that, I had it in Surinam, remember? I was really ill.'

'*I'm* really ill, Tanis! I haven't eaten for twenty-four hours and all I fancy is a piece of dry bread and some cold mineral water.'

'Aah, I know you are. God, Bilharzia sounds dreadful, listen to this: "The adult male and female worms live in pairs in the veins of the abdomen and their eggs, which have spines, work their way through the tissues into the bowel or bladder. Very often eggs fail to reach the exterior or lose their way".'

'What are the symptoms?'

'That's odd. "Acute vomiting and diarrhoea lasting twenty-four hours, followed by irrational cravings for carbonated water and bread".'

'WHAT?'

'I'm joking. Hey, here's one that fits: "Sudden in its onset, characterised by profuse purging, vomiting, muscular cramps and rapid collapse . . . because of the large loss of fluid, the patient rapidly becomes dehydrated and in fact . . ." Oh!'

'In fact what? Come on, what does it say, I'm definitely dehydrated, that sounds exactly right, what is it?'

'You look a lot better now, how do you feel?'

'I feel lousy, Tan, now what does it say after "in fact"?'

'Nothing much at all really.'

'Read out what is says.'

'Are you sure you want to know?'

'Yes, I'm sure.'

'OK. It says: "In fact, it is dehydration that is the immediate cause of death." It's cholera. Would you like a cup of tea?'

'Tan, go and clean the boat or something, and throw that book in the river.'

A week later, in a spotlessly clean boat, we sailed down the Manu. Everywhere mountains of logs twenty feet high, trees toppled by bank erosion caused by the rising, falling river. Driftwood lurked near the surface, sharp branches waiting for a vulnerable inflatable to pass by. Past the women, now only two, and back to Pakitsa.

Dear Mum,

It's eleven thirty in the morning and pouring with rain. It rained all night, the boat filled with water and this morning our shoes and gear were floating in it. I'd planned to do the washing today. Typical!

There are two guards here at Pakitsa, Jorgé and Daniel. We shared a meal last night, they stand up to eat, they reckon they don't get bitten so much. On the Pucacungayo we ate most of our meals walking up and down, you couldn't stand still for a second, if you did you got a mouth full of insects. Not pleasant. They have a saying here that you arrive with eight pints of blood but leave with four.

It took a bit of getting used to, not carrying a gun on this trip. Not that we'd want to use one, but it does give a feeling of security. Guns aren't allowed in Manu.

For some obscure reason, we carried the packing case from the engine with us upriver. It's a large polystyrene box, we had the idea that when we resell the engine, it would look better in its box.

Campsites near beaches are not too good for hammocks here. The jungle is fronted by a twenty foot tall plant, with a long stalk and a fan of sword-like blades with serrated edges. It's called caña brava and apart from being impenetrable for about thirty feet, breeds insects by the millions. Where there are no beaches, the bank is high and very muddy, sometimes we sink to our knees in sludge. The other day we were walking along the bank and Martin (being Martin) dived off to chase a crab and immediately sank to his hips in the mud. I was laughing until I realised that he was actually in trouble, he was sinking fast! As I gingerly stepped towards him, I began to sink too! It was like quicksand. By the time I'd found some driftwood long enough to reach him, he was up to his chest. It wasn't quite like the movies, glugging and sucking him under but he was well and truly stuck, if he'd been alone, who knows?

The other day we were motoring along counting the caimans on beaches. Every beach has a few, sometimes dozens. They're wonderful to see. At least they're fairly safe here, not like most of their relatives who end up as bags, shoes, wallets and belts. People shouldn't buy those things, it's a disgusting trade.

We decided to see how close we could get to them. As we drew nearer, one by one they slid into the water, not even bothering to stand up properly, just slithering on their bellies. All except one. He (or she?) was about eleven feet long and just looked at us as if he simply couldn't be bothered to move.

'They're very slow and sluggish aren't they?' I said. We were almost on the beach then and I had visions of walking right up to him. Then he stood up (on surprisingly long legs) and ran down the beach so fast that he skimmed across the water, right to the middle of the river before he stopped and sank. I was flabbergasted. I never dreamt they had such a turn of speed. They never bother us though.

I'm washing my hair in the Peruvian equivalent of floor soap, it's turning a peculiar shade of yellow. I'm getting brown, though we can rarely take any clothes off, due to the insects. The soles of my feet are getting tough again, my nails are all broken, I'm covered in hundreds, no, thousands of bites; yesterday I found three ticks burrowing into my legs. My cough is taking ages to go. We have fungus growing on our feet, clothes and almost everything else. I know that when we get home we'll forget how bad the insects were, we always do. The kit bags and shelter are standing up to life here very well.

My stomach, which suffered so badly in Lima and Cuzco, is fine now. Martin tells me that in one night, I passed out four times and had such convulsions he thought I was dying! Never again will I eat a fish omelette in a sleazy café. It bears out my theory that we're safer in the jungle than the town.

Did I tell you that they eat guinea pigs in Peruvian restaurants? In some, they live in the kitchens, running free around the floor, you choose the one you want, they kill it and cook it. In Cuzco they were for sale, cooked with a bright green pepper stuffed in their mouths, they also have guinea pig races in the Plaza in Lima!

The next part of our trip should be great. It was nice being with Brigitte, Michael and Manolo but we prefer to be alone. Michael was lovely, he muddles his v's and w's and talks about how 've wisited the vild willage'. He asked us to correct his English and when we do it's always 'thank you, wery good, wery fine'.

So, we'll travel downriver about twenty-five miles to the Pinquen River. A few miles up is a cabin, very old and deserted according to the guards, and after that is unexplored river, they say that nobody has been very far past it. We want to travel right up until the river forks and then we'll continue up a tributary known as the Dinquira. There are Machiguengas and Yaminaguas there but I don't think they'll bother us.

I hope all is well, it's funny when I think of home you're six hours ahead of us, if I think about you in the evenings you'd be asleep. I say to Martin, Oh, it's midday in England, Mrs so and so will just be being shampooed. Lots of love, hope the G. Pigs are fine, (don't show them this letter!). Love T & M.

THWUMP!

It was midnight and the peculiar noise came from the direction of the river, like someone beating a hollow log with a wet towel.

THWUMP!

'That's a new one, Tan, haven't heard that before, wonder what it is?'

THWUMP!

'Dunno, Mart,' she yawned, 'sounds like rubber being whacked, . . . RUBBER!'

In the glimmering moonlight, the boat floated peacefully in the deep water where we'd moored it. Then it bounced. Eleven caimans surrounded it. Leading the gang was a beast ten feet long and clenched between its grizzly jaws was the painter. It shook its head, one side of the boat flipped out of the water, the engine shuddered on the transom.

'Martin, make it let go of the rope.'

'How?' I asked, and practical as ever she replied.

'Go and bop it on the head with something.'

With Tanis close behind me, I climbed down the bank. 'Shine the torch on it and get ready to run the minute I hit it,' I whispered, wishing I'd found a longer piece of wood. As I crept towards it, the creature swished its body out of the water and viciously walloped the boat with its tail. We gulped, the ten feet we had estimated had been only part of it, it was much longer than our boat, nearer fifteen feet. Nothing less than the seriousness of the situation could have induced me to commit a violent act against such a creature. We'd be in for some fine adventures without a boat or provisions.

I charged down the beach and hurled the wood straight at it, hitting it fair and square on the snout. There was a powerful splash behind me as I scrambled up the bank in Tanis's slipstream, imagining the gaping jaws snapping at my ankles. 'Perhaps he thought the boat was a rival male and was beating him up,' Tanis remarked as we stood puffing with relief on top of the bank.

'Good job he didn't think it was a sexy female,' I said, 'he might have climbed aboard and screwed the engine.'

The caimans had departed but we felt compelled to spend a sleepless night guarding the boat.

At the mouth of the Pinquen stood a tapir, up to her belly in the shallows. The size of a donkey, with a tube-like snout and small, shortsighted eyes, she would wriggle from side to side, splashing water about, stop for a minute to whistle and squeak contentedly to herself, then start splashing about again, totally unaware of our presence. Minutes later we came upon eight capybaras swimming in midstream, who dived beneath the surface as we went near. The Pinquen promised to be a good river.

On the second day we reached the guard post, a badly neglected cabin perched precariously on the edge of a forty foot high bank, almost obscured by rampant greenery. No one had been there for a year or two, and it had become a home for furry spiders, scorpions, and the biggest cockroaches I'd ever seen. Tanis evicted them all, quite mercilessly. There, in our house on the Pinquen, we spent a blissful two weeks, with only the forest and its creatures for company. Then, when we'd tired of a roof above us and wooden boards beneath our feet, we reloaded the boat and set off upriver into the unknown.

The Dinquira River was a noisy place. As we made camp in the forest, a troupe of howler monkeys clambered through the trees. Seeing us below, they began to roar. These animals have a voice amplification mechanism that would be the envy of a rock group, enabling them to produce sound of greater volume than the trumpeting of an elephant or the roar of a lion. In the distance, a troupe of howlers sound like a wailing wind, but directed as it was at us, from a distance of forty feet, the noise had us plugging our ears and made our heads ring for half an hour afterwards.

There was an abundance of cicadas. At precisely a quarter past five in the afternoon they would begin to whirr, erratically at first like a stuttered sentence, but soon warming up into a continuous, screaming whine like a circular saw cutting through logs. Parties of long-limbed orange frogs with inflatable balloons on their throats assembled in forest clearings and with the high-pitched electronic tone of robots would demand. 'Who are you? Who are you?' A toad wandered around beneath our hammocks during the night saying, 'Ho, ho, ho!' in a deep grunting bass. At night, too, there were disturbing sounds of a more dramatic nature, when great slabs of eroded sediment would slide away from the bank and crash into the water. Trees would sometimes be undermined and tumble over. Occasionally a whole section of riverbank forest would collapse with an almighty, thunderous roar.

There were other surprises. At irregular intervals, cold air masses descended from the Andes and the temperature would drop dramatically, as low as fifteen degrees centigrade and remain there for a couple of days. For lowland tropical rainforest it was very, very cold. We huddled in blankets and with the sky grey and jungle silent of frogs, insects and birds, it was like being on a river in England on a dismal winter day.

The boat was stuck solid. In an attempt to avoid a portage Martin had the idea of partially deflating the tubes and we were forcing it between two fallen trees, one above and one beneath the water. Wallowing in the water, we shoved and pushed until with an ominous crack, the boat sprang forward. The piercing cry of a screaming pia rang through the trees like a long, slow, nostalgic wolf-whistle; a birdsong as much a part of the forest as the sight of blue morpho butterflies. From far away another screaming pia answered. And then another. On the water's surface, foam and bubbles drifted past the hull, looking like detergent scrum and warning of turbulent water ahead. But for the moment, all was peace, the Dinquira ran gentle and smooth. Riverside trees were in bloom, explosions of purple and yellow in the green, and in places russet, orange and red, like some exotic, autumnal vision.

'It's fantastic here,' I murmured, lost in reverie. Then I noticed the water that was slowly creeping up to my ankles. By the time we'd found a place to stop, it was six inches deep. A lump of wood two feet long had punctured the boat and was wedged firmly under the bow.

Our enforced campsite was a splendid beach, a quarter of a mile of fine chalky sand. But the jungle was awful, mucky and wet, full of palms, thorny vines and clumps of stinging razor grass that lacerated skin. The beach was too tempting. 'Don't look round,' I called to Martin as I set to work, 'I'm going to surprise you.' Half an hour later I'd finished.

'Oh, is it supposed to be a tent?' he said, surveying the makeshift construction that was my interpretation of a ridge-tent.

'It'll be great,' I enthused, 'look, I've rigged up the mosquito nets inside.'

'It's wonderful, Tan, wonderful.'

'You sound disappointed.'

''Course I'm not, it's just that I thought you were doing something to eat, I felt sure you'd got a treat hidden away, and I was looking forward to it.'

That night under the shooting stars we sat by the fire. Night noises added to our tranquillity.

ZZZZ, splutter, cough. 'Martin? Mart, you're snoring, turn over.'

Silence.

Snort, splutter, grunt. 'Martin,' I prodded him in the ribs.

'Eh, what, what's wrong?'

'You were snoring, making a terrible noise.'

'Oh sorry, 'night.'

'Goodnight, sleep tight.'

Grunt, grunt, snort. 'Marti . . .'

'Shhh, it's not me, it's something outside!'

We lay rigid with the effort of listening. A large creature was prowling around the camp. 'Where are the machetes?' Martin whispered.

'I don't know, outside somewhere.'

'Great. We deserve to be eaten alive by a family of jaguars you know, that'd teach us.' Next morning we found fresh, deep, pad prints made by a very large cat which had circled our shelter two or three times, then padded into the forest.

For two days we stayed, but into our thoughts crept a niggling remembrance of Manolo's words. 'Never stay more than a single night in one place.' On the third day at dawn, we heard the sound. It was like a drum being struck at ten second intervals. First we ignored it, then we listened with rising anxiety and eventually we talked about it, speculating that it must be an Indian beating something with a stick, to inform all the others in the vicinity of our whereabouts. After twenty minutes, unable to bear the suspense any longer, we were compelled to go into the forest and discover who was causing it.

Through the forest we crept, hearts throbbing like bongo drums. The knocking continued and drew us to a hollow tree. As we stood beneath it, there was another loud knock. Fifteen feet above us, a pigeon-sized, chestnut-coloured woodpecker clung to the trunk. It looked quizzically at our ashen faces before returning its attention to more important things. Drawing back its head, it waited for a count of ten, then struck the tree a resounding, skull-vibrating blow.

The narrow Dinquira widened unexpectedly into a lagoon, half a mile long and a hundred yards wide. After the confines of the forest it was like arriving at the seaside. In the middle of the lagoon was a shelf-like island of sand, with a dozen caimans lined up side by side, rigid and glinting golden in the sunshine like huge, surreal, brass ornaments. 'Look!' said Martin excitedly, pointing into the water. Beneath the boat were scores of two foot long, carp-like fish. We turned off the engine and drifted. The entire lagoon was as densely packed, there were thousands of them. We'd stumbled upon a spawning ground.

Beyond the lagoon the river was dark and mysterious. A

grey head, the size of a fist, popped out of the murky water, opened and closed its mouth a few times, then writhed its snake-like body across the surface, looking like a small Loch Ness monster: an electric eel coming up for air. Electric eels are related to catfish and can produce a shock powerful enough to knock out a human being. Paradise has its drawbacks. Electric eels usually frequent deep, stagnant pools, the kind of places we'd be unlikely to swim in. A more real danger came from the possibility of one of us stepping on a stingray, a flat fish with a barbed tail, capable of delivering an agonising wound taking months to heal. The most worrying thing about stingrays was their habit of lying on the river bed in the shallows where we had to wade, when dragging the boat round obstacles. Half buried in sand, mud or gravel, they become almost invisible and move only with great reluctance – nothing less than a vigorous prod with a stick will induce an unresponsive stingray to shift into gear. Whenever we saw clouds of sediment rising in otherwise clear water, it was invariably a stingray, digging itself in.

Driving our boat onto a sandbank, we disturbed the biggest stingray we'd ever seen, a monstrous creature with a three foot 'wing-span', which took off with commendable agility when a quarter of a ton of inflatable boat landed on top of it. It was a sobering moment, for had we parked a couple of feet to left or right, one of us might have stepped out onto it.

Sunset, strolling along the beach, thinking about nothing in particular Martin spotted the most beautiful lizard we'd ever seen. Three feet long with a purple head and green and yellow body. 'Nip back and get the camera Tan, I'll try to catch it.' As I left it scurried into the bushes with Martin hot on its tail.

I raced back with the camera and met Martin lizardless, and looking serious. 'I think we're being followed,' he said quietly. 'When I rushed into the bushes just now there was a man in there. He'd been following us, creeping through the bushes, I don't know who got more of a shock, him or me. He couldn't possibly have anticipated that without warning I'd suddenly rush into the forest straight at him.'

'What did he do, what was he like?' I pressed.

'What would you do if someone came charging straight at you? He ran away.'

Two things worried us about the incident. We now knew for certain that we were not alone on the river. And he might interpret the incident as aggressive, that Martin had charged into the bushes to attack him. That night lying on the beach under the shelter, our imaginations ran riot. Every sound became human. A hoot was no longer a bird, it was a man, answered by others on the far side of the river, drawing closer by the minute. At three in the morning we rose, and in the cool darkness chased away the caimans that lay half out of the water and lit a massive fire of driftwood by the river edge. If, as Manolo said, Indians attack at dawn, perhaps seeing us so obviously awake and alert might put them off. We couldn't sleep anyway.

As soon as it was day, we loaded the boat – if necessary we could make a fast getaway – but left the shelter up on the beach. The rising of the sun dispelled our fears and we faced our indecision. Would it be foolhardy to continue upriver? We'd been lost in the magic of the place, was it now necessary to rush off downstream? We didn't know what might lie ahead, the place was full of unexpected rewards. If we turned back now, we would be beginning the long journey home. 'What do you want to do, Tan?'

'I don't know, I don't really want to go back yet, do you?'

'No, definitely not, but I can't help feeling it's a bit chancey to go on.'

'Do you think they'd mind if we just stayed here?'

'I'm pretty sure that if they do, they'll let us know!' he joked.

Another restless night, up at three for another bonfire. We decided to continue but our peace of mind had gone. Two days later came the second encounter. Far upstream, on the other side of the river, two men emerged from the forest and stood facing us for a minute or so with the obvious intention of being seen. Too far away for us to determine any expression, even this event was open to interpretation. Were they being friendly, curious, warning us to proceed no further or intimating that we leave? There was nothing on which to make an objective assessment of the situation.

Somehow we hadn't expected direct contact with Indians. But in the event, we presumed it would be like that with the three women on the Manu. That they'd come out and greet us and we might have the opportunity to show them that we were nice, friendly people. The knowledge that we were being followed and observed, certainly for days, possibly for weeks, was unnerving, like being hunted. We couldn't avoid the fear that we might unwittingly do something wrong, something that could make them see us as enemies.

By travelling so far upriver we'd moved a lot closer to the valley in which the English journalist Bob Nichols and his two French companions were killed by Machiguengas in 1971. Reports at the time were conflicting – they were killed with arrows – they were stoned to death – the Indians wanted their possessions – they'd been eating from the Indians plantations. Nineteen seventy-one wasn't *that* long ago and the people who did it, for whatever reason, would still be around.

Intuitively, we felt it was time to go. We packed the shelter into the boat and motored away downriver. Twenty minutes later, we got stuck across a barrier of trees, ripped a hole in the bottom of the boat and it rapidly filled with water. There was no alternative but to unload, repair the damage and camp for another night while the glued patch set. We stayed up all night, dragging driftwood onto a fire which blazed into the sky like a Guy Fawkes night celebration and next morning reloaded the boat in four minutes flat and set off with a feeling of tremendous relief.

CHAPTER TWENTY-ONE

Progress downstream was tediously slow. With no rain for two weeks the river had dropped considerably, fallen trees and hills of timber dammed the stream and blocked our way. Once having made the decision to return, we were taken over by a feeling of urgency, the need to get far away as quickly as possible. Tense with the frustration of stopping every five minutes to hack away at branches and drag the boat through shallows, we sweated and cursed in the relentless heat of a cloudless day, while being eaten alive by blackflies. With the heat had come a new insect, a microscopic menace which invaded our hair and bit our scalps, like hundreds of red hot needles.

By late afternoon we felt satisfied that we were finally safe. The air was still and breathlessly hot but on the western horizon storm clouds were piled on the mountains, producing a dramatic sunset, red and gold with patches of green. To the east, a purple and black sky, perpetually illuminated by lightning, the rumble of thunder came and went with the wind. With the possibility of a rainstorm arriving during the night, we made camp on the highest beach we could find, twenty yards from the river, at the very edge of the forest. For additional protection, Martin covered the boat with a layered thatch of *caña brava* fronds and secured it to a fifty foot long tree trunk that lay half-buried in the sand.

At eleven-thirty I woke with cold feet. The air was still, it wasn't raining and moonlight shone from a clear sky. But something was very wrong. There were plopping sounds of fish jumping very close by, and the slap and lap of water. 'Mart, I think. . . .'

'Oh no!' he yelled, jumping up with a squelching splash, 'we've done it *again*.'

In a tangle of blankets and nets, we struggled from the shelter to be confronted by a nightmarish sight. The river had risen fifteen feet in three hours and was now a powerful torrent. In the moonlight, trees floated silently past at alarming speed.

'The boat!' Martin cried, he was beside himself. Both of him splashed into the river. The boat had disappeared along with the tree it was tied to, carried away in the flood. Behind me the shelter collapsed, pegs uprooted, and was being tugged away by the flow. In a desperate panic I clutched it up along with our sodden blankets. Martin floundered along the beach through waist deep water. Snagged in the bushes on the next bend was the mighty tree trunk with the painter still attached to it. He hauled it in madly and I hardly dared look to see if the boat was still attached to the other end, for it was still invisible in the black shadows of the riverside. 'AAAGH!' yelled Martin, 'there's a sodding great THING on the boat!'

Like a horrible, supernatural apparition, the boat appeared from the shadows with a giant creature sitting on top of it silhouetted against the river, a creature that looked like a bat with a twelve foot wing span. It swayed and trembled and flapped its massive wings as if, like a demon of the woods, it would leap at him and tear open his throat. Then one of its wings fell off. As it drew nearer the myopic vision became the pile of *caña brava* he'd covered the boat with the previous evening. 'I reckon by the time we've made another ten expeditions, we'll have learned not to camp on beaches,' said Martin. Rain high in the mountains had craftily flooded our valley.

It was a miserable, interminable time till dawn. Rain came and we huddled in the boat beneath the shelter, soaking wet and cold, with the mosquitoes sucking us dry. 'We're incredibly lucky you know, Tan,' said Martin, attempting cheerfulness.

A mass of unknown creepy crawlies had fallen into the boat from the *caña brava* and were scurrying up my legs. Rain poured down my neck and a vicious mosquito bit me on the eyelid. 'Oh, we are, Martin, very lucky indeed, we might have camped in the jungle, we might be asleep in warm dry hammocks now. I mean, just think, we might have missed all this!'

'No, I mean we could have lost the boat, and now we'd be facing a long walk out. It would take weeks, with no food, nothing, imagine that.'

'Martin, we're trying hard aren't we? There's still time, if we continue like this and do our best, I'm sure we'll manage to lose the boat or kill ourselves before the trip's out!'

Gone were all our cooking and eating utensils, not one pot, plate, cup, fork or spoon remained, I'd left them on the beach. The rusty tin can we used for baling out the boat was the only thing left to cook in and eat from. But at this stage in the journey it was nothing more than a minor inconvenience. Living standards were getting low. Our rations were dwindling, all sugar, flour, beans and milk used up. The last treat, creme caramel made with water, had been gobbled up on the Pucacungayo. Tomato sauce, herbs and spices were just delicious memories. Saccharin instead of sugar sweetened our coffee. We'd smoked most of our cigarettes and were both rolling tobacco in air mail paper. Clearly we were going to run out, but my threat to go home when that happened no longer had teeth – we were going home anyway. We'd be back among people in a week or so.

The flood was a great help in one respect. Sailing down the swollen river on a speedy current, in eight hours we covered a distance that would have taken us three or four days picking a route through timber-clogged shallows. That evening we were light-headed with fatigue, it had been days since we'd slept properly. Too tired to do more than fix up the shelter and nets we lay on the forest floor wrapped in our hammocks and slept fitfully. I dozed off just as it was getting light. Half an hour later I opened my eyes to see a pile of rich, moist animal droppings a foot from my nose, between shelter and net. An unknown nocturnal visitor had passed through.

We reached the hut on the Pinquen. As we unloaded the

boat, a herd of peccaries, a hundred strong, burst squabbling and squealing from the forest on the opposite bank and trotted down to the river. Spotting us, the front-runners turned, but too late, the ranks charged onwards till the bank was a confusion of panicked pigs, falling over each other in the mud. That night we boiled rice in the tin can and went to bed desperately tired but fully expecting to be woken at midnight by peccaries rampaging through the room, for the cabin to catch fire or slide over the bank into the water.

We set sail for the Manu River, breakfasting as we went along on cold porridge eaten with our fingers. At night we slept in our clothes and tied a rope from the boat to Martin's foot, just in case.

At the mouth of the Manu River, in a clearing high on a bank lived three miserable Government employees, checking boat traffic up and down the river, perhaps banished to this remote outpost in punishment for some misdemeanour. We climbed the bank and presented our papers to a gaunt, nervous, unshaven man who gave the impression of having been interrupted during a suicide attempt. As we stood there, muddy and wild-looking, scratching our insect bites, two canoes arrived with men who looked European. They stared at us with curiosity but we rudely ignored them. We didn't want the outside world yet and were in no hurry to talk to people. Once again we took the irrational attitude that Manu Park was ours.

One of the men approached us and offered his hand. 'Hello, I'm Mike Andrews from the BBC, we're going to film in the Park. Have you just come from there? What's it like?'

Now we babbled like idiots about Indians, jaguars, caimans, snakes, storms and floods, trying to condense all our experiences into five minutes. 'I'll let you know when the film will be broadcast,' said Mike as we exchanged addresses. 'It'll be called *Flight of the Condor*.'

Downstream, two Indian families lived in board shacks. We wanted food but more urgently, we needed tobacco. They grew it there, but it was still green. Seeing the desperation on our faces, a man presented us with a piece of paper containing about an ounce from his private supply, but would take no payment for it. Another said he had food to sell and we asked if we could buy bananas. '*Si*,' he nodded his head enthusiastically, '*No hay platanos*.'

'Did he say what I thought he said?' I asked Martin, 'yes, we have no bananas.'

'I don't expect he's got broad beans and onions, or cabbages like bunions either,' he said. But he did have plenty of yucca, a large root vegetable with white flesh which, when boiled, tastes like a cross between potato and sweet chestnut.

Now we sailed down the wide, fast-flowing Madre de Dios River, where parties of gold miners dug caves out of the riverbanks, flushing the sediment down crude wooden chutes and trapping gold particles in sacking. From this originates the legend of the 'Golden Fleece', when sheepskin was used for the same purpose. Once over the first shock of seeing us in our boat, they waved and called us in to drink with them.

There were no animals to be seen. Those that had not been shot had moved away, or were developing nocturnal habits, a typical reaction to men with guns. No caiman who valued his hide would dare to sunbathe on the Madre de Dios. We pulled onto a beach and I put up the shelter, while Martin cooked the yucca. 'Hey, look,' I called, pleased with myself, 'there were poles already cut over there so I used them.'

'Tan, that's a goldminer's claim you've just demolished, they mark them with those poles. They'd probably kill you for that.'

It was my birthday, the next day would be Tanis's, and it would be the fourth time we'd celebrated birthdays in the jungle, though on this occasion we were almost out of it. For Tanis, I'd secretly made a card, with cartoons and daft rhymes. She'd done the same for me, but as well as this she gave me a gift-wrapped present that astonished me, a bar of chocolate which had been purchased before the trip, the last time we'd seen a shop. Across the Andes, through the jungles, up and down unexplored rivers that bar of chocolate had remained hidden. I thought what a very lucky man I was, and not just for the chocolate.

We had a map of the Madre de Dios and as we slid past the mouths of rivers, read their names. Rio Blanco, Rio Azul, Rio Colorado (white river, blue river, coloured river). Just past the Colorado was a goldminers' trading post where we sold everything we no longer needed and bought tins of cheese, pots of jam and cigarettes. The proprietor, a fat man with a shrewd eye, presented us with a free teaspoon as we left.

Now life was easy. We sat in the boat, drifting with the current to conserve the last of our petrol. The Madre de Dios widened by the hour as we travelled downstream in mid-channel. The sky was gloriously expansive, horizons unfamiliarly distant, giving us a feeling of space we'd been deprived of for months. The vastness of it thrilled me in the same way it had when, as a child, I'd read of the exploits of Percy Fawcett, struggling through his green hell in search of his dreams. The waters of the Madre de Dios eventually join the Madeira River and then the Amazon. The Madeira is over two thousand miles long, the longest of the Amazon's network of fifteen thousand feeder rivers, which drain an area of nearly three million square miles.

'It must have looked pretty much the same as this sixty million years ago, when dinosaurs were wandering around,' I said.

'It's hard to believe it could all be gone in thirty years,' said Tanis. She'd been sharing my thoughts. The thrill was replaced by a chilling vision of the twenty-first century, when the land would be criss-crossed by roads, rivers dammed and polluted, forest cleared for farms and ranches, valleys dotted with towns. Buildings, machines, noise, dirt and people everywhere. Fervently I hoped that the ambitions of politicians, multinational companies, planners and developers would never be realised. Deeply I feared that no amount of vision and intelligence would be permitted to get in the way of demands made by an insanely expanding human population, coupled with industrial nations insatiable desire for hardwoods and cheap beef.

'How far to Laberinto?' I called to some miners.

'A little further, maybe one hour,' they replied. We spent that night on a beach.

High on a distant bank stood a multi-coloured cluster of buildings, so many reds, greens, purples, yellows and blues that it looked like an international flag day. As we drew closer, we saw the place for what it really was, a shanty town of tin-roofed hovels with walls made of coloured plastic sacks, opened out with the names of the products they'd once contained printed on them in bold letters; fertilizers, pesticides, poisons. Dreadful pop music blared from loudspeakers fixed in the branches of trees. It looked horribly squalid. Tough-looking, gun-toting men and a few women and children emerged to stare at us stonily. But as soon as we waved, smiles broke out and everyone waved back enthusiastically, calling to us above the din. 'Come, gringos, come and take coffee with us.'

'Sorry, we can't stop. How far to Laberinto?'

'Not far, not far, one hour. Just around the bend. Go with God, gringos.'

'Just think,' I said, 'a few days upriver are people who've never seen a gun or an outboard engine, or for that matter a piece of metal or plastic. I wonder what they'd make of this lot?'

'Let's hope they never have to find out,' said Martin. 'Give these miners half a chance and they'll move into Manu Park in their thousands.'

We spent that night on a beach.

Daily we passed more and more miners. Every hundred yards were workings, and traffic on the river seemed like the London rush hour. This must be what the Carrao in Venezuela was like in the gold boom, I thought, but there was nothing threatening about these men.

'Wonder what Rudy's doing now?' I said.

'Funny, I was just thinking about that,' Martin said, between spoonfuls of jam. 'That was a good trip, wasn't it, I wonder if we'll ever go back to Angel Falls?'

'Never return to a place where you were happy. I don't know where I heard that, but it's probably good advice.'

'Remember Tarhit? Standing on top of a sand dune?' Hesitating for less than a second before opening the last jar of jam.

'Martin, you'll make yourself sick. We were going to drive across Africa then.' I opened the second tin of cheese.

'I can't imagine not making trips now, can you?' Martin said, spreading jam on chunks of cheese.

'No, it's just something we do, isn't it?' I replied, dipping cheese into the jam.

'I enjoy being home though, especially painting, there's such a lot I want to do when we get back.' Putting the empty jam jar down.

'I'm going to learn Spanish fluently,' I said vehemently, looking at the empty cheese tin. The end of a trip was our time for resolutions.

'You always say that, but you never do.' Martin reminded me. 'I'm going to give up smoking.'

'Ha! *You* always say that. You ought to find it easy, you've done it often enough.'

'Yuk, I feel a bit sick now.'

'Ugh, so do I.'

Had there ever been a life without South America?

'How far to Laberinto?'

'You're nearly there, one hour more.' It was not from any Machiavellian desire to mislead us, just that they thought it was what we wanted to hear. We spent that night on the beach.

For much of the hundred miles to Laberinto we'd drifted and it had taken six days. Six days of fragile, misty mornings merging into blazing afternoons, evening camps on shingle beaches where we talked incessantly about comfortable beds, cold beers, fresh food and letters from home.

Among a maze of islands we asked again. 'How far to Laberinto?'

'It is there,' pointing downstream, 'an hour.' In the far distance, there it was.

'OK, Tan, it's time for a decision.'

All the way downriver we'd pondered the question, devoting our sole attention to the seriousness of the matter. We'd remember this decision for a long time to come. Whenever we thought of Peru.

I looked at Martin, he'd made his decision, and then, I had my answer. 'Martin, I'm going to have cheese, tomato and onion salad, *and* fried eggs with pizza and spaghetti, *and* three freshly boiled corn on the cob!'

In the afternoon we arrived at Laberinto, a small frontier settlement with a road connection to Puerto Maldonado, a town with an airfield and flights to Cuzco. We moored our boat among a row of dugout canoes watched by a large crowd, more people than we'd seen together in months. Martin stayed with the boat and I entered the dusty heat of the little town of dilapidated shacks, hardware stores and bars. A red dirt road disappeared into the jungle. There were trucks and motor-bikes, dogs, pigs, chickens and children. Indians and miners stood in noisy groups, many of them reeling drunk. Piles of refuse lay everywhere: rotting fruit, broken bottles, rusty cans and the overwhelming stench of fuel, alcohol and garbage.

There was a truck leaving for Puerto Maldonado in half an hour and he would take us. Hurriedly we stuffed things into kit bags and sweated back and forth from boat to truck, until everything was loaded. Last item was the boat itself and with that aboard we were ready to depart. We felt disappointed, as if we'd been snatched from the river without our consent. It had all happened so fast. Suddenly, too suddenly, our river trip was over. I could have cried. Martin looked miserable too.

'Think of all the things we've been missing for the last three months,' I said. 'Are you looking forward to them?'

'Not very much,' he replied. 'What about you?'

'I'd rather be back on the river.'

EPILOGUE

The chef and his staff had emerged from their smoky, steam-filled dungeon of a kitchen to watch us eat. The waiter summoned them when we'd each ordered our third main course and out they came to stand around our table while we tucked in, smiling their appreciation and politely murmuring encouragement. On this, the evening of our return to Lima, with gargantuan appetites yet to return to normal, we were making up for months of hard living.

Another bottle of wine arrived, this one on the house. We were enjoying Lima. We were enjoying Peru. So much so that we'd decided to remain for a couple more months, visiting a few of the places this utterly fascinating country has to offer: the Inca ruins of Machu Picchu, the ancient, mysterious desert drawings at Nazca, massive Lake Titicaca more than two miles high in the Andes.

It was an exciting prospect, but exciting in a gentle, unchallenging way that could never match the raw adventure of a jungle river trip. From now on we'd be tourists in well-toured places. Already our minds were leaping ahead to the more distant future. 'Do you remember Nicholas Guppy's book about the Wai-Wai Indians in Brazil?' said Martin, looking thoughtful. 'What was that river called?'

'The Mapuera?'

'That's right. The Mapuera.' Now he looked very thoughtful.

' I wonder where we can get a really good map of Brazil. . . ?'

CHRISTINA DODWELL

A TRAVELLER ON HORSEBACK

Horseback, Christina Dodwell's favourite form of travel, gave her the freedom to venture alone through some of the wildest parts of the world. Her journey, which took her from Eastern Turkey, to Cappadocia, Iran, Pakistan and back, kept within the confines of the Persian Empire. She visited ancient cities such as Persepolis and Pasargad and travelled through varied countryside, among snow caps, salt lakes and paddy fields. She also stayed with and met many local people including some ranchers who bred the once extinct miniature Caspian horse.

It was on her return to Eastern Turkey that she bought her favourite horse, Keyif, a fine grey Arab stallion. Together they rode from Erzurum to Lake Van, up the Russian border to Mount Ararat in search of Noah's Ark.

A TRAVELLER ON HORSEBACK is a breath-taking account of an enthralling journey, told by one of the most intrepid women explorers writing in the world today.

A Royal Mail service in association with the Book Marketing Council & The Booksellers Association.

Post-A-Book is a Post Office trademark.

DEREK NIMMO

UP MOUNT EVEREST WITHOUT A PADDLE

A little travelling music, maestro, please ... Derek Nimmo offers an in-flight feast of traveller's tales with the maximum duty-free allowance of laughter.

Travelwise enough to avoid such hazards as playing in *There's a Girl in My Soup* in Papua New Guinea, the long-distance Nimmo is no stranger to the traumas of travel. Indeed, his first flight on a Jumbo was sadly marred when he was told: 'I'm sorry, sir, you can only see a dirty movie if you're a smoker.'

His gloriously funny global guide is spiced with such gems overheard as the American lady's complaint on ascending the Parthenon – 'You'd think with all these tourists about, they would build an elevator ...'

HODDER AND STOUGHTON PAPERBACKS

PETER SOMERVILLE-LARGE

TO THE NAVEL OF THE WORLD
Yaks and Unheroic Travels in Nepal and Tibet

Combining the traditions of Robert Louis Stevenson's TRAVELS ON A DONKEY with the humour of Gerald Durrell's MY FAMILY AND OTHER ANIMALS, Peter Somerville-Large ventured to uncharted lands on that most uncompromising of beasts, the yak. The result is an extraordinarily engaging travel book, offering unusual glimpses of the Himalayas, the Forbidden City and the Tibetans, Chinese and Nepalese.

'Peter Somerville-Large is the most congenial sort of travel writer: witty, modest, observant, stoical, compassionate without being sentimental, unobtrusively knowledgeable and deliciously dotty'
Dervla Murphy in *The Literary Review*

'A wonderful adventure which brings us — like all great armchair travel books — through a largely uncharted landscape . . . a terrific book; a small classic of pure travel'
Douglas Kennedy in *The Irish Times*

HODDER AND STOUGHTON PAPERBACKS